FROM SERF TO RUSSIAN SOLDIER

Elise Kimerling Wirtschafter

PRINCETON UNIVERSITY PRESS

PRINCETON, NEW JERSEY

Copyright © 1990 by Princeton University Press
Published by Princeton University Press, 41 William Street,
Princeton, New Jersey 08540
In the United Kingdom: Princeton University Press, Oxford

All Rights Reserved

Library of Congress Cataloging-in-Publication Data

Wirtschafter, Elise Kimerling.
From serf to Russian soldier
Elise Kimerling Wirtschafter.
p. cm. Bibliography: p. Includes index.
ISBN 0-691-05585-8 (alk. paper)
1. Russia. Armiia—Military life—History—19th century.
2. Soviet Union—Armed Forces—Military life—History—19th century
3. Serfdom—Soviet Union—History—19th century. I. Title.
U771.W57   1989   306.2'7'0947—dc20   89-10522

This book has been composed in Linotron Sabon and Gills Sans

Princeton University Press books are printed on acid-free paper,
and meet the guidelines for permanence and durability of the
Committee on Production Guidelines for Book Longevity of the
Council on Library Resources

Printed in the United States of America by Princeton University Press,
Princeton, New Jersey

10 9 8 7 6 5 4 3 2 1

Designed by Laury A. Egan

To my grandfather
Max Lionel Kimerling

From Serf to Russian Soldier

CONTENTS

LIST OF TABLES	ix
ACKNOWLEDGMENTS	xi
INTRODUCTION	xiii
ONE Conscription	3
TWO Military Society and the State	26
THREE From Peasant to Soldier: Education and Training	55
FOUR The Limits of Bureaucratic Regulation: The Regimental Economy	74
FIVE Justice with Order: Autocratic Values and Military Discipline	96
SIX Soldiers in Service: Expectations and Realities	120
CONCLUSION The Semi-Standing Army	149
NOTES AND LIST OF ABBREVIATIONS	153
SELECT BIBLIOGRAPHY	199
INDEX	209

LIST OF TABLES

1.1	Age and Social Origin of Recruits	10
1.2	Recruits Sent to the Azov Infantry Regiment in 1795 and 1811	11
1.3	Physical Inadequacies among Recruits	24
2.1	Mortality among the Lower Ranks	30
2.2	Illness and Mortality in the Active Army	31
2.3	Rates of Illness, Mortality, and Desertion	32
2.4	Illness, Mortality, and Desertion in the Pskov Infantry Regiment	33
2.5	Married Soldiers, 1841–44	37
2.6	Family Ties among Recruits	37
2.7	Infantry Noncommissioned Officers in 1807	44
2.8	Jager Noncommissioned Officers in 1805	45
2.9	Noncommissioned Officers in 1813	46
2.10	Garrison Noncommissioned Officers in 1816	47
3.1	Level of Skill among Recruits	63
4.1	Artel and Economic Sums per Soldier	80
5.1	Rate of Desertion	111
5.2	Crime among Lower Ranks of Non-Noble Origin	112
5.3	Types of Crimes Committed by Non-Noble Lower Ranks	113
5.4	Crime among Lower Ranks of Noble Origin	114
5.5	Crime Rate (Ratios of Accused Officers and Lower Ranks)	115
5.6	Crime among Officers	116

ACKNOWLEDGMENTS

This book has benefited from the patience and professionalism of many people. I am particularly indebted to the staff of the Central State Military Historical Archive (TsGVIA) in Moscow; the Central State Archive of the October Revolution (TsGAOR), also in Moscow; and the Central State Historical Archive (TsGIA) in Leningrad. Without their efforts, completion of this study would have been impossible. I am also grateful to the staff of the Lenin Library in Moscow, the Slavonic Library in Helsinki, and the New York Public Library. On two occasions (1980–81 and 1984) grants from the International Research and Exchanges Board and the Fulbright-Hays programs for research abroad allowed me to conduct essential research in the USSR and Finland. I would also like to thank two teachers, Leopold Haimson and Isser Woloch, who, as instructors and readers, offered suggestions for expanding and improving my thesis.

Two other teachers, Marc Raeff and Gregory L. Freeze, have provided ongoing guidance and inspiration. Despite their own very demanding schedules and unusual productivity as scholars, they have always had time and wisdom to share. Special thanks are also due to my parents, Rita and Sol Kimerling. Most of all, I want to thank my husband, Gary, whose enduring patience, flexible personality, and parental skills have allowed me to continue my work, while caring for our two children.

Los Angeles, 1988

INTRODUCTION

Throughout the European continent, the effective imposition of tax and conscription obligations signaled the rise of the centralized state.[1] In Russia these intrusions into local life began in the early eighteenth century, when Peter the Great established a standing army and introduced the poll tax. For the common soldier, the experience of entering the army was comparable to that of a peasant or artisan moving into the mechanical routines of factory life. At times discipline was lax, but generally speaking, daily life in the army contained a high degree of routinization. Roll calls occurred twice a day. Formal inspections were less frequent, though when the troops gathered as units, training was also a daily affair. The production and maintenance of uniforms and equipment required regular attention. Attendance at church services, the daily recitation of prayers, observance of the sacraments, and religious fasts served to remind the lower ranks of their country's Orthodox heritage.[2] Finally, for those stationed along borders or in towns and garrisons, guard duty was a frequent activity. A strict system of subordination and discipline enforced these routines, so that the soldiers' activities were regulated in ways unthinkable in peasant society.

The Russian army before the Great Reforms was both a society in itself and a reflection of Russian society as a whole. Because the *Polizeistaat* of imperial Russia could regulate military society, with its relatively finite boundaries, more effectively than the larger, more amorphous civilian society, the army provides a rich arena for understanding the relationship between the state and society. An analysis of this relationship raises important questions concerning the modernization of the old regime, particularly the problem of promoting bureaucratic rationality and professional performance within the framework of the traditional social arrangements based on serfdom. The social history of the lower ranks suggests that the government's need to mobilize society's resources for military purposes created an ongoing systemic stimulus for reform and for equality in the treatment of society. Thus the state sought to meet its military and administrative needs by molding the moral and social development of its subjects.[3] In addition, through bureaucratic regulation, enlightened officials tried to institute an autocracy of procedures with clear delimitations of arbitrariness.

The government's ability to achieve these professed and implicit goals was far from successful. This military society always suffered from a discrepancy between governmental intentions and the resources available to achieve offical goals. To fill this gap, officers enjoyed extensive discretionary authority—that is, the informal right to interpret laws, carry out instructions, and execute official policies by whatever means they deemed necessary. Discretionary authority was especially visible in the regimental economy where, because of chronic shortages, the government repeatedly tolerated violations of law, as long as they served the state interest. Discipline was another area where commanders possessed broad powers of interpretation within specified legal norms. There were limits to discretionary authority, but they were vague and changeable, depending on the circumstances and the individuals involved. Moreover, the discretionary authority that admitted open violations of the law inevitably degenerated into arbitrariness. The resulting confusion in social and legal norms had important implications both for the condition of the lower ranks and for the achievement of the army's professional military goals.

Aside from contradictions between official policy and the underlying socioeconomic structure, harsh environmental realities affected the condition of the lower ranks. The struggle to survive in a very basic physical sense was a constant factor in the life of the army. The absence of modern communications was not unique to Russia, but because of the empire's vast geographical reaches and low population density, the effects were felt more acutely than in other European countries. This accounts for the government's sensitivity to the manpower problem, which, along with the desire for order and efficiency, prompted measures to protect soldiers from economic and physical abuse.

State policy and material realities explain much about the social condition of the common soldier, but it is also important to recognize the soldier as an autonomous actor on the stage of history, as a vital element of the society in which he lived. Too many historians treat the soldiers (and the lower classes in general) either as passive victims or as latent revolutionaries. The soldiers were neither. Rather, they were survivors who adjusted their expectations and behavior to the realities of military life and the dangers of combat service. This does not mean that social conflict was absent, for the underlying social tension easily erupted into acts of rebellion or desperation. Soldiers took to heart the professed goals of the autocracy and expected both fair discipline and economic security from their commanding officers.

Historians recently have begun to recognize the importance of standing armies in the development of modern European society—and nowhere was this more apparent than in imperial Russia, where obligatory conscription and the standing army developed simultaneously. Russia's role

INTRODUCTION

as a great power, combined with the demands of an expanding imperial administration, made the army an institution of special importance. The lower ranks of the pre-reform army provide a clear example of the close relationship between status group (*soslovie*) and governmental institution (*vedomstvo*) in imperial Russia. All social classes came under the regulation of a particular administrative domain, a situation that promoted the organization of society to serve the interests of the state. Russian historians have devoted serious studies to the classic status groups (nobles, peasants, townspeople, and clergy), but there is no work that examines the lower ranks of the pre-reform era as a social class or the army as a social institution.

Recent forays into the social history of the military either cover later periods (Bushnell and Kenez) or provide broad chronological and thematic syntheses of primarily printed sources (Beyrau and Keep). Dietrich Beyrau (*Militär und Gesellschaft im vorrevolutionären Russland*) has ably analyzed the relationship between the army and society in the eighteenth and nineteenth centuries. Although his book includes valuable chapters on training and the regimental economy, it is primarily an institutional history that examines the dysfunctioning of the military system (both before and after the military reforms of the 1870s) in the broader context of civilian society and economy. John Keep's recent study (*Soldiers of the Tsar: Army and Society in Russia, 1462–1874*) is a highly readable, skillful synthesis of mostly printed sources. Although he places significant emphasis on the common soldier, the absence of a broad archival base has limited the analytic scope to essentially a descriptive account. Professor Keep tends to echo the publicistic sources by focusing on the harshness and lack of improvement in the soldier's life. John Bushnell takes a more sociological approach (*Mutiny amid Repression: Russian Soldiers in the Revolution of 1905–1906*), but he is concerned with a structurally changed army (and society) in the revolutionary period. The Soviet literature touches on some aspects of the army's social life (conscription, rebellion, and folklore), but there is no work that examines soldiers as a social class. The major Soviet studies generally address questions of military theory, organization, and tactics (Beskrovnyi, Zaionchkovskii, Bogdanov, Zolotarev et al.).

This study represents the first attempt to write a social history of the common soldier based on extensive archival research. The first task is to describe concretely the social condition of the lower ranks, to identify the basic parameters of the soldier's daily life. What were the physical and psychological factors defining his existence? What did service mean for the individual recruits, for society as a whole, and for the state in particular? This study then seeks to fit the details of the soldier's daily life into a more general conception of "military society" by examining the patterns of control, cohesion, and conflict in that society. The second task is to define the norms of "military society," to explore the mental characteristics of the soldier—his attitudes, expectations, and behavioral patterns. Finally, by analyzing the dynamics of authority and social relations in the pre-reform army, this study provides insights into the relationship between the state and society, especially the problem of modernization in the context of a traditional, though highly fluid social structure.

The concept of "military society" first appeared in the pioneering works of the French historian André Corvisier. Regardless of the specific national context, important features of administration, culture, and social organization were common to all the major European armies. Since I have approached this study as a social historian with little technical knowledge of the military, specifically Russian themes predominate. In Russia the presence of serfdom and the obligatory nature of conscription created social issues much different from those found in England, France, Austria, or Germany. It is precisely the effects of serfdom that make Russia so suitable for a study of military society: service was obligatory, lasted for twenty or twenty-five years, and brought with it a fundamental change in juridical status. Conscription implied a very sharp and complete break with one's native environment. The lengthy term of service and the change in social status thus provided the foundation for a separate "military society."

The first half of the nineteenth century is significant for several reasons. In this period the Petrine system of service classes reached its fullest point of development and maturation. The basic contradiction between the government's desire to promote military efficiency and its commitment to preserving the traditional social order became increasingly visible. The army's professional performance was crucial to the survival of the state, and official efforts to ensure adequate military performance strikingly revealed all the inherent contradictions and weaknesses of the Petrine system. The period thus provided the backdrop for the Great Reforms, the most comprehensive attempt under the old regime to restructure Russia's social institutions. Although the military system survived until the 1870s, the Crimean War represented the psychological break after which it became clear that fundamental reform was imminent. Also in this period Russia's perceived military might and her role as a great power reached a peak—a peak shattered in the Crimean War and not regained until almost a century later. All three emperors who ruled Russia during the first half of the nineteenth century (Paul, 1796–1801; Alexander I, 1801–25; and Nicholas I, 1825–55) took an active personal interest in the condition of the troops—a fact that reveals the army's central importance. Finally, the first half of the nineteenth century, and especially the reign of Nicholas I, witnessed a rapid growth in the size of the state bureaucracy—a growth that reflected the government's increasingly "modern" efforts to mold society's development. The period is therefore particularly important for understanding the relationship between the autocratic state and pre-reform Russian society.

Historians know very little about concrete conditions in the pre-reform army. Because this book represents the first attempt to delve deeply into archival sources relating to the social history of the lower ranks, it is limited to "normal" peacetime conditions. War brought dramatic changes in daily expectations, military laws, the rules of discipline, and economic possibilities. This study relies primarily upon official governmental sources. The most important are courts-martial records, which allow soldiers to speak for themselves and which provide direct evidence of their responses to specific situations. Only three memoirs from this period were actually written by soldiers, and officers generally were not concerned with them in their personal reminiscences.[4] This fact underlies the importance of soldiers' judicial testimonies, even if reported secondhand. Irregularities in the administration of military justice no doubt affected the reliability of judicial records. As late as 1854, an order of the war minister reminded officials that during the investigation of crimes, it was illegal to subject the accused to "biased interrogations, tortures, and cruelties."[5] For both the authorities and the witnesses, judicial testimony had an express purpose that often cast doubt not only on their veracity, but also on the accuracy of official conclusions. Despite these shortcomings, the judicial records remain the richest source of information on social behavior and the organization of daily life. Studies of deviance have proven especially important to social historians, contributing enormously to our understanding of popular mentalities at a time of mass illiteracy.

Other valuable sources of information are the Inspectors' Department (*Inspektorskii Departament*) of the War Ministry and the *Voenno-uchenyi arkhiv* of Main Headquarters. These provide statistical materials on manpower and conscription, as well as inspectors' reports on the general condition of the troops. Service lists (*formuliarnye spiski*) give important data on the careers of noncommissioned officers, a key group for understanding the question of social mobility. The service lists examined to date are inadequate for a purely quantitative analysis. But used in conjunction with other descriptive sources, they can serve as useful indicators of sociological patterns. The personal papers of well-known military figures such as P. D. Kiselev and the Decembrists P. I. Pestel and V. F. Raevskii also provide revealing, often critical evaluations of conditions in the army. Finally, information on resistance to conscription and discussions of official policy are available in the proceedings of the Recruitment Committee attached to the Second Department of His Majesty's Personal Chancery.

The basic legislation affecting the army is found in the *Polnoe sobranie zakonov Rossiiskoi imperii* (first and second series) and the *Svod voennykh postanovlenii* (1838) with subsequent supplementary volumes. Another important legislative source, *Prikazy voennogo ministra*, contains orders issued by the war minister beginning in 1809. Memoirs and regimental histories also provide interesting materials for purposes of illustration, though the data they contain on the common soldier is quite limited. There are several nineteenth-century military journals that offer useful information on social conditions in the pre-reform army; *Voenno-meditsinskii zhurnal*, for example, provides data on illness and mortality. Once discussions of reform began after the Crimean War, *Voennyi sbornik* published numerous articles on education and training, the possibilities for promotion, and economic conditions.

Sources on the social history of the lower ranks in the first half of the nineteenth century present a frustrating problem. For the latter part of Alexander I's reign, the papers of P. D. Kiselev figure heavily, reflecting the sporadic, regional character of the sources. As enlightened servitor, Kiselev articulated basic problems about conditions in the army, but reliance on his views inevitably introduces a bias in the sources. In general there is both a quantitative and qualitative improvement in the sources beginning with the reign of Nicholas I, which leads to a certain imbalance in the source base. There is little one can do about the lack of symmetry, but since the social system did not change fundamentally in this period, the imbalance seems less disturbing. Moreover, since the purpose of this study is to describe the daily life of the common soldier under normal peacetime circumstances, to discover the most typical and ordinary features of social life in the pre-reform army, it is perhaps appropriate that the sources are weighted toward the reign of Nicholas I, a time of relative peace compared with the period of the Napoleonic Wars that lasted from the late 1790s until 1815. Also because of the emphasis on routine conditions, this book does not directly examine periods of war or the Decembrist movement (and on the whole avoids the very minor problem of rebellion in the army). Because of changes in regulations, procedures, and the actual conditions of daily life, warfare requires separate study.

The main difficulty for a systematic study of the pre-reform army is the absence of a closed comprehensive body of sources. Regimental records are scattered and fragmentary, and the sources for some militarily significant regions like the Caucasus are inaccessible. The records for the military colonies, garrisons, and Guards regiments are better, but these troops

INTRODUCTION

are exceptional by nature and could not provide the basis for a study of the regular standing army. There are to date no complete service lists for the lower ranks of any army regiment. Isolated lists appear, but nothing comprehensive. Given the general inadequacy of statistical sources for pre-reform Russian history, this situation is not surprising. Aside from tallying the number of men, horses, and guns and the quantity of money, supplies, and equipment, the central bureaucracy showed little concern for the concrete conditions of daily life. Detailed accounts of local conditions tended to result from extraordianry circumstances—flagrant abuses by officers or disobedience by soldiers—that prompted special investigations. It was possible to overcome these limitations by relying on a wide variety of quantitative and descriptive sources that are not necessarily continuous in time and place. Because of the volume and breadth of these sources, a relatively comprehensive (albeit exploratory) picture of the life of the common soldier has emerged.

This study tries to pay particular attention to the attitudes and behavior of the lower ranks in an effort to examine the social history of the army "from below." The results have been mixed. One can analyze military society in terms of the soldiers' daily experiences and present the many aspects of military life as they impacted on the lower ranks. Still, the soldiers themselves have not spoken; one observes only indirectly their behavior and responses to specific circumstances. The top-heaviness of the autocratic state system has inevitably made itself felt. Official documents present the government's point of view, so that the social history of the army in many ways emerges as a history of state policy toward the lower ranks. To the extent that soldiers speak at all, they must do so through a framework defined by the state.[6] This is due partly to the conscious social goals of the imperial government, partly to the illiteracy of the general population, and partly to the nature and availability of the archival sources. This study thus represents an initial excursion into previously uncharted territory. Only further and more comprehensive research in the archival holdings can correct biases in the sources.

From Serf to Russian Soldier

CHAPTER ONE

Conscription

One son is not a son.
Two sons are half a son.
Three sons are a son.[1]

Of all the obligations imposed on the poll-tax population, none was more terrible or feared than military service. Nowhere was coercion in the relationship between the state and society more visible. For the Russian empire, the years from 1796 to 1815 were a time of almost continual warfare. The Napoleonic Wars were the most devastating, but Russia also became embroiled in conflicts with her traditional enemies: Sweden, Turkey, and Persia. From the Congress of Vienna until the Crimean War, Russia enjoyed relative peace and did not participate in any major European conflict. Despite the publicity it has attracted, the Hungarian campaign of 1849 was largely symbolic. There were full-scale wars with Persia (1826–28) and Turkey (1828–29). Closer to home were the Polish rebellion of 1830 and the continual fighting in the Caucasus. These engagements did not even approach the scope or importance of the Napoleonic Wars, but Russia still needed a large standing army to secure the empire's extensive landlocked borders and to support imperial expansion into Europe, the Caucasus, Siberia, and Central Asia. Patterns of recruitment in the first half of the nineteenth century reflected the steady increase in the size of Russia's armed forces. Between 1796 and 1815, eighteen levies produced 1,616,199 recruits. From 1816 until 1855, forty levies provided 3,158,199 recruits.[2] In its role as the great land power of Europe, the Russian state effectively mobilized society's resources for military purposes, maintaining one of Europe's largest armies.[3]

CHAPTER ONE

Popular Attitudes toward Conscription

> As I drove into this village [Grodnya], my ears were assailed not by the melody of verse, but by a heart-rending lament of women, children, and old men. Getting out of my carriage, I sent it on to the post station, for I was curious to learn the cause of the disturbance I had noticed in the street.
>
> Going up to a group of people, I learned that a levy of recruits was the cause of the sobs and tears of the people crowded together there. From many villages, both crown and manorial, those who were to be drafted into the army had come together here.[4]

Unlike young nobles destined for service as officers, the typical recruit from the poll-tax population entered the army, not with the anxious anticipation of glory and adventure, but rather with a feeling of profound sorrow and dread. Conscription meant a sudden and final break from home and family with little chance of return. Depriving peasant society of able-bodied men, it could bring economic ruin to individual families. In 1825 M. M. Speransky noted that conscription was burdensome not just for the individual household, but for the country as a whole. In his view, every family ruined by conscription increased the number of orphans, promoted impoverishment, and harmed agriculture and industry.[5] No wonder village youths regarded recruitment as a horror comparable to death. In an 1811 memorandum submitted to Alexander I, the noted admiral N. S. Mordvinov reported that upon learning of a levy "any young man will try to hide; [and] for this reason his relatives place him under guard, shackle him in irons, [and] treat him like a villain."[6] An 1829 judicial decision also revealed the popular view of conscription as a familial tragedy. In 1828 Lieutenant Larionov accompanied a party of recruits from Penza province. During that time he granted brief leaves to eighteen recruits, who in return gave him money and gifts. At his trial Larionov admitted that

> Although he knew it was strictly forbidden to grant recruits leaves to go home, their own and their relatives' earnest entreaties forced him to release a few for a short time—however, not out of cupidity, but solely out of a feeling of compassion for their tearful petitions. And who would not have done so, seeing before him petitioners wallowing in tears, evoking the name of God to allow them to bid farewell to wives, children, and relatives and to receive from them the assistance expected for the coming journey?[7]

Whatever Larionov's real motives, the sense of personal loss suffered by the recruits and their families is clear.

Not surprisingly, outright resistance to conscription was a persistent problem. Whether one examines administrative corruption or trickery by clever peasants, all reveal society's desire to escape military service. Throughout the first half of the nineteenth century, officials complained about popular flight in response to the call for levies. A Senate ukase of 1798 attributed flight among recruits to the insufficient manpower available to guard them. Consequently, the Senate empowered governors to have the communities responsible for delivering the recruits supervise them until the military escort arrived.[8] Even during Napoleon's invasion of 1812, flight from conscription continued. A prerevolutionary study of Riazan province suggests significant resistance to conscription, despite the threat to Russia's national existence.[9] While there is evidence of popular loyalty to the tsar in this period, one cannot equate such loyalty with patriotism. For pre-reform society, military service was an obligation imposed upon the servile population by the state, and it reflected the coercive nature of service in the Petrine system.

Legislation from the reign of Nicholas I showed that flight from conscription remained a problem. In 1828 the State Council ruled that local authorities should send state peasants who hid to avoid service to recruiting stations, as soon as they reappeared or were caught. These men would then count toward their community's next quota of recruits. Even if such a man had passed the maximum legal age, he was still subject to service.[10] Broadening this provision, an 1831 statute ruled that temporary exemptions from physical requirements, sometimes introduced to increase the number of recruits, also applied to runaways who were later found and handed over to the army.[11] A law of 1845 penalized families and communities that concealed recruits, requiring them to provide two recruits instead of one. If no suitable man could be found, the head of the household was to be flogged or fined and resettled in Siberia.[12] Despite efforts to make the family responsible for runaway recruits, flight from levies persisted, reflecting popular opposition to conscription.

Discussions in the War Council revealed just how seriously the government regarded the problem of flight. Concerned about the time it took to conduct a levy and deliver new recruits to their assigned regiments (about one year), in 1832 Nicholas I proposed a levy of reserve recruits. The proposal divided levies into two periods: in the first, recruits would return home to their usual occupations, so that in the second, when additional manpower was needed, authorities could quickly outfit them and send them to the army. But the War Council was so fearful of an increase in flight and self-mutilation, if recruits were permitted to return home for an unspecified time, it decided that the proposal would only further aggravate existing problems. According to the Council, large numbers of men vanished at the earliest rumors of a levy, forcing landlords and village communities to keep recruits under close guard until their delivery to the military.[13]

Popular hostility toward conscription remained a major problem, but it is wrong to assume that the majority of eligible men fled at the prospect of military service. Most people accepted conscription obediently, if only because they had little opportunity to escape. It was in the interest of landlords and local communities to enforce the obligation; otherwise they had to deliver replacements or bear the cost of finding the runaway. In border regions where it was easier to flee abroad and where ethnic peculiarities made enforcement more complicated, the danger of flight was greater.[14] Consequently, some border areas enjoyed special exemption from conscription.[15] While Russia's military might provided positive proof of the absolutist state's ability to impose service upon society, officials identified popular flight as a basic reason for the inefficiencies and shortcomings of the recruitment system, attributing this flight to the long term of service and the harshness of military life.

Faced with the prospect of permanent separation from home and family, many potential recruits resorted to self-mutilation to avoid military service.[16] There are no precise data on this problem, but legislation and discussions held in the Recruitment Committee revealed its seriousness. Catherine the Great's General Statute on Recruitment (1766) specified that persons guilty of self-mutilation be "mercilessly" punished.[17] Subsequent laws continued this policy.[18] In the reign of Alexander I, concern developed about punishing the innocent. As a result, sentences were lightened and the rules on verification tightened.[19] The repeated appearance of new legislation suggests that self-mutilation persisted throughout the pre-reform era.

The popular imagination showed great ingenuity in developing methods of mutilation. As early as 1809 officials in Simbirsk province reported that in families with five or more laborers, underaged males and those eligible for service all suffered from injuries "which cannot be attributed to the natural effects of illness, but are absolutely premeditated."[20] In 1813 the governor of Pskov province informed St. Petersburg that economic peasants in that province had mangy heads. Artificially transmitting this disease from generation to generation, they freed themselves from conscription.[21] Fifteen years later the local medical board conducted an investigation and discovered that ten times fewer women suffered from mange than men and that men over thirty-five almost all had clean heads. Moreover, families with one or two laborers and serfs on neighboring estates rarely contracted the disease. The Ministry of Interior concluded that the only way to eliminate the disease (which could be cured in two or three months anyway) and, more important, to eliminate such deliberate evasion, was to accept recruits with mange. This proposal became law in 1828. The government could fight this stubborn resistance to conscription only by lowering physical standards.[22]

The recruitment regulation of 1831 systematized the legislation combating mutilation.[23] If a potential recruit injured himself, he was supposed to report his injury within three days and, if possible, present witnesses. If he did not report the injury, and twelve members of his community testified under oath that he intended to escape conscription, the police were to conduct an investigation.[24] In cases involving private serfs, the landlord had only to report the crime. The law also specified the punishment for self-mutilation: twenty-five to fifty blows with lashes and assignment to service. Men unfit for service faced exile in a convicts' company or settlement in Siberia. To encourage enforcement, offenders who would have been fit for service counted toward the quota of recruits demanded from the landlord or local community.[25] Providing a more systematic definition of the rules on self-mutilation, the recruitment regulation introduced stricter standards of verification.

Punitive measures still had scant effect, and self-mutilation continued. In 1836 a gendarme officer who observed two levies in Riazan province reported that recruits consciously mutilated their limbs to avoid service.[26] Officials at the recruiting station also repeatedly found substances such as beeswax, lard, seeds, flies, and even arsenic in the ears of recruits. These objects produced a discharge indicating infection, which was sufficient grounds for rejecting a recruit. Similarly, high-level officials supervising the levy of 1843 noted the use of self-inflicted wounds to avoid service and claimed that among the recruits rejected for aural discharge, many had marks on their cheeks caused by pouring sharp vodka into their ears.[27] This particular method of evasion was impossible to prevent and extremely difficult to prove. Other artificially induced physical disabilities reported in the early 1850s included prolopsus of the intestine, sores, and swelling of the face, neck, chest, and scrotum.[28] This obvious willingness to inflict bodily harm in order to avoid military service revealed a high degree of popular despair in the face of service obligations.

The numerous legal enactments and continued evidence of self-mutilation show that the government was virtually powerless to control this popular action. National minorities were especially resistant to service demands. The Russian authorities claimed that Tatars, Jews, and other ethnic minorities automatically mutilated their children, so that it became impossible to prove any connection with conscription.[29] The only way to prevent self-mutilation, officials argued, was to accept recruits who suffered from diseases and injuries (whether self-inflicted or not) like mange, deafness in one ear, and damage to the right eye or index finger. In a report of 1847, the minister of state domains argued that "whenever the government has permitted the acceptance of recruits with such diseases and physical defects, the diseases have disappeared in the people."[30] A law of 1828 had permitted the acceptance of recruits with mange.[31] Similarly, legislation from 1849 sought to combat ear wounds and feigned deafness and muteness.[32] Authorities were to accept recruits "who have a simple outflow of purulent matter from the ears, without signs of a general diseased condition which could cause suppuration, as long as there is no localized pain in the parts of the auditory organ." During the Crimean War, when the army's need for manpower became especially acute, official instructions to doctors permitted the acceptance of recruits missing an index finger (without which a soldier could not fire his musket) or suffering from ear diseases that did not produce deafness or interfere with movement.[33] Officials were not happy about accepting these recruits, who, they felt, would lower the moral and physical quality of the troops.[34] In addition, they risked spreading infectious diseases among the already disease-ridden lower ranks.

According to official sources, the incidence of self-mutilation declined in the 1840s.[35] The government attributed this to the lighter punishments for self-inflicted injury and, more important, to the practice of granting communities and landlords receipts for recruits proven guilty of self-mutilation. This practice, instituted in the 1830s, gave local communities an incentive to prosecute and prevent self-mutilation.[36] Less plausible was the explanation offered by the minister of state domains, who claimed that the new lottery system effectively reduced both self-mutilation and flight from conscription.[37] Once a man participated in the lottery, regardless of whether his number was drawn, he was freed from subsequent levies; hence peasants were less likely to maim themselves or their children and unnecessarily deprive the family of a fully able laborer. But the lottery was never applied to the whole empire, and whatever its benefits, it failed to ensure the administrative regularity that was supposed to reduce popular resistance to conscription. In wartime the need for recruits meant that peasants already subjected to the lottery might face recall and even be drafted out of turn. The continued inability to cope with evasion again found expression in 1851, when the Medical Department of the Ministry of Interior declared that the only effective way to combat self-mutilation was to establish the "sanctity of obligations to the fatherland" and "to instil in potential recruits feelings of duty about the high importance of the calling for which they are destined."[38] Such a solution was hardly viable in pre-reform Russia, where the peasant's primary identification lay with the local community and where the fulfillment of service obligations by the poll-tax population depended on coercion and force.

Distributing the Burden of Conscription

The long term of service (twenty or twenty-five years) and the harsh conditions of military life made it very unlikely that a recruit would ever return home. In most cases conscription meant a sudden and final break with one's family and village community. Consequently, peasants were willing to risk permanent bodily injury and maim their children in order to avoid the clutches of the imperial army. High-level official discussions identified the long tour of duty and inequalities in distributing the burden of recruitment as the main reasons for evasion and the popular dread of service. As early as 1811, N. S. Mordvinov advocated reducing the term of service to twelve years and broadening the social base of recruitment. Mordvinov argued that the harshness of military obligations not only prompted flight, but also lowered the moral and fighting qualities of recruits.[39] More significant, in the early 1850s the War Ministry examined the possibility of ending special exemptions from conscription among the poll-tax population. Although the Ministry was concerned more to enlarge the sources of manpower than to guarantee equality, most provincial governors responded negatively to the suggestion, noting that the government should honor traditional rights and privileges. In contrast, the governor of Novgorod curtly proposed that "all classes (*sosloviia*) without differentiation and including the nobility" should fulfill recruitment obligations in kind.[40] This view was rare among high-level officials, who generally accepted exemptions and distinctions based on social origin as natural and just. What disturbed them was inequality of treatment within the poll-tax population itself, especially the inequality that resulted from deliberate evasion. In 1847 the minister of state domains reported that "to avoid conscription, Tatars damage fingers and auditory organs, so that they develop suppuration of the ears, and also [they] feign hernias and spread wounds over [their] bodies, as a result of which the recruitment obligation becomes unequal and arouses indignation among people who do not violate the law."[41] The authorities painfully acknowledged this issue, for they could justify the terrible burden of military service only if it was apportioned equally among the lower classes.

This professed moral dilemma loses some credibility, if one considers the numerous exemptions from military service. Most soldiers came from the poll-tax population of manorial serfs, state peasants, and townspeople (see tables 1.1–1.2).[42] Since the reign of Peter the Great, the obligation

Table 1.1. Age and Social Origin of Recruits[a]

Year and Province	Size of Sample[b]	Average Age	Social Origin (%):[c]			Single Householders	Ethnic Minorities	Foreigners	Vagrants	Other
			Serfs	Peasants[d]	Urban[e]					
1814										
Voronezh	1,186	24	39	18	1	41	(4)			(2)
1827–28										
Iaroslavl	282	24	73	22	5					
Kiev	568	21	80	7	3		11[f]			
Kostroma	354	23	67.5	29	2.5					(3)
Kursk	607	20	48	7	2	42				
Novgorod	269	23	64	33	3					(1)
Pskov	251	22	67	29	3					
Riazan	403	23	69	20	2	9				(1)
St. Petersburg	679	27	76	17.5	5		(1)	(3)		(7)
Saratov	429	23	51.5	34	3	6	4.2	(1)		
Smolensk	395	23	77.5	18	4	(1)				(1)
Tomsk	116	22	(1)	81	18					
Voronezh	551	22	35	11	1	52	(1)			(3)
1835–36										
Smolensk	1,066	23	70	22	4	(4)	(2)		3	(4)

SOURCE: TsGVIA, f. 395, op. 318, d. 6, 10, 21, 22, 25, 28, 29, 30, 33, 37, 43, 45.

[a] These data do not include criminals and other recruits who did not count toward a community's quota.
[b] For 1827–28 the sample is one-quarter of the recruits listed and for 1814 and 1835–36, one-half.
[c] For categories with small numbers, the absolute figures are given in parentheses.
[d] State peasants include all categories of nonseigneurial peasants.
[e] The urban category includes *meshchane, posadskie,* and factory workers.
[f] Includes 5.5 Jews and 6 Polish *szlachta*.

to provide recruits and pay the poll tax signified the inferior status of these groups. Other less important sources of manpower included soldiers' sons, criminals, vagrants, and persons sent to the army for punishment by the landlord or local community.[43] Finally, after 1827 the state also required that Jews supply recruits in kind rather than make a monetary payment. The government explained this policy as a desire to establish social uniformity among the diverse ethnic groups within the empire, so that "the recruitment obligation, for the relief of our subjects, should be equal for all social categories."[44]

Formal exemptions from conscription reflected the highly differentiated social structure. L. G. Beskrovnyi has estimated that in the first half of the nineteenth century, exemptions based on social origin removed up to two million men from the pool of possible recruits. In addition, there were territorial and ethnic exemptions, so that at midcentury five to six million individuals were either altogether free from service or allowed to make a monetary payment.[45] Nobles, merchants, and clergy were exempt from service on a social basis.[46] Peter the Great had forced the nobility to serve, but in 1762 they were emancipated from this obligation. Merchants, small in number and distinguished by their economic importance,

Table 1.2. Recruits Sent to the Azov Infantry Regiment in 1795 and 1811

Year	1795	1811
Size of sample	198	547
Average Age	23	22
Married (%)	50	56
Fathers (%)[a]	22	35
Literate[b]	3	9
Trained in a craft[b]	0	1
Social origin (%):		
Serfs	74	37
State peasants	24	53
Townsmen	2	1.6
Minorities[c]		8
Others		.4

SOURCE: TsGVIA, f. 489, op. 1, d. 15 and 17.

[a] Recruits who left pregnant wives are counted as fathers.

[b] Recruits who were both literate and trained in a craft are counted in both categories.

[c] Includes Votiaks, Tatars, and Cheremis.

were also exempt, though until 1807 they made monetary payments.[47] Only a very small segment of the population avoided conscription on the basis of social origin, but like the poll tax, recruitment obligations clearly separated privileged Russia from the masses.

Within the poll-tax population, exemption from active service was possible on grounds of physical disability, public office, and legally specified economic or demographic conditions. The recruitment regulation of 1831 continued earlier provisions that exempted families with only one male laborer between the ages of eighteen and sixty-five or with two laborers consisting of a father and son. In addition, state peasants who served nine years in public office were also freed from conscription.[48] Some groups paid a monetary sum, rather than supplying recruits in kind. These included possessionary factories and recruiting districts of peasants and townspeople with no more than twenty souls.[49] As an 1853 report of the Inspectors' Department noted, serfs whose master owned no more than twenty souls in a single province fulfilled recruitment obligations with a monetary payment, because of the difficulty in finding physically suitable recruits on small estates.[50] The last thing the government wanted was for conscription to bring economic ruin to families and villages; for how then would they pay taxes? In allowing these exemptions, the state pragmatically responded to economic and demographic realities and to the actual capacity of some groups to provide recruits.

The 1831 recruitment regulation also granted some exemptions that allowed members of the poll-tax population to perform various public services and to establish themselves after resettlement or changes in juridical status.[51] In addition, there were numerous ethnic and geographic exemptions that often had an economic basis. Beginning in 1797, members of artisan guilds in the Baltics and Finland owed a monetary obligation.[52] In 1816 some peasants in Estland province gained exemption on the basis of wealth and productivity.[53] Descendants of the original citizens of Kiev were exempt on the basis of traditional privileges granted by Tsar Aleksei Mikhailovich.[54] Other geographic exemptions aimed to combat desertion and underpopulation. This was especially evident in borderlands containing non-Russian populations; to prevent desertion, an ukase of 1801 prescribed that communities located within 100 versts of the border from the Black Sea to the Baltic pay a monetary sum for each recruit.[55] That same year Kurland province was also freed from conscription in kind.[56] Then in 1811 the government exempted Georgia from service obligations, and beginning in 1815, Bessarabia.[57] There is some question as to whether landlords and local communities could avail themselves of the opportunity to make a monetary payment instead of providing a recruit. In an

1802 report the governor of Lithuania claimed that landlords preferred to supply a recruit rather than pay 360 rubles.[58]

Underpopulation also brought exemption from recruitment. Always striving to colonize the Siberian provinces, in 1812 the government ordered residents to make a monetary payment.[59] Similarly, in Arkhangel'sk province, where the fishing industry kept some inhabitants away from home for long periods, an ukase of 1820 required a monetary payment.[60] Laws of 1820–21 also granted this right to private estates in areas where military colonies existed.[61] Then in 1825 the government granted landlords in the Caucasus region the right to make a monetary payment.[62] The ostensible reason was the small size of the serf population, but subsequent legislation suggests that the desire to prevent flight abroad was also a consideration.[63] Whether to combat flight or preserve communities in underpopulated areas, official policy often reflected pragmatic considerations.

The recruitment regulation of 1831 confirmed and systematized the numerous ethnic and geographic exemptions.[64] Some groups paid a monetary sum for each recruit owed: residents of Arkhangel'sk province and of areas within 100 versts of the Austrian and Prussian borders and manorial serfs in the Caucausus and parts of Tauride province. Others were entirely freed from conscription obligations: inhabitants of Siberia and Muslims or pagans who converted to Orthodoxy. The law also identified a number of poll-tax groups that were exempt or fulfilled a monetary obligation on the basis of special statutes issued in the previous two centuries.[65] Although the legislation failed to mention Georgia and Bessarabia, subsequent recruitment manifestos indicate that they remained exempt.[66] The numerous exemptions from military service reflected the ethnic and social diversity of the empire—conditions making it extremely difficult to forge national unity or to impose a uniform administrative order throughout the country. More important, exemptions undermined the moral justification for conscription, which was necessary to thwart evasion and assure good morale among the troops.

During the first half of the nineteenth century, especially in the reign of Nicholas I, as the size of the bureaucracy and the functions of government expanded, exemptions based on education became increasingly important. The government actively promoted the development of semiprofessional groups in response to its increasingly complex administrative and military needs. These exemptions fully revealed the value placed on men with specialized training and skills. Thus the Kiselev reform of state peasants freed some semiprofessional elements from military service.[67] Other state peasants with special skills were allowed to make a monetary payment.[68] The extension of exemptions based on education to the lowly state peasants vividly reflected the growing importance of education in determining social status.

Even the more troublesome ethnic minorities enjoyed economic and educational exemptions. Exemptions granted to Jews encouraged Russification through education and the pursuit of farming.[69] Following the Polish rebellion of 1831, the Russian government limited exemptions by reducing the number of petty landowners (*szlachta*) enjoying noble rights. All szlachta who had not proven their nobility paid taxes to support the troops and provided recruits, though their term of service was only fifteen years. Some urban residents made a monetary payment: a privileged stratum of townspeople and professionals such as doctors, teachers, artists, and lawyers.[70] Although the Russian government clearly lowered the status of the Polish szlachta, it once again recognized the value of professional skills.

Finally, extraordinary circumstances stemming from war, crop failures, or epidemics also justified exemption from recruitment, though such relief was temporary and the areas affected usually had to provide additional recruits during subsequent levies.[71] Cholera caused the postponement of levies in 1830, 1831, and 1847.[72] Crop failure led to temporary exemption for numerous provinces in 1833, 1840, 1845, and 1849.[73] During subsequent levies, the government collected the recruits owed by these provinces, so that the amelioration offered was only temporary.[74] Such exemptions represented an interruption in the process of conscription, not a lightening of obligations.

War also caused disruptions in recruitment precisely at a time when additional manpower was desperately needed. During a levy in August 1812, the government exempted provinces declared to be on a war footing. Estland and Pskov provinces also did not supply recruits because of "various heavy obligations" (presumably the supply of provisions and transport) they were fulfilling in connection with the war.[75] In addition, noble estates that organized militia units escaped conscription.[76] Finally, in January 1813 provinces that had suffered major devastation at the hands of Napoleon's army were freed from conscription for one year.[77] But then in July 1813, in the name of "equity" and uniformity in the treatment of society (which was often only a pretext to extract the last recruit or kopeck out of the Russian people), the government began a series of "equalizing" levies from provinces that enjoyed exemptions during 1812. The scope of the levies varied, depending on the number of recruits that a particular province supplied during 1812.[78] As in cases of epidemic or crop failure, exemptions during wartime constituted a temporary concession to deal with a crisis situation. Once the crisis subsided, the government moved to demand additional recruits.

Sometimes the government completely exempted provinces close to a theater of war. During the Turkish war of 1828–29, six provinces avoided conscription altogether, because they supplied the army with provisions and transport.[79] More often than not, however, exemptions due to war were only temporary.[80] The Crimean War also brought exemptions from service. A general levy declared in October 1855 excluded five provinces and also Jews in Bessarabia.[81] In November the townspeople of Grodno were allowed to make a monetary payment in the eleventh partial levy, for the city recently had suffered a loss of population, and according to local authorities, there was not a physically suitable candidate available.[82] Precisely when the government most needed extra recruits, it was forced to exempt some areas from service—a graphic demonstration of the delicate balance between local socioeconomic stability and the manpower requirements of the armed forces. War brought immediate disruptions to the system of conscription.

The physical requirements for military service also had implications for "equalizing" the burden of service. The authorities viewed conscription in terms of manpower and resources: what percentage of the population was eligible for service and how many of these were suitable? How, indeed, should one define "suitable"? The large number of men pronounced unfit for military service was astounding. In 1850 the Inspectors' Department reported that of 20,712,756 males subject to personal conscription, only 6,900,000 were in fact suitable for military service.[83] Health requirements were particularly difficult to define. Men weakened by chronic disease could hardly survive the rigors of military life, nor did it make sense to draft men with infectious illnesses that would spread among the troops. Similarly, the army had little use for soldiers with missing limbs and other severe physical disabilities. Height requirements, significant enough, were highly arbitrary and partly subject to change. While the authorities considered height a general criterion of good health, it was also clear from official discussions that height requirements created inequities in the system of conscription.

The 1766 recruitment statute established a height norm of 5 feet, 3 inches, and an age norm of seventeen to thirty-five.[84] Showing the strains of the Napoleonic Wars, between 1805 and 1815 height norms were reduced four times (1805, 1806, 1811, 1812) and raised twice (1808 and 1815). Age norms were lowered in 1811 and 1812, and while the minimum age was raised to nineteen in 1813, the maximum age was extended to forty.[85] Physical requirements reached a nadir in 1812: the minimum height was fixed at 4 feet, 11½ inches, the minimum age at twelve.[86] It was not until September 1815 that the government restored the statutory height requirement of 5 feet, 3 inches, and set an age norm of nineteen to thirty-five.⁸⁷ These requirements survived until August 1827, when war once again led to lower standards in new legislation in 1827–29—a minimum height of 5 feet, 1 inches, and a minimum age of eighteen (see tables 1.1–1.2).⁸⁸ In 1831 the government reduced the minimum height to 4 feet, 11½ inches, but raised the minimum age to twenty.⁸⁹ Reacting to shortages of manpower in extraordinary circumstances, laws governing levies in 1831–32 even permitted officials to accept recruits who were missing two front teeth or part of the left index finger or were blind in one eye.⁹⁰ Only in 1836 did the government return to peacetime norms.⁹¹ These repeated adjustments in physical standards suggest that the resources of the poll-tax population were often insufficient to meet the wartime needs of the state. Russia succeeded in fielding large armies, but only at the cost of lowering physical standards.

A law of 1854 systematized the ad hoc adjustments traditionally made to ensure adequate manpower during war.⁹² The new law defined three types of levies: normal, auxiliary, and extraordinary. In normal levies (fewer than seven recruits per thousand souls in a two-year period), recruits twenty-two and older were supposed to measure 5 feet, 2½ inches, and those under twenty-two, 5 feet, 2⅛ inches.⁹³ In auxiliary levies (seven to ten recruits per thousand souls in a two-year period) persons of all ages with a height of 5 feet, 2⅛ inches, were acceptable. Among state peasants, who were drafted in a lottery system, officials could recall men who participated in the previous lottery, if the number of suitable candidates in the current lottery did not suffice. Finally, in extraordinary levies (over ten recruits per thousand souls in a two-year period), the law set a minimum height of only 5 feet, 1¼ inches, for all age groups. Throughout the Crimean War the authorities subjected men as old as thirty-five to the lottery.⁹⁴ In May 1854 the rules on extraordinary levies went into effect, meaning a height requirement of 5 feet, 1¼ inches. In addition, officials could accept persons aged thirty-six and thirty-seven from peasant and urban communities not employing the lottery system.⁹⁵ Whether the government used the line or the lottery system, it found that manpower needs in wartime demanded lower physical standards, a practice regarded as harmful to the condition of the army.

It was not just in wartime that height requirements caused problems for officials. In 1841 the Recruitment Committee concluded that the required height of 5 feet, 3 inches, was "one of the main reasons for inequality in the fulfillment of recruitment obligations."⁹⁶ In 1842 the minister of state domains reiterated this view, noting that height requirements freed many families from service, violated the egalitarian goals of the conscription system, and prevented the application of regularized procedures and rules during levies.⁹⁷ As a result, small families of only two laborers often bore the burden of conscription, while large families with perfectly healthy members did not serve for decades, simply because they did not meet height standards.[98] The consequences were sometimes disastrous: for a small family or one with young children, the loss of even one laborer could spell economic ruin.[99] Sensitive to the harshness of service obligations, the minister of state domains explained that the only consolation for the people came with awareness of a "just and equitable distribution" of the service burden, which was supposed to be inescapable for every family.[100] But because of the failure of the law to apportion military burdens equally, it could no longer "instil in the people a moral belief in the justice of the obligation imposed upon them."[101] Consequently, evasion had increased to such a degree that all measures against it were ineffectual. In its effort to maximize manpower by imposing uniform obligations, the unequal distribution of the burden caused the government considerable discomfort. It regarded this inequality as a disruptive factor that interfered with conscription, harmed the national economy, and promoted evasion.

The discussions on height requirements revealed the difficulty of imposing bureaucratic uniformity upon highly diverse social elements. Information examined by the Recruitment Committee in 1841 indicated that the difficulties were increasing.[102] Officials were most concerned that in provinces where Great Russians lived among ethnic minorities, the burden of conscription sometimes fell exclusively on Russian families.[103] Local authorities in Kazan, Viatka, and Perm provinces reported that otherwise healthy men from the Chuvash, Cheremis, Tatar, Votiak, and Zyrian peoples avoided military service because of insufficient height.[104] Similar difficulties were reported among Ukrainian cossacks.[105] Already by 1841 the government had lowered height standards to 5 feet, 3/8 inch, for several districts in Arkhangel'sk and Vologda provinces.[106] Similarly, the law permitted Cheremis in one district of Perm province to deliver recruits as short as 4 feet, 11½ inches, for appointment as craftsmen in mining enterprises.[107]

After 1839 in areas where the government introduced the lottery system, difficulties arose because men aged twenty and twenty-one were not always full grown. Thus authorities rejected potential recruits who might still grow to the required height.[108] This problem was solved in 1844 by lowering height requirements to 5 feet, 2⅛ inches, for recruits no older than twenty-one. The law also applied to Votiaks, Cheremis, Chuvash, and Zyrians no matter what their age.[109] It was virtually impossible for the autocracy to impose a uniform system of rules upon the ethnically, socially, and geographically diverse regions of the vast Russian empire. Despite constant concern for the quality of recruits, a reduction in height requirements was the only way the government could satisfy its desire for uniformity in the treatment of servile society.

Height requirements reflected the full complexity of conscription in pre-reform Russia, highlighting both its moral and practical aspects. Forced upon society by the state, conscription could only be justified, according to high-level military officials, if all segments of the poll-tax population bore the burden equally. Although the state did not hesitate to grant exemptions from service on social or economic grounds, there was some practical and moral rationale for these privileges. Merchants fulfilled a necessary economic function that benefited the entire national economy, the clergy looked after the spiritual needs of the people, and the nobility tended to serve anyway. In addition, the number of men receiving these privileges was probably small compared to the number who avoided service because of height. In 1843 the Recruitment Committee calculated that for every 100,000 recruits delivered, 34,000 would be rejected on grounds of height.[110] This situation made it difficult to mobilize adequate manpower for the army and also threatened the security of individual families by giving unfair advantages to those who happened to be smaller in stature. Still, concern for the physical quality of recruits prevented the government from changing the statutory norm for height. Instead, it made adjustments only for specific ethnic groups or in wartime circumstances, thereby undermining its own desire for administrative regularity.

Popular evasion was another important factor preventing the equal distribution of service obligations. The extreme act of self-mutilation was one method effectively employed. The notorious corruption of Russia's local officials also intensified inequalities by increasing the possibilities for evasion. Bribery was an endemic feature of imperial administration, and its role in conscription is no surprise. In June 1855 one noncommissioned officer was found guilty of accepting bribes from the relatives of eighteen soldiers' sons who hoped to postpone or altogether avoid military service.[111] There were other less extreme ways for the poll-tax population to avoid conscription. In 1807 the Senate forced indebted townspeople to serve, after discovering that they declared themselves in debt only to evade service.[112] Townspeople also joined with relatives to form a common capital that allowed them to register as merchants. They avoided conscription and paid lower taxes, while continuing to work and live separately. To fight these practices, an ukase of 1809 permitted only parents and children to register together. Moreover, a townsman could enroll in a guild only if the community freed him from his service obligation.[113] Another popular form of evasion was division of a large household into smaller units.[114] These inventive methods of evasion show how the people took advantage of every possible loophole to avoid military service.

There is significant evidence that the rich consistently escaped service, while the poor usually were drafted. The rich could bribe an official, hire a substitute, or make a monetary payment directly to the state.[115] According to state peasants in Viatka province, in 1807 rich settlers bribed officials to release them from the militia. As a result, only the poor were sent to the army.[116] Similar incidents occurred during the Crimean War. Religious schismatics delivered to Riga during a levy in 1855 reported that their prosperous neighbors paid off the local police in order to escape military service, so that "this obligation falls only upon the poor."[117]

The practice of hiring substitutes no doubt benefited the wealthier elements of peasant society.[118] In Arkhangel'sk province state peasants who hired substitutes had to pay their taxes until the next census.[119] The hiring peasant not only made a significant payment to the substitute, but in some cases also clothed and supported him until his acceptance by the military authorities.[120] Whether a peasant paid the 300 silver rubles allowed in Arkhangel'sk province in place of a recruit or hired a substitute, he usually went into debt to obtain the necessary funds. The most common way to repay this debt was to work for his creditor. This led to indentured servitude, as the debtor sold control over his labor and person.[121] Hiring substitutes was widespread in Arkhangel'sk province, and local officials believed that the contracts concluded for this purpose were a major cause of impoverishment.[122] The implications of conscription for economic and social development were significant. But given the evidence currently available, it is impossible to know whether these private agreements were characteristic of all Russia.

Better documented is the widespread trade in recruits handled by professional middlemen. Many of these traders used illegal means to obtain substitutes. Some bought the freedom of serfs and then sold them as substitutes for exorbitant prices.[123] One peasant trader from Iaroslavl province bought serfs for 1,200–1,500 paper rubles and then sold them as substitutes for 3,000 rubles.[124] The serfs apparently did not know they were free, but believed that their landlord had sold them as recruits.[125] An 1849 memorandum of the Inspectors' Department revealed other pernicious abuses associated with hiring substitutes. Single householders (*odnodvortsy*) and urban residents (*grazhdane*) in the western provinces were permitted to sell themselves to Russian townspeople and state peasants as substitutes. There was a flourishing trade in recruits in Kovno province where ninety-eight substitutes were hired over nine months. It turned out, however, that the majority of these so-called *odnodvortsy* were runaway serfs or deserters from the army.[126]

In an effort to stem abuses and control the moral quality of substitutes, the government of Nicholas I tried to replace the private trade with a state system. For every volunteer entering the army, the government sold a receipt that could be presented in place of a recruit.[127] Since there were never enough volunteers, most substitutes continued to come from the private trade. Reportedly, these substitutes were more prone to crime and desertion than other soldiers.[128] In 1848 the government attacked the problem by outlawing middlemen.[129] But officials immediately questioned the value of this measure. In 1850 Moscow's military governor general argued that because conscription was such a tremendous burden for the people, middlemen were a necessary evil.[130] They provided the only amelioration of this hardship, the only chance for a peasant to prevent the loss of a family member. Without the help of middlemen, peasants would not be able to find substitutes and would become vulnerable to deception. Moreover, since the government had forbidden middlemen, their numbers had actually increased in Moscow.[131]

Overall, the evidence suggests that the government failed to eliminate abuses associated with the private trade in recruits. As long as the popular dread of service remained, the middlemen would conduct an active business. There is no question that any peasant with adequate means sought to avoid conscription. Although a richer peasant could hire a substitute more easily, his poorer neighbor achieved the same result by going into debt. Economic inequalities, administrative corruption, and the prevailing popular attitude toward service combined to make an equitable distribution of the burden impossible. In the diverse conditions of the Russian empire, the application of uniform rules and procedures always proved elusive. Ethnic and social pluralism impeded bureaucratic regularity and reinforced personal charismatic rule, consistently undermining the autocracy's ability to govern and reform.

The Process of Conscription

Conscription began in the peasant village or urban community with significant variations that depended on the condition of the population, the honesty of local officials, and, on private estates, on the landlord. In the pre-reform era the line system (*ocherednaia sistema*) served as the basic mechanism for conducting a levy. It relied upon a rotational order of families defined by the number and ages of male laborers and dependents in the household.[132] Not codified until 1831, the line system incorporated peasant practices dating back to the early eighteenth century.[133] In a statute of 1805 (applied in Petersburg, Moscow, Novgorod, and Tver provinces), the government began to regulate more closely the selection of recruits in urban communities and state and crown villages.[134] Conscription was based upon districts of five hundred male souls, and communities belonging to different domains did not mix.[135] Hence state peasants, manorial serfs, crown peasants, and townspeople comprised separate districts. Each district formed a rotational order of families determined by the size of the household and the number and ages of able male laborers. The largest families stood first in line to provide recruits, while families with only one laborer were exempt. The law thus took account of the family's general economic potential. In this way the government hoped to avoid ruining individual households.

The recruitment regulation of 1831 codified the line system more precisely.[136] To determine the number of laborers in a family, the law counted men between the ages of eighteen and sixty, although recruits were supposed to be no younger than twenty and no older than thirty-five.[137] When two families were the same size, the one with more laborers provided a recruit; and if two families had an equal number of laborers, the one with a larger number of older laborers sent a member. Finally, if the families were equal in all respects, they drew lots to decide who would supply the recruit. By contrast, families composed of one laborer or of a father and only son were exempt from conscription altogether. The law preferred bachelors to married men, and among bachelors, the older over the younger. If all the suitable laborers in a family were married, then those without children were supposed to serve. If all had children, the decision was made by the parents, voluntary agreement, or the drawing of lots. Subsequent rules issued in 1837 and 1850 preserved these basic guidelines for selecting recruits with some minor changes in formulation. The most important changes involved a precise definition of disabled men who were not counted as laborers.[138] Clearly, the law incorporated egalitarian principles of communal justice and aimed to minimize disruptions to social and economic life.

The legislation suggests that the main purpose of the line system was to preserve the economic viability of the individual households comprising the commune. Actual peasant practice, however, varied significantly.[139] Consistent with legislative norms, many communes and landlords demanded that large families provide recruits.[140] Others preferred to rid the community of economically weak peasants who were landless or had fallen behind in paying dues.[141] According to V. A. Aleksandrov, as the purchase of substitutes and exemption receipts became increasingly widespread in the early nineteenth century, poor and middle peasants who could not afford these options tended to land in the army, while rich peasants managed to escape service.[142] In general, before even employing the line order, the commune would draft criminals, drunkards, and the lazy.[143] In 1823 Baron Korf reported that before they applied the rotational order, urban communities first drafted vagrants who lacked a home and trade and then disorderly men guilty of repeated drunkenness, theft, and brawling.[144] Conscription thus offered the local community an effective means for purging undesirable elements.

Despite the egalitarian beauty of the line system, it failed to guarantee fairness or the economic viability of individual households. For any family, conscription could spell economic ruin. When a family's last laborer was drafted, the commune's support for dependents left behind was often inadequate.[145] Even where it was possible to apply the legislative norms in full, they did not necessarily guarantee the intended protection. An 1839 report from the western provinces noted that in families with an equal number of laborers between the ages of eighteen and sixty, the one whose members were older stood first in line. Consequently, families with two older men and only one member suitable for the army could lose their only young and healthy worker. Left with two old workers, these families were quickly ruined.[146] The corruption of local officials and the division of families created problems with the rotational lists based upon parish records. Deliberate or inadvertent errors in these records allowed manipulation and caused misunderstandings about the order of selection.[147] Since house serfs were exempt from the rotational order, landlords could change that order just before a levy by assigning a physically suitable peasant to domestic work.[148] Clearly, the line system did not function according to the letter of the law. Legislative norms and actual practices shared an egalitarian bent; but administrative corruption, the difficulty of finding physically fit men, and the desire of local communities and landlords to rid themselves of unwanted elements prevented the efficient and just distribution of the service burden.

Abuses and inequalities in distributing the burden characterized conscription throughout the reign of Nicholas I. Beginning in the 1830s reform of conscription became a constant concern. The Ministry of State Domains took the lead in 1838, when it began to introduce the lottery system (*zhereb'evaia sistema*) as part of a general administrative reform among the state peasants.[149] The new system retained many features of the old, especially the rules on exemptions. At the time of a levy, authorities called to the lottery all men aged twenty and twenty-one, dividing them into three groups determined by the number of laborers in their families. Men from the first group were drafted first and on down the line. If the number of suitable recruits from this age group was insufficient to meet quotas, authorities included men as old as twenty-five. By 1852 the new system applied to state peasants in all the provinces of European

Russia. The reform became law in 1854 and required that all males who turned twenty by January 1 of the year in which a levy was declared participate in the lottery.[150] By the time of the Crimean War, only private serfs and a few non-Russian areas did not provide recruits on the basis of the new system.[151] Through administrative uniformity, this reform aimed to thwart evasion and ease the economic burden of military service by increasing regularity and predictability in conscription.

Reports from the 1840s and 1850s indicate that the government considered the lottery system a success.[152] One observer even claimed that flight by peasants to avoid conscription had ceased. The selection of recruits also occurred with more publicity and equity: fewer recruits were rejected for physical reasons, and rich peasants were finding evasion impossible. The new system was more effective in delivering recruits and eliminating abuses.[153] Despite official claims, the lottery brought few benefits to the people: administrative corruption, manipulation of the family lists, and the shortage of suitable recruits (especially in wartime) led to repeated violations of law.[154] During the Crimean War the army drafted men as old as thirty-seven who should have been exempt.[155] The lottery system thus failed to solve the basic problem of arbitrariness in conscription.

Once the available recruits had been gathered, they were transported to military authorities at the nearest recruiting station. Here they underwent medical examination, and those accepted joined parties that journeyed to their assigned regiments. Men from the same province tended to serve in the same regiments, though by the nineteenth century they were not necessarily sent to adjacent areas.[156] The community bore the cost of outfitting and provisioning recruits for three months (or until they reached the regiments).[157] At the time of a levy, an imperial ukase stipulated the amount due for uniforms. The cost of provisions also varied, since the local community had to provide for recruits, replacements, and escorts.[158] Along with the personal loss suffered by the families of recruits, the local community as a whole paid a heavy economic price.[159]

As fair as the legislation governing conscription seemed to be, the burden placed upon Russian society was simply too great to guarantee efficiency and justice. Even in the best circumstances, the discrepancy between the needs of the state and society's meager resources made conscription a difficult and arbitrary process. Due to administrative corruption and popular evasion, those families most capable of providing recruits often avoided the sacrifice. Considerable manipulation accompanied conscription, and peasants would do anything within their power to evade service. Thus the poor and the weak tended to answer the call to arms. Peasant complaints and official reports repeatedly exposed administrative irregularities. In placing unreasonable demands on some segments of society, the system of conscription lacked the moral authority to counteract evasion or attract the best-qualified personnel.

The Manpower Problem in Conscription

By far the most serious factor reducing the pool of potential recruits was the physical condition of the population. Concerned about the health and physical attributes of soldiers, the authorities rejected large numbers of recruits for medical reasons.[160] In December 1848 the Recruitment Committee reported that in the four preceding levies, few men between the ages of twenty and thirty-five were found suitable for service: out of 100,000 recruits, 34,000 were rejected for height, 20,000 for chronic diseases, and 31,000 for physical inadequacies.[161] Figures from the seventh partial levy in 1847 showed that about 32 percent of state peasants subject to conscription were unfit because of height and other physical disabilities (see table 1.3).[162] These data are astounding, even if one allows for the likelihood of administrative abuse.

Because of the large number of recruits rejected for health reasons, the government was repeatedly forced to adjust physical requirements in order to satisfy the army's manpower needs. Physical standards also aggravated inequities in distributing the burden of conscription. Large families

Table 1.3. Physical Inadequacies among Recruits[a]

Year	Delivered	Accepted	Rejected for:			
			Height	Age	Physical Disabilities	Chronic Diseases
1839		52,161	16,951	7,991	15,527	12,638
1840		92,591	31,128	10,702	28,053	16,918
1841		55,409	22,298	5,531	18,319	11,447
1842		44,964	12,906	5,488	14,385	8,841
1850	139,002	66,544	15,595	3,975	16,928	10,080
1851	182,187	72,811	19,188	5,976	16,548	11,843
1855	347,281	175,204	16,988	13,616	31,197	15,907

Sources: TsGIA, f. 1262, op. 1, d. 27, l. 17ob.; d. 183, l. 3; TsGVIA, f. 395, op. 213, d. 21–22.

[a] These data contain obvious mathematical errors and should be treated only as imprecise indicators. The difference between the number of recruits delivered and the number accepted or rejected is the number of replacements sent but not needed.

lacking even one suitable recruit could avoid service, whereas the last worker of a small family might be selected. In most cases chance and arbitrariness, rather that "equal apportionment," determined the order of selection.[163] For the state, the guarantor of national integrity, conscription was a matter of the highest order. Not surprisingly, the government's main purpose was to maximize the manpower resources available to the army. Russia's policymakers were concerned that all segments of the servile population carry their fair share of the burden. But in the ethnically and socially diverse Russian empire, the application of uniform procedures proved elusive.

The most significant military reforms of the pre-reform period addressed conscription. Speransky expected the military colonies to eliminate levies altogether. Combining military training and farming, the colonies were supposed to increase the sources of manpower by preserving family life and placing military service on a secure economic foundation.[164] The lottery system aimed to reduce evasion by promoting regularity and fairness in the selection of recruits. The division of the empire into two spheres for purposes of conscription also sought to equalize distribution of the burden. Finally, the introduction of indefinite leaves after twenty years of service was designed to reduce costs, lighten the burden of service, and create a trained reserve ready for call-up in wartime.[165] Some high-level officials regarded a shorter term of service as the best way to reduce the social and economic dislocations caused by the long tour of duty. But the juridical definitions of serfdom precluded this solution. Service brought emancipation. Hence only with the end of serfdom could the government introduce universal conscription, which would ensure a more equitable distribution of the service burden.[166] The government was disturbed by inequities, but not sufficiently disturbed to attempt fundamental reform. There was no pressing need for change, since the army undoubtedly served well the military and foreign policy goals of the state.

CHAPTER TWO

Military Society and the State

When a young man entered the service, the parameters of his life changed dramatically. He was now part of a distinct social institution with its own particular functions and laws. New recruits immediately confronted two factors that continuously affected military society: one was the formal legal structure of the army defined by the state, and the other was the constant threat to physical survival. In the first, the government actively sought to legislate its own bureaucratic vision of military modernization, and in the second, it was forced to react to the limitations imposed by pre-industrial material life.

In an age of pre-industrial warfare, the integrity and fighting capacity of the army depended upon the government's ability to feed, clothe, and generally maintain the troops.[1] Good health was crucial to the effectiveness of the army. Sick and disabled soldiers, too enervated to perform their service obligations, represented a significant drain on the already scarce resources of the military economy.[2] The constant threat of losses from illness, death, and desertion had a significant impact on official policy toward the troops. Thus the government's approach to economic problems, to military discipline, and to training exercises all revealed the paramount importance of preserving manpower.

The harsh physical realities of military life began the moment a recruit entered the service. Officials considered new recruits particularly vulnerable to death and disease. Subject to tremendous psychological and physical stress after separation from their families, recruits also had to march long distances to reach their assigned units. Contemporary observers depicted the harmful physical effects of prolonged marches. Exposure to the elements and inadequate supplies of food brought recruits to their regiments in a weakened physical state that was exacerbated by grief at separation from their loved ones.[3] Unaccustomed to military life, they were less hardy than seasoned soldiers and more likely to fall victim to infectious diseases.[4]

Official sources regarded illness and mortality as primary threats to the effectiveness and physical integrity of the army. Many reasons were given for poor health among soldiers. Inadequate material resources, especially poor nutrition and housing, represented a major threat to the troops. In 1850 the inspector of reserve battalions of the Third Infantry Corps attributed the "healthy and cheerful" appearance of the lower ranks to their being quartered in Poltava province, where residents provided "good, nutritious, and abundant food."[5] Good food meant good health, while a poor diet brought physical weakness.[6] Dingy, dirty, poorly ventilated quarters also caused illness and poor health. Barracks and towns were particularly conducive to the spread of disease. From a health standpoint, soldiers were much better off living in more open, even if poor, rural surroundings.[7]

Considering the backwardness of medicine in pre-reform Russia, it is not surprising that experts considered climate and environment the most important reasons for ill health.[8] Good health required good hygiene. Dirty clothing, linen, and utensils clearly promoted the spread of disease.[9] Officials also encouraged regular bathing as essential for good health. In proposed instructions for camp gatherings, P. D. Kiselev recommended that soldiers of the Second Army bathe twice a week.[10] Through regulations and official publications, the government intervened to impose the most basic rules of hygiene on military society.[11]

The effectiveness of governmental policy (and intentions) depended on the attitudes of those officers who directly administered the troops. The situation at the Tobol'sk Half-battalion of Cantonists illustrates the difficulties encountered. In 1840 the battalion commander received a severe reprimand for abuses discovered during an investigation into reports of excessive illness.[12] He was responsible for the cantonists' sloppy dress, the dirty conditions in which they lived, and the poor quality of the food they ate. According to the final judicial report, the floors in the cantonists' quarters were filthy and the air oppressive. The cantonists' personal and bed linens were neither changed on schedule (i.e., weekly) nor properly washed. Their food was sometimes spoiled, and they did not receive enough soap to wash their hands daily. In a similar case the commander of the Voronezh Cantonist Battalion received two severe reprimands in

January and February 1842, because of high mortality among his charges. The authorities attributed this problem to the appearance of scorbutic disease caused by bad food.[13] As these cases indicate, the central government had little control over actual conditions and had to rely on the officers in charge to implement official policy.

The possible ill effects of corporal punishment (the prevailing means of discipline in the pre-reform army) on the health of soldiers were obvious to all. The authorities generally recognized that physical punishment, especially when excessively severe, could cause illness and inflict permanent internal damage to the body.[14] In an 1810 circular to generals, Minister of War Barclay de Tolly attributed an increase in illness and mortality to the habit "of basing all [martial] science, discipline, and military order on corporal punishments."[15] It was clear to high-level officials that corporal punishment exacerbated health problems, but no one considered eliminating it altogether.

Training also bore directly on the soldiers' health.[16] Reporting on summer camp gatherings from 1819 until 1824, P. D. Kiselev noted that in an effort to "conserve the men," no more than three hours each morning were devoted to the difficult drills used in closed-order formation, while the afternoons were spent in less taxing activities such as marksmanship and drills in extended order.[17] According to Kiselev, excessive training harmed the service "by exhausting the men and depriving them of any desire to perform their duties."[18] In 1841 a more critical observer blamed mortality and disability not just on excessive drills, but on the very method of training and the movements practiced in the pre-reform army.[19] Recognizing a relationship between health and training, the government tried to regulate the extent of drill and was especially concerned that soldiers not be unduly punished for mistakes. But aside from limiting exercises and some forms of corporal punishment, it did nothing to ease service demands.

An institutional infrastructure (infirmaries, hospitals, and medical schools) for delivering health care to the Russian troops had existed since the reign of Peter the Great.[20] The first half of the nineteenth century witnessed an increase both in the number of hospitals and in expenditures for the sick.[21] Between 1826 and 1850, hospital beds for the lower ranks increased from 28,025 to 50,890, while expenditures to support the sick rose from 1,454,871 rubles to 3,371,623 rubles.[22] The number of beds for military personnel in town hospitals also grew from 4,079 in 1826 to 13,556 in 1850.[23] The government steadily increased the resources allocated for the army's medical needs.

Improvements in medical care based on better scientific knowledge had some effect. Clothing was changed to enhance hygiene. An official military history from 1850 attributed an improvement in the health of soldiers partly to the looser uniforms introduced under Nicholas I, claiming that various ailments—aneurisms of the large vessels (caused by moving in tight clothes), as well as constipation and other abdominal diseases attributed to excessive tightening of the stomach, had become rarer. It likewise asserted that the helmet (which had replaced the shako) reduced head, eye, and ear disease. Finally, dangerous bone growths on the ribs and sternum—the result of repeated contusions of the chest caused by carrying weapons—almost disappeared after changes in the manual of arms.[24] Whatever the scientific basis of such conclusions, they did testify to a conscious policy of protecting the health of soldiers.

The Medical Department of the War Ministry also periodically issued regulations to combat specific diseases. In the 1830s and 1840s, the authorities prescribed treatment for inflammation of the eyes.[25] Food poisoning was another area of concern; in 1850, for example, the Medical Department published rules "on protecting the lower military ranks from the toxic effect of damp salted fish and on aid for persons poisoned by it."[26] The pre-reform government (especially in the reign of Nicholas I) consciously expanded its medical role by providing more resources and tightening regulation from the center.

If the picture of increased concern for medical problems is accurate, its effectiveness is another question. The data on illness and mortality are inadequate for meaningful statistical analysis. There is no single source of statistical information, so the available figures tend to be contradictory or unsuitable for comparison.[27] It is possible that better and more complete statistical materials quietly repose somewhere in the archives; for now, however, the data provide only a general point of departure for impressionistic analysis.

There were no significant changes in the types of diseases that afflicted the troops in the first half of the nineteenth century. Variations in rates of mortality and illness stemmed more from the ravages of particular wars and epidemics than from any permanent progress in health services, though hygienic measures and better medical knowledge may have helped to counteract a few diseases. Whatever the improvements, epidemics nevertheless repeatedly threatened the troops. Official sources mention bubonic plague, cholera, and various types of fevers as the most common killers.[28] Because information on the frequency of disease before 1825 is so limited, it is impossible to determine whether medical care actually improved during the reign of Nicholas I. The troops certainly did not become less vulnerable to contagious disease. Indeed, at midcentury one high-level official even expressed concern about previously unmentioned chest diseases.[29] There was, then, no long-term success in fighting disease (see tables 2.1–2.4).

The data on mortality also do not indicate any overall improvement (see tables 2.1–2.4). Local variations were still significant. Illness and death rates tended to vary sharply, fluctuating in response to a host of environmental factors. Like any other subsistence society, the pre-reform army experienced demographic crises due to climatic conditions, natural disasters, famines, and epidemics. War also affected mortality, but throughout Europe, more wartime deaths resulted from illness than from actual combat.[30] The failure to achieve tangible improvement in military health was candidly admitted in Russia's first medical journal. Although Russia's problem was depicted as universal, the message was clear: "The history of military hygiene and diseases in armies shows that, beginning

Table 2.1. Mortality among the Lower Ranks[a]

Year	Total Number of men[c]	Total Died	Dead from: Suicide	Dead from: In Battle or from Wounds	Dead from: Disease	Rate of Death (%)
1801[b]	337,923	21,645				6
1818		23,381	195[d]			
1820	879,165	22,596	195[d]			3
1827	1,027,416	18,515	117			2
1836	829,785	26,033	157	265	25,611	3
1837	821,889	27,222	273	572	26,377	3
1838	853,603	30,059	278	254	29,527	4
1847	918,206	37,878	180	312	37,386	4
1848	955,913	47,554	192	707	46,655[e]	5
1849	955,351	43,273	217	917	42,139	5
1850	926,209	43,270	263	194	42,813	5
1851[f]	994,317	40,450	245	347	39,831	4

SOURCES: TsGVIA, f. 395, op. 325, d. 5, 10, 19–22, 31–35; *Imperatorskie ukazy i prikazy voennogo ministerstva za 1809.*

[a] Figures do not include reserve troops.
[b] Data are missing for eight regiments.
[c] Figure represents the number of men on the service rolls January 1.
[d] These figures are from TsGVIA, f. Voenno-uchenyi arkhiv, d. 825, and include military orphanages. It is not known whether reserve troops are included.
[e] Figure includes 12,904 men who died in the cholera epidemic. (TsGVIA, f. 395, op. 325, d. 32, l. 5.)
[f] It is not known whether reserve troops are included.

Table 2.2. Illness and Mortality in the Active Army[a]

Year	Men on the Service Rolls[b]	Fell Ill[c]	Recovered(%)	Died(%)
1835	231,099	173,892 (75)	95	5[d]
1836	214,057	144,893 (68)	95	5
1837	226,576	148,632 (65)	95	5
1838	231,491	142,887 (62)	95	5
1839		135,788	97	3
1840		112,298	94	5
1841	229,007	140,793 (61)	96[e]	4[f]
1842	216,129	145,725 (67)	97	4
1846–47[g]		193,140	96	5
1850[g]		294,633	87	7
1851[g]		255,060	88	5
1851		212,903	95	6
1852[g]		216,663	88	5
1852		196,038	87	6

SOURCE: *Voenno-meditsinskii zhurnal*, 1837–53.

[a] Unless indicated, data are for hospitals (*gospitali*) and field hospitals (*lazarety*) and do not include dressing stations (*okolodki*).
[b] Data include lower ranks, officers, noncombat personnel, regular and irregular troops.
[c] Figure in parentheses is the rate of illness.
[d] Alternative figures show a death rate of 6%.
[e] Alternative figures show a recovery rate of 94%.
[f] Alternative figures show a death rate of 5%.
[g] Data include dressing stations.

with the wars of the first years of this century until the present, there has been no significant improvement in the hygienic [i.e., health] conditions of the soldier's life."[31]

Whatever the precise numerical dimensions, the health problem was a basic fact of military life with implications for the army's manpower resources. The army functioned under the continual threat of physiological collapse. While disease and mortality were the most obvious results of the army's precarious material condition, the threat to physical survival also affected social life. Thus official policy toward discipline, economic organization, and relations between soldiers and their commanders all reflected health considerations. In order to understand the social condition of the common soldier, it is essential to keep in mind the extreme fragility of his physical existence.

Table 2.3. Rates of Illness, Mortality, and Desertion[a]

	Year	Illness	Mortality[b]	Desertion
Guards Corps:	1838	46	3	.2
	1839	45	3	.2
	1840	45	3	.2
	1841	40	3	.1
	1842	33	2	.1
	1843	33	2.5	.1
	1844	32	2	.1
	1845	no data	2	.1
Grenadier Corps:	1841	28	1.5	.4
	1842	26	1	.4
	1843	27	1	.3
	1844	25	1	.3
	1845	no data	1	.2
Sixth Infantry Corps:[c]	1841–42	3	3	1
	1842–43	3	3	.7
	1843–44	2	2	.3
	1844–45	2	1	.4
	1845–46	1.6	1	.4

SOURCES: TsGVIA, f. 395, op. 101, d. 111, 228; f. Voenno-uchenyi arkhiv, d. 17542, ch. 2–3.

[a] Computations are based on the average number of lower ranks on the service rolls. Figures for the Guards and Grenadier Corps in 1845 are based on the number of men present at the time of inspection.

[b] Mortality rates include suicide and murders.

[c] Data for the Sixth Infantry Corps run from July to July. The data on illness do not include dressing stations, which may account for the extremely lower figures. It is also possible that the figures represent the number of men who were ill only at the time of inspection.

The Structure of Military Society:
Soldiers and "the *Soslovie* Paradigm"

Gregory L. Freeze has characterized the first half of the nineteenth century as a dynamic period of *soslovie* formation in which the groups comprising Russian society were becoming more numerous and more distinct. To meet the needs of state and society, new social categories were created and older ones redefined.[32] The development of soldiers as a social class

Table 2.4. Illness, Mortality, and Desertion in the Pskov Infantry Regiment
(per 1,000 men on the service rolls)

Year	Ill as of 1 July	Died	Deserted
1834	41.6	35.4	13.3
1835	40	35.4	17.2
1836	50.1	31	16.8
1837	73.9	33.8	14.8
1838	67.9	28.6	12.2
1839	65.6	26.8	14.7
1840	88.1	43.9	14
1841	52.4	40	8.7
1842	11.7	29.6	9.1
1843	56.2	30	6.7
1844	164.1	31.9	5.9
1846	45	33.5	8.1
1847	30.8	16.5	11.4
1848	77.7	27	10.4
1849	37.9	54.2	9.9
1850	54.6	43.2	11.7
1851	67.8	34.5	2.6
1852	75.6	61	1.1
1853	85.9	48.3	6.1
1854	94.5	69.9	6.9

SOURCE: Kapitan Geniev, *Istoriia Pskovskogo pekhotnogo Generala Fel'dmarshala kniazia Kutuzova-Smolenskogo polka, 1700–1881* (Moscow, 1883), pp. 290–91.

falls squarely into this process. Like all the *sosloviia*, soldiers were identified by their obligations to the state and by their legally defined rights and privileges.[33] As a social category, they occupied an ambiguous status between the poll-tax population and the privileged classes. The very obligation to serve indicated inferior status, but once in the army a soldier was legally "free," and as a serviceman he was in a position to rise through the ranks. Although there was little chance of achieving noble status, social mobility remained a theoretical possibility.

Most soldiers were not born into that status, but the long term of service and the juridical emancipation brought by conscription separated the soldier from his *soslovie* of origin. In the eighteenth century common soldiers served for life and beginning in 1793 for twenty-five years (the exception was the elite Guards, who, beginning in 1818, served for twenty-two years).[34] A few special groups like the *odnodvortsy* and *voiskovye obyvateli* served only fifteen years.[35] Then in 1834 the army began to grant "indefinite leaves" to soldiers who had served irreproachably for twenty years. These soldiers could return home or resettle, but for five years they would still be subject to military call-up.[36] In 1855 official statistics reported that 215,197 men held indefinite leaves.[37] Surely the establishment of indefinite leaves represented an improvement in the terms of service. The army also apparently granted indefinite leaves to soldiers who had not yet served twenty years: a statute of 1841 required that soldiers on indefinite leave who had not completed twenty years of service return to the army once each year for training.[38]

An 1842 ukase of Nicholas I explained the reason for indefinite leaves:

> Having established indefinite leaves, I always hoped to lighten state expenditures by reducing the number of troops under arms without undermining the basic strength of an army, that corresponds to the territory, needs, and dignity of the Empire. I also wanted to shorten the term of real service for meritorious soldiers and to give them the chance to return home before old age and be useful among their families.[39]

The emperor expressed satisfaction with the new system. He noted that the men released always appeared for training and that only 116 of the 150,000 soldiers affected had been tried for crimes committed while on leave.

Indefinite leaves did shorten the term of service (for men who survived that long) but failed to reduce state expenditures or return soldiers to civilian status and family life. Because they might be called to service at any time, the soldiers affected could not establish stable sources of income. Instead, they remained homeless and alien to peasant life.[40] As the Crimean War showed, from a purely military point of view, indefinite leaves did not solve the basic problem of mobilizing auxiliary manpower in time of war.[41] After twenty years of service it was unlikely that many of the released soldiers actually were fit for combat duty.[42]

The long term of service and changes in juridical status account for the soldiers' social separateness, which made reintegration into civilian society difficult. The plight of retired soldiers revealed the full extent of the problem. These men formed a "homeless class" living in a condition of vagrancy and poverty. Cut off from family and community at the time of conscription, those who returned home might encounter strangers who regarded them as aliens.[43] Because most retired soldiers were exempt from feudal dues and taxes, they were of no use to either the landlord or the peasant commune. They also had no property rights and hence depended on relatives or the village community for access to land and sustenance.[44] From the landlord's perspective, retired soldiers constituted a potential threat to social order, for there is evidence that they became involved in peasant uprisings.[45] Considering the economic vagaries of retired soldiers, that would hardly be surprising. If they chose not to go home, they had the right to settle on state lands, but that meant they had to live in distant provinces. Many did not consider this desirable and gravitated toward urban areas, where they could work as day laborers or artisans.[46] It seems, then, that for the relatively few soldiers who reached retirement, "freedom" meant dependence, wandering, and poverty.[47]

Some soldiers obtained employment in local state institutions, but this only reflected the serious problems of reintegration. In December 1829 the emperor enjoined provincial governors to take active measures to relocate soldiers who wandered about, begging alms.[48] If possible, they should receive employment in governmental offices.[49] In 1832 the Saratov governor reported that because retired soldiers were orderly and disciplined, they made better firemen than hired freemen.[50] Another option was to provide them with fifty paper rubles and sufficient land from town holdings to build a house and plant a garden.[51] Regardless of occupation, retired soldiers and those on indefinite leave were among the poorest residents of any town.[52] Ad hoc governmental measures did little to alleviate their plight. As late as 1856, not even the disabled and infirmed received adequate care.[53] A few retired soldiers fared well in petty urban trade, but overall, their material condition was precarious and their reintegration into peasant society virtually impossible.[54]

Like other *sosloviia*, the status of soldier was inheritable. The juridical "freedom" attained by a recruit once he took the oath to the tsar was also conferred on his wife and on any children born to him after he began active service.[55] The wife of a soldier was "free" in the sense that she no longer belonged to the landlord or local community. Hers was not, however, an enviable status. Deserted at a young age, soldiers' wives were suspected of promiscuity and loose morals.[56] Their economic position was also uncertain. They could remain in the village, dependent on the generosity of relatives, the peasant community or the landlord. According to one observer, the soldier's family often viewed his wife as a hired laborer.[57] The commune generally provided land for soldiers' sons, but not for daughters, childless wives, or the illegitimate children of soldiers' wives.[58] In state villages, soldiers' wives were probably better off, since the law promised them land and public assistance if needed.[59] Theoretically, soldiers' wives enjoyed the option of joining their husbands, who could also give them permission to obtain passports that allowed them to settle in towns.[60] Free from the control of their former masters, free from the authority of their native villages, these women were thrown into the world and forced to make their own way.

Information on the activities of soldiers' wives is extremely fragmentary. At the end of Catherine the Great's reign, the law directed them to earn a livelihood among the troops by making tents and by sewing, washing, and mending clothes. In addition, Potemkin encouraged their employment in hospitals.[61] The 1838 military code allowed them to work as sutlers and instructed regimental commanders to provide them with "various female occupations" for which they should be paid.[62] Regardless of whether they lived with their husbands, soldiers' wives enjoyed all the privileges of "free" social classes (*svobodnye sostoianiia*), including the right to engage in urban trades (*posadskie promysly*).[63] By the mid-nineteenth century many found employment in factories.[64] Finally, it is known that soldiers' wives were active in prostitution and in the trafficking of unwanted children between the countryside and the Moscow and St. Petersburg foundling homes.[65] There were several alternatives available to this group, but for a young woman who *de facto* lost her husband forever, but could not remarry without proof of his death, it must have been a difficult life, full of hardships and struggle.

In general, soldiers' families represented an enormous welfare problem. Consequently, the army tried to restrict the possibilities for family life. An 1821 statute forbade soldiers' wives to join their husbands among field troops, except in the Caucasus Corps. Henceforth only women who had their own means of support could follow their husbands. The law noted that the presence of these women was inconvenient and burdensome for the civilians who quartered soldiers. When the troops were mobilized, the women were left without sustenance, and the state incurred significant expenses transporting them to their husbands.[66] Since a soldier could marry only with the permission of his regimental commander, it was not too difficult to limit family life.[67] The commander's main concern was whether regimental resources were adequate to support additional families.[68] As a result, there was significant variation, depending on the individual commander and local conditions.

There is no detailed information on family arrangements in the army, so it is not known precisely how many soldiers were married, lived with their wives, or fathered children. The limited data available indicate that married soldiers were a minority (though at times a substantial one) and that the number of these with children was considerably smaller (see tables 2.5–2.6). Family life was probably more widespread in garrisons and distant places, where the troops led a sedentary existence or in areas where an urban economy offered employment. In 1820 the State Council decided there was a sufficient number of wives in the Sevastopol barracks

Table 2.5. Married Soldiers, 1841–44[a]

	Number Married	% Living with Wives
Rank		
Privates	142,618	9
Noncommissioned Officers	10,832	36
Musicians	3,324	34
Noncombat	12,430	27.5
Branch of Service		
Infantry	124,341	9
Cavalry	27,092	28
Artillery	14,372	10
Sapper	3,399	17

SOURCE: TsGAOR, f. 672, op. 1, d. 81, ll. 1–10.
[a] The precise dates of these data are not known.

Table 2.6. Family Ties among Recruits

Year and Province	Married (%)	Fathers (%)[a]
1814		
Voronezh	65	31
1827–28		
Iaroslavl	53	34
Kiev	19	8.5
Kostroma	56	29
Kursk	53	30
Novgorod	41	23
Pskov	42	19
Riazan	64	28
St. Petersburg	39	10
Saratov	59	32
Smolensk	44	22
Tomsk	37	12
Voronezh	51	29
1835–36		
Smolensk	44	28

SOURCE: TsGVIA, f. 395, op. 318, d. 6, 10, 21, 22, 25, 28, 29, 30, 33, 37, 43, 45.
[a] Figure includes recruits who left pregnant wives.

to establish a separate women's section at the local naval hospital.[69] If there was a shortage of space in state buildings, married soldiers in Sevastopol were quartered in private homes, though after 1839 they no longer received governmental assistance for rent.[70] A law of 1821 limited monetary support to married soldiers in the Caucasus and military colonies.[71] But then in 1826 support was restored for garrison regiments and for infantry and transport guard units located in Siberia.[72] In the Siberian provinces, there were sufficient barracks for soldiers and their spouses, so that local residents were not inconvenienced. A significant number of Siberian soldiers even owned their own homes.[73] At midcentury, married soldiers in the Kinburn Artillery Garrison actually lived in houses in the suburbs, rather than in barracks.[74] Guards units quartered in St. Petersburg also had a greater chance of maintaining a family life.[75] Still, space was a prime consideration, and a law of 1844 forbade soldiers to marry unless there were vacancies in the barracks.[76]

Whether soldiers' families lived in state barracks or private homes, they maintained a separate economy, at least partly independent of the regiment. The 1838 military code indicated that married soldiers could not participate in the collective funds that formed a basic component of the regimental economy.[77] Sometimes several families shared rented quarters and formed their own private artel.[78] Since married soldiers returned to their barracks before the evening roll call, these arrangements benefited the wives, who otherwise had to look after children and manage the household alone. Soldiers could visit their families only during their free daytime hours, so without collective arrangements, domestic burdens fell solely on the wife. If she was busy shopping or working, the children were neglected.[79] Because soldiers could not live with their families in rented quarters, they preferred to have them in state barracks, despite the lack of privacy and the crowded conditions, which created animosity and bickering.[80] Still, there was never enough space in state buildings, and most families lived in rented quarters. The army provided some money for rent (*kvartirnye den'gi*), but the allowance was so small that many could afford to rent only part of a room.[81] Like retired soldiers and wives who tried to make it on their own, soldiers' families lived in the most squalid and impoverished conditions.

The existence of the juridically defined social category *soldatskie deti* (soldiers' children) revealed the presence of some family life in the army. From 1719 until 1856 soldiers' sons and the illegitimate children of soldiers' wives, girlfriends, and daughters belonged to the "military domain" (*voennoe vedomstvo*) and were destined for a life of military service.[82] These children could live with parents or relatives until age eighteen, when they began active service, or they could enter special military schools from age seven.⁸³ In 1797, 12,000 soldiers' sons were studying in the military schools, and when the category was abolished in 1856, there were 378,000.⁸⁴ Most became soldiers or noncommissioned officers. Others learned handicrafts, worked as copyists, or acquired special technical and administrative skills needed by the army.⁸⁵

The education provided for soldiers' sons gave them the opportunity to rise socially. Among officers promoted from the lower classes, soldiers' sons were the largest group.⁸⁶ They were especially important as a source of noncommissioned officers.⁸⁷ Despite these possibilities for advancement, parents tirelessly strove to conceal their children from the army.⁸⁸ Just as the promise of juridical emancipation failed to make conscription a desirable fate, so too the chance for education and mobility did not affect the natural desire of parents to keep their children at home. The Decembrist P. I. Pestel described the status of soldiers' children as slavery (*kabal*) to the state.⁸⁹ Separated from their parents at an early age, forced to endure physical privation and harsh discipline in the military schools, they still faced twenty-five years of active service beginning at age eighteen.

Much less is known about soldiers' daughters, who supposedly lived with parents or relatives until marriage. There were a few schools for these girls in St. Petersburg, but nothing on the scale of the schools for soldiers' sons. The 1820 annual report of the Inspectors' Department noted that three Guards regiments in the capital maintained schools for soldiers' daughters.⁹⁰ The girls learned reading, writing, and various "female handicrafts." The Moscow and St. Petersburg Foundling Homes also accepted soldiers' daughters under age fourteen who had lost either parent. These girls were raised in villages and then acquired positions in state institutions or private homes.⁹¹ Very few soldiers' daughters received any formal education. Boys represented a valuable resource for the army, but girls were simply a welfare problem that the government could not completely ignore. Thus, needy sons could receive state support until they began active service, while orphaned daughters were eligible for assistance only until age twelve.⁹² In general, policy toward soldiers' children combined welfare considerations with the military and administrative needs of the state, reflecting the status of soldiers as a juridically distinct group.

The significance of the soldier's family lies in its distinctive juridical status. Even if juridical distinctions did not always correspond to actual conditions, they did serve as the basis for official policy and to a large extent defined the activities legally open to an individual. One should not underestimate the psychological and social implications of a serf, his wife, and his as yet unborn children becoming "free." Although the soldier remained closely tied to civilian society economically and was probably no better off materially than a peasant, he was still a "free" man in a country of serfs. At the very least, this suggested the possibility of a change in the social identity and expectations of recruits. Most significant in this respect was the status of soldiers' sons whose military education created the possibility of real social mobility. Except for his special military functions, the soldier may have continued to live much like a peasant, but his relationship and that of his family to the state, to the landlord, and to the local community changed dramatically.

The implications of a soldier's "freedom" are difficult to assess. In the bureaucratic, hierarchical structure of the army, he was even more accountable to his social superiors than a farming peasant would be. In addition, his life was regulated in a new and relatively strict fashion. For the soldier himself there was no realization of his "free" status as long as he remained in the army. By contrast, "freedom" was of immediate significance for his family. His wife was free to engage in urban trades, and his son began to climb the ladder of upward social mobility. The soldier was separated from the poll-tax population by his juridical status, military functions, and institutional associations. Popular attitudes toward service reflected this separation. Young soldiers were mourned as dead. Their wives became outcasts from peasant society, and upon retirement they found reintegration virtually impossible. Although soldiers in active service were rarely isolated from civilian life, they and their families possessed the legal and social attributes of a distinct *soslovie*.

The Formal Structure of Military Society

Although closely connected to civilian society, the army was a separate entity. It had its own peculiar legal system and professional functions, its own social divisions, and its own unique set of problems. Military society was highly differentiated. Different branches of the service and different kinds of troops enjoyed different privileges and performed different tasks. These arrangements stemmed primarily from the requirements of war. There were four branches of service in the regular Russian army: infantry, cavalry, artillery, and engineering troops. Within each branch were different types of units distinguished by their weapons, uniforms, and military functions. Sometimes these distinctions gave a unit elite status. Thus the most privileged troops were the Guards regiments, which included units from each of the service's four branches.

Formal social divisions also existed in the Russian army. The most obvious divisions depended on rank, but the attainment of rank derived from social origin, in accordance with the ascriptive organization of Russian society. Education, performance, service record, seniority, patronage, and the support of one's superiors all affected promotion.[93] But no matter what level of excellence a man achieved, he could rise above the limits set by his social origin only in exceptional circumstances. For the poll-tax population, the chances of rising were greater in military than in civilian society, but here too the channels of upward mobility were severely constricted. More often than not, social divisions and definitions in military society corresponded to and reflected those in society at large.

The elite of military society were the officers, who came primarily from the nobility. According to Peter the Great's Table of Ranks, military ranks 1–5 comprised the Generalitet, ranks 6–8 the field officers (*shtab-ofitsery*), and ranks 9–14 the senior officers (*ober-ofitsery*). Achievement of the first officer rank (i.e., rank 14) automatically conferred noble status.[94] Officers in Guards and artillery units formally enjoyed a higher status than officers in the line army. The Petrine structure of military ranks survived until 1884 with one important change: after 1845 only rank 8 conferred noble status, while ranks 9–14 granted personal nobility. Personal nobles enjoyed all the rights and privileges of the hereditary nobles, but their children were not automatically ennobled.[95] This more limited access to the nobility revealed the fundamental contradiction between military efficiency and a social order based on ascription. At the same time that the government was making education an increasingly important determinant of social status, it was also restricting access to the nobility and, therefore, the rewards of performance.

The lower ranks (*nizhnie chiny*) consisted of privates and noncommissioned officers. Although official sources often treat them as a single group, there were significant differences. The mass of lower ranks were privates (*riadovye*), called cannoneers (*kanoniry*) in the artillery.[96] Socially, they were a homogeneous group, conscripted primarily from the Great Russian Orthodox peasantry. But even among the lowly privates, social divisions existed—divisions based on age, experience, performance, and skill. Older soldiers enjoyed a prestige and authority reinforced by the government, which considered them more disciplined and reliable. In the infantry, cavalry, and engineering troops, the older and better soldiers received the title of lance corporal (*efreitor*; *bombardir* in the artillery). When the noncommissioned officers who commanded the platoons (*otdeleniia*) and subplatoons within a company were absent, the lance corporals replaced them.[97] Another basic division existed between combat and noncombat soldiers. Men physically unsuitable for combat served as wagonmasters, supervisors of the sick (*nadzirateli bol'nykh*), drivers, feldshers, copyists, sacristans (*tserkovniki*), infirmary staff, barbers, craftsmen, orderlies, or barrack and camp cleaners (*profosy*).[98] Noncombat lower ranks could be privates or noncommissioned officers, depending on the position and availability of manpower.

The noncommissioned officers were the real enforcers of the army's military goals. Exercising the most immediate control over the soldiers, they served as the army's primary agents of discipline. The status of noncommissioned officer brought significant responsibilities that increased the chances of punishment and disgrace. Judicial records show that the government held them responsible for the performance and behavior of the soldiers they commanded. The noncommissioned officer escorted his men to their assigned duties and supervised the execution of daily routines. He directed the soldiers' military training, taught them basic combat skills, and led them in battle. Equally important, the noncommissioned officer was supposed to deflect discontent and prevent outbreaks of disobedience. His position was not an enviable one, and one wonders whether the onerous burden of increased accountability did not outweigh the benefits of promotion. Although the noncommissioned officer's way of life was not that different from the soldier's, he still wielded significant authority over his subordinates.[99] This power often became arbitrary and abusive. Like their superiors, noncommissioned officers were eager to apply the stick as the primary means of discipline.[100] Because they themselves were punished for infractions by their subordinates, their closeness to the soldiers' milieu did not translate into leniency.

Among the noncommissioned officers, there was also a hierarchy of rank, status, and privilege. The most elite group of noncommissioned officers was that from the nobility. Formally separated from the mass of noncommissioned officers, beginning in 1800 the future officers from this group were called "subensigns" (*podpraporshchiki*) in the infantry, and starting in 1802, junkers in cavalry, artillery, and jager (light infantry) units.[101] An imperial ukase of 1796 gave them clear priority over nonnoble elements in promotion to officer rank.[102] The most senior noncommissioned officer was the sergeant-major, who closely assisted the company or battery commander in general administration, economic affairs, and the maintenance of discipline. During an officer's absence, the sergeant major performed his duties.[103] The bulk of noncommissioned officers were called either "senior" or "junior."[104] As commanders of the five groups of ten soldiers (*desiatki*; sg., *desiatka*) who comprised each of the four platoons (*otdeleniia*) within a company, these noncommissioned officers were supposed to be literate, possess excellent records of conduct, and a sound knowledge of military drill. As the commanding element always on the spot, they were an important source of discipline and control.

For most soldiers promotion to noncommissioned officer represented the only path to social advancement. The military regulation of 1796 required that soldiers promoted to noncommissioned officer be literate and distinguished by their bravery.[105] To provide these skills, an imperial order of 1809 ruled that in addition to the noncommissioned officers educated in special training troops (*uchebnye voiska*), regimental commanders should prepare privates in their units for promotion. They should teach them literacy and promote those who mastered the rules of service and the correct military paces and those who were of "good and sober behavior." Commanders should also give priority in promotions to decorated soldiers.[106] The 1838 military code identified three grounds for promotion to noncommissioned officer: the existence of a vacancy, completion of the legal term of service, and demonstration of excellence.[107] The code also confirmed previous educational requirements, emphasizing the role of noncommissioned officers as teachers. The regiments were supposed to train well-behaved candidates in the rules of combat and garrison service and teach them reading, calligraphy, and computations.[108]

The term of service required before promotion to noncommissioned officer was unclear. The military regulation of 1796 required four years of service, but by 1809 the legal norm was three years.[109] In reality, the average promotion took longer, though some also occurred in less than three years (see tables 2.7–2.10). An 1837 order of the war minister noted that in some units, privates who served no more than one year became noncommissioned officers. The order then confirmed that soldiers should serve at least three years before promotion.[110] By the 1830s the government was already trying to restrict mobility. This policy would become increasingly apparent in the 1840s, as a result of changes in the rules on promotion to officer.

In principle, noncommissioned officers were chosen for their exemplary conduct and military skills. The engineering troops, followed by the artillery, boasted the best-trained noncommissioned officers. Beginning with the reign of Nicholas I, both of these branches maintained special schools to educate noncommissioned officers.[111] Noncommissioned officers were distinguished from soldiers by a higher rate of literacy and proportionately more diverse social origins. They were the progeny of peasants, sacristans (*tserkovniki*), soldiers, and various other social elements. Many nobles also entered the army with the rank of noncommissioned officer, but they rose quickly to officer status and did not regard their colleagues as peers. The social composition of the noncommissioned officers suggests the importance of education in social mobility: lower-class elements with minimal access to schools were heavily represented.

Although there were significant social differences between the noncommissioned officers and the mass of privates, the conditions of military

Table 2.7. Infantry Noncommissioned Officers in 1807[a]

Size of Sample[b]	1,993 (1,750)
Average age[c]	29
Average length of service before promotion[c]	9 years
Social origin (%)[d]	
Peasants	44
Soldiers' children	23
Nobles[e]	13
Sacristans	8
Single householders	4
Urban	3
Cossacks	1
Ethnic minorities	1
Clergy	.7
State officials	.45
Other	.6

SOURCE: TsGVIA, f. 489, op. 1, d. 7212

[a] Data are from eighteen musketeer regiments.
[b] Figure in parentheses excludes all *podpraporshchiki* and nobles if their number exceeds ten in any one regiment.
[c] Figure excludes all *podpraporshchiki* and nobles if their number exceeds ten in any one regiment.
[d] Figures include all *podpraporshchiki*.
[e] Nobles include hereditary nobles, senior officers' children, officers, Polish *szlachta*, and other foreign nobles.

service did not promote the translation of these differences into a special way of life: because most companies were billeted in scattered villages, the noncommissioned officers did not live together in a common society. Dispersed along with their men, they had few opportunities to gather as a group. The term of service also played a role. Noncommissioned officers in the French and Austrian armies were distinguished from the enlisted men by the permanent, and in that sense professional, nature of their service.[112] By contrast, all the lower ranks in the Russian army represented a permanent element. Lengthy service with its inevitable adoption of a military way of life characterized both noncommissioned officers and soldiers.

In military society the noncommissioned officers represented the upwardly mobile group from the poll-tax population. If they could survive

Table 2.8. Jager Noncommissioned Officers in 1805[a]

Size of sample[b]	1,311 (1,085)
Average age[c]	32
Average length of service before promotion[c]	9 years
Social origin (%)[d]	
Peasants	40
Soldiers' children	21
Nobles[e]	18
Sacristans	9
Single householders	7
Urban	2
Volunteers	.45
Ethnic minorities	.7
State officials	.5
Clergy	.45
Other	.8

SOURCE: TsGVIA, f. 489, op. 1, d. 7205.

[a] Data are from fourteen jager regiments.
[b] Figure in parentheses excludes Junkers.
[c] All Junkers are excluded. Nobles are excluded if their number exceeds ten in any one regiment.
[d] Figures include Junkers.
[e] Nobles include hereditary nobles, field and senior officers' children, Polish *szlachta*, and other foreign nobles.

(both physically and professionally), there was a possibility that they—but more likely their sons or grandsons—might attain officer rank.[113] Still, the chances of this happening were in reality not great, for the channels of upward mobility were extremely narrow. Social origin and the traditional juridical divisions of pre-reform society largely determined the terms of service and the possibilities for promotion.

Social Mobility

The rules for promotion in the army reflected the growing tension between the autocracy's desire at once to restrict social mobility and to improve bureaucratic efficiency and rationality by rewarding performance. Social origin directly affected promotion to officer rank; the military

Table 2.9. Noncommissioned Officers in 1813[a]

	Regiment				
	Azov Infantry	Suzdal Infantry	Uglich Infantry	Lubenskii Hussar	Jager No. 35
Size of sample	130	116	121	129	124
Average age	35	36	28	20	29
Average length of service before promotion (years)	9	8	5	4	6
Literate (%)	21	58	39	91	45
Married (%)	19	24	21	5	17
Have children (%)	5	9	10	2	6
Decorated (%)	35	0	16	8	10
Served in military campaigns (%)	91	72	37	67	46
Social origin (%)					
Serfs	25	34	44		30
State Peasants	41	24	30	5	29
Soldiers' children	8	10	7	8	23
Single householders	12	12	3	4	2
Sacristans	5	10	2		6
Urban		4	7	7	6
Cossacks	5				
Nobles		3	2	9	
Vospitanniki				3	
Raznochintsy				11	
Clergy				18	
Minorities				7	
Free status groups				10	
Foreigners				8	
State officials				10	
Other	2	3	5		5

SOURCE: TsGVIA, f. 489, op. 1, d. 17, 897, 1014, 2285, 7225.

[a] For all regiments except the Jager No. 35, data include an insignificant number of *podpraporshchiki*.

Table 2.10. Garrison Noncommissioned Officers in 1816

	Riazan		Voronezh	
	Garrison Battalion	Veterans' Unit	Garrison Battalion	Veterans' Unit
Size of sample	40	65	33	45
Average age	40	45	43	44
Average length of service before promotion (years)	10	13	11	11
Literate (%)	50	18	no data	no data
Married (%)	70	69	no data	no data
Have children (%)	35	17	no data	no data
Decorated (%)	2	9	no data	no data
Served in military campaigns (%)	62	78	no data	no data
Social origin (%)				
Serfs	22	58		
State peasants	20	26	51[a]	49[a]
Soldiers' children	10	5	18	27
Single householders	7	1	15	7
Sacristans	17	8	3	2
Urban	15	1		2
Nobles	7		3	7
Cossacks			6	2
Other			3	4

SOURCE: TsGVIA, f. 489, op. 1, d. 5267 and 5876.

[a] These data do not distinguish serfs and state peasants.

regulation of 1796 specified that prior to promotion, nobles serve three years as noncommissioned officers and non-nobles twelve years.[114] A law of 1797 further accelerated promotion for nobles by granting them the right to enter service as noncommissioned officers, even if vacancies did not exist.[115] The rules on promotion at retirement also reflected traditional social divisions. A law of 1802 permitted nobles to retire with promotion to rank 14 after twelve years of service if they had served three years as noncommissioned officers. "Volunteers" could retire with promotion to rank 14 after fifteen years of service, including four as a noncommissioned officer.[116] In contrast, lower ranks from the soldiers' children, *raznochintsy*, and recruits were required to be literate and to serve twelve years as noncommissioned officers before they became eligible for promotion.[117] Although the type of service affected promotion, social origin was by far the main determinant.

Education also played an increasingly important role in social advancement, especially from the reign of Alexander I. An imperial ukase of 1804 ordered inspectors to promote noncommissioned officers on the basis of "behavior, knowledge, and ability," and not because of "any personal circumstances" or a desire "to please relatives."[118] Then a law of July 1806 allowed nobles who graduated from a university to serve only three months as privates and three months as subensigns before elevation to officer rank; the promotions were to occur regardless of whether vacancies existed.[119] More significant still was a decree in November that extended these rights to students of non-noble origin.[120] From 1818 these privileges also applied to graduates of the Iaroslavl Demidov School of Higher Education, the gymnasia in Kiev and Petersburg, and the boarding schools attached to Moscow University and the Main Pedagogical Institute in St. Petersburg.[121] The army placed clear emphasis on education, which conformed to the state laws requiring a civil service examination for high-level advancement in the bureaucracy.

The government of Nicholas I further expanded the interest in education. New legislation raised additional barriers to social mobility, while accentuating even more the importance of education and skill for social advancement. In the late 1820s the authorities already were expressing concern about the effects of promoting noncommissioned officers from the poll-tax estates to officer rank, even after ten or twelve years of active service. In 1828 the commander of the Corps of the Internal Guard complained about the illiteracy of garrison officers promoted from the poll-tax population.[122] A decree of 1829 explained the full dimensions of the problem:

> Experience shows that a large portion of the lower ranks [promoted from the poll-tax population], after irreproachable service for the legally specified years, prove unworthy to hold the title of Officer, which confers noble status, because they do not have the appropriate education and are barely literate. Their immediate commanders—lacking alternative awards for umblemished service, and not wanting to weaken the other noncommissioned officers' desire to fulfill their service duties—immediately promote them to officer [rank] as soon as they have served the required years, as long as their behavior has been beyond reproach. At the same time, commanders transfer many of them to the Internal Guard, because they do not want them under

their own command as officers. In this way the Army and Garrisons are filled with Officers who lack the appropriate education, and the noble *soslovie* is filled with people for whom this status becomes a burden once they have finished service.[123]

Although this decree revealed official misgivings about the quality of officers from the lower classes, it did not significantly amend the rules of promotion. Promotion for nobles became somewhat easier. They were now eligible for promotion to officer rank after two years as noncommissioned officers. Non-nobles were also freed from corporal punishment and from demotion to private without a court decision confirmed by commanders-in-chief or commanders of separate corps. This law clearly demonstrates the contradictions in state policy, which at once sought to limit social mobility and encourage performance with the promise of promotion.

The 1838 military code systematized the qualifications for promotion to officer rank. As before, a specified term of service as noncommissioned officer preceded promotion: twelve years for common soldiers, six years for *odnodvortsy* who entered service with the rights of "volunteers," four years for candidates who held the first postgraduate degree (law of 1835), and six months for students of the universities.[124] To attain officer rank, the law required literacy of all social groups. Nobles and "volunteers" began service as noncommissioned officers, only if they were literate and knew basic grammar and arithmetic. The illiterate, even if noble, entered the army as privates.[125] This represented a significant departure from previous laws that allowed nobles to begin service as noncommissioned officers regardless of literacy. The code also placed additional restrictions on promoting noncommissioned officers from the lower classes. These men were supposed to have served in combat or campaigns. Noncommissioned officers in the Internal Guard who were literate, but had not served in the army or in combat, could attain officer rank only after eighteen years of service as noncommissioned officers. In the Separate Orenburg and Siberian Corps, the requisite term of service was fifteen years. In contrast, noncommissioned officers in Guards units might reach officer rank after only ten years.[126] Finally, soldiers who suffered corporal punishment with or without a trial for serious infractions recorded in the service lists could never achieve officer rank.[127] According to the law, basic literacy, general performance, the type of service, and especially social origin determined the conditions for promotion.

In the 1840s the government further restricted access to the nobility, but also tightened educational standards for promotion to officer rank. As before, nobles and "volunteers" who graduated from any formal school could enter service with the rank of noncommissioned officer, only if they passed an examination in reading, writing, grammar, and arithmetic. Otherwise, according to a law of February 1840, they entered service as privates and could not receive noncommissioned officer status (leading to officer rank after two or four years) without passing this examination.[128] Subsequent legislation again raised educational standards and specified the subjects covered by the officers' examination.[129] Although social origin was a crucial factor in access to schools, the new laws on promotion made educational qualifications a necessity for all classes, including the nobility. The nobility could still advance faster than other groups, but not unless they attained the educational level specified in the law.

The new educational standards also affected the lower classes, though the government was aware that it could not expect the same qualifications from this group as from nobles and "volunteers." Previously, after twelve years of service as noncommissioned officers, those who could read and write from dictation were eligible for officer status. But subsequent legislation raised the educational requirements.[130] Given the mass illiteracy of the time, the enforcement of this law could only hurt a soldier's chances for promotion. The most serious barrier to social mobility was raised in 1845, when a statute authorized ennoblement only at field officer, rather than senior officer, rank (i.e., rank 8 rather than rank 14). Although the educational requirements for promotion affected all social groups and in this sense loosened *soslovie* boundaries, their value as a force for change was offset by the fact that real social mobility came only with noble status, which had become significantly more difficult to attain. Moreover, access to education still depended to a large extent upon social origin. Thus, within the context of the traditional social structure, higher standards of education for promotion meant less social mobility and greater official reliance on the nobility and middling military semiprofessionals.

During the eighteenth and early nineteenth centuries, it became increasingly difficult for non-nobles to attain officer rank.[131] Tsar Paul I actually forbade the promotion of non-nobles to officer rank in 1798. But this prohibition broke down under the pressure of the Napoleonic Wars, when the demand for officers rose dramatically.[132] In general, promotions were more rapid in wartime. At the start of the Crimean War in 1853, the government was forced to promote noncommissioned officers who had not served the specified period for advancement or passed the examination.[133] The government's main purpose in promoting noncommissioned officers was to reward worthy servicemen and supply the army with competent officers. The low educational level of the lower ranks and the primacy of *soslovie* distinctions made this a contradictory policy.

In an effort to overcome this problem, the government conferred special privileges on noncommissioned officers who were eligible for promotion but chose to remain in their previous rank. These men received a silver sword-knot and chevrons of gold or silver galloon, two-thirds the pay of an ensign or cornet, and exemption from corporal punishment and demotion to private without a trial.[134] They were also entitled to a pension after five years of additional service, whereas those who became officers had to serve another twelve years to obtain a pension.[135] Clearly, the government intended to make nonpromotion more economically attractive than officer rank, which entailed new and significant expenses.[136] Consistent with the government's desire to limit mobility and upgrade professional standards, the privileges granted for refusing promotion sought to reward performance without allowing real social advancement.[137]

The effects of governmental efforts to restrict mobility are evident in the small number of non-nobles who achieved officer rank. Official data from 1863 show that only 5.9 percent of 12,652 officers originated from the poll-tax population.[138] Even these low figures may have been inflated by the impact of the Crimean War. Not surprisingly, there were more officers from the servile classes in the army, especially the infantry, than in the Guards.[139] Officers promoted from the poll-tax population also tended to be concentrated in the junior ranks and usually commanded noncombat units such as garrison battalions and veterans' companies.[140] They were considered useful as officers because of their proximity and familiarity with the soldiers' life, their firsthand knowledge of military drill, and their combat experience. But as one commentator pointed out, most of these officers had served as noncommissioned officers in noncombat positions.[141] Because of their educational and administrative background, noncombat noncommissioned officers were better prepared to pass the examination for promotion to officer rank.[142] As officers they were not highly regarded. Many were functionally illiterate, and in general they had a reputation for cruelty and moral depravity.[143] Transition to officer status was difficult. According to contemporaries, those promoted from the poll-tax population were never fully accepted into the society of officers. Rather, they remained isolated from the mass of noble officers. In pre-reform Russian society, professional roles and identities could not yet transcend the distinction between noble and non-noble. The formal separation of noble and non-noble noncommissioned officers after 1800 helped preserve *soslovie* differences and prevented interaction as professional peers. Nobles moved in their own social circles, and officers from the servile classes remained very close to the soldiers' lifestyle.[144]

Although significant social mobility came only with promotion to officer, awards and decorations represented a limited source of advancement. The most common decoration was the Order of St. Anne, awarded to combat soldiers for twenty years of irreproachable service.[145] A manifesto of 1807 established the Military Order of St. George for bravery against the enemy. Soldiers acquired this decoration only on the field of battle, in the siege and defense of fortresses, and in naval engagements.[146] Both decorations included monetary awards in the form of additional pensions (St. Anne) or higher pay (St. George).[147] Holders of both decorations were exempt from the poll tax at retirement. Designed to motivate the lower ranks, these orders clearly rewarded meritorious behavior and performance.

More important, the orders of St. Anne and St. George brought to their recipients a significant change in juridical status. Beginning in 1800, criminal cases involving soldiers who held the order of St. Anne were referred to the capital.[148] Only the emperor and commanders-in-chief could strip soldiers of this decoration.[149] Legislation from 1807 to 1809 deprived recipients of the Order of St. George of their decorations for serious crimes; but for less important offenses, such as drunkenness and rudeness toward superiors, they were to be arrested and fed on bread and water without corporal punishment.[150] The demotion of noncommissioned officers holding either decoration was not possible without a trial.[151] And lower ranks could not be deprived of these decorations without the emperor's approval.[152] The 1838 military code specifically stated that recipients of both orders were freed from corporal punishment without a trial.[153] This was implicit in earlier legislation, but never so clearly stated. Then an imperial order of October 1843 significantly broadened the scope of these exemptions from corporal punishment. For a first crime, recipients of the Orders of St. Anne and St. George might lose their awards with imperial approval, but they were still exempt from corporal punishment; only for a second subsequent offense could they suffer such punishment.[154] In a serf society where corporal punishment was the norm, this exemption represented a fundamental improvement in the juridical and social status of poll-tax elements.

Despite the government's desire to restrict mobility, military efficiency required some reward of performance. The 1838 military code defined the diverse possibilities. Starting in 1825, all lower ranks (combat and noncombat) who served irreproachably for ten years received a gold stripe, and for each additional five years of unblemished service, they received another stripe.[155] The government also awarded gold and silver medals for heroism and for humanitarian acts like saving a life. Stripes and medals awarded for specific military campaigns or battles were largely honorific, bringing few material benefits.[156] Only in 1843 did recipients of these distinctions also become exempt from corporal punishment for minor crimes upon retirement from military service.[157] Recipients of medals for saving lives and for zealousness were freed from corporal punishment on the same basis as recipients of the orders of St. Anne and St. George.[158] Freedom from corporal punishment was possibly the most desirable privilege, other than promotion to officer rank, that a soldier could attain.

Soldiers could also benefit from various monetary awards. Beginning in May 1808, noncombat soldiers who served irreproachably for twelve years as noncommissioned officers received double pay, but only if they served in the army for twenty years.[159] Then a law of 1809 insisted that only persons eligible for promotion to officer were entitled to double pay. Consequently, anyone who was illiterate, convicted by a court, or demoted to private was not entitled to this award.[160] In July 1828 the government extended these provisions to all noncommissioned officers, but the additional pay was not to exceed 120 rubles.[161] Finally, beginning in 1831 those who remained in the army after completing a full term of service received triple pay and wore a stripe of gold galloon.[162] The government also awarded combat soldiers who served irreproachably in the Guards for twenty-two years and in the army for twenty-five years and then elected to stay in the service. In 1825 they received pay and a half, and beginning in 1829 they got double pay or two and a half times their legally allotted pay, though a law of 1849 limited the supplementary pay to 34 silver rubles a year. Finally, starting in 1826 these soldiers wore an additional gold or silver chevron and beginning in 1854 they received silver medals "for zealousness."[163] Additional pay represented a continuous award permanently distinguishing a soldier from his peers.

Monetary awards were also granted on special occasions. Guards regiments received additional pay for name days, weddings, christenings, and at holiday celebrations. Sometimes for inspections, parades, maneuvers, military exercises and the daily posting of sentries the monarch granted monetary awards, or extra portions of wine, meat, and fish.[164] Finally, the emperor granted monetary sums to soldiers who performed humanitarian and other commendable acts.[165] Military law and tradition clearly rewarded soldiers who distinguished themselves with irreproachable behavior, good performance, or acts of heroism and zealousness.

The structure of the pre-reform army vividly revealed the particularism of the Petrine social and institutional order. The broader structure of Russian society manifested itself in the patterns of social stratification and mobility found in the army. But the army's organization and the state's military needs implicitly threatened the existing social system. The government was naturally concerned with the efficiency and performance of its fighting machine. Consequently, it found itself in the uncomfortable position of actively promoting social advancement, while at the same time upholding a social order that explicitly restricted mobility. The problem became especially acute during the reign of Nicholas I, when the government began to focus on education and greater professionalization as the answer to its increasingly complex military and administrative needs. The tremendous expansion of schools that began in the reign of Peter the Great made stricter educational requirements a reasonable possibility by the time of Nicholas I. Still, the contradiction between rewarding achievement and maintaining the traditional social order was a paramount feature of tsarist social policy. In the immediate future, this issue would play a significant role in the formulation and implementation of the Great Reforms. As a social institution that performed essential professional functions and developed its own special interests, the army repeatedly came into conflict with existing social norms. The government promoted this tension by sanctioning and codifying possible patterns of social mobility. Codification was extremely important as a guarantee of any newly acquired legal status.[166] Yet in practice, the legal possibilities did not translate into a significant challenge to traditional social arrangements. Social mobility remained extremely limited; even when possible, the persistence of *soslovie* subcultures prevented real social integration on a professional basis.

On the eve of the Great Reforms, social origin had become a negative force in structuring Russian society. Birth was an impediment to mobility, but it was neither the sole determinant of social status, nor a guarantee of advancement. Despite its roots in the traditional social order, the army's professional functions and special interests created new tensions in the structure of social relations without, however, changing its essential character. The Russian experience of military modernization is suggestive for European history as a whole. It indicates that social change that was often attributed to the impact of the French Revolution, the advent of liberal politics, and the rise of the bourgeoisie to a significant extent originated in the bureaucratic state of the old regime.[167]

CHAPTER THREE

From Peasant to Soldier: Education and Training

[This is] an army than which, there is none more brave, and with which no other can march, starve, or suffer physical privations and natural inclemencies.
　　　　—Sir Robert Thomas Wilson, 1817

The [soldiers'] oath is a vow, given before God, to serve God and Sovereign with faith and truth, to obey commanders uncomplainingly, to bear patiently cold, hunger, and all the needs of a soldier; to spare not even [one's] last drop of blood for Sovereign and Fatherland, to go to battle boldly and cheerfully for the Tsar, [for] Holy Rus, and [for] the Orthodox faith.
　　　　—*Chtenie dlia soldat*, 1857

Professional training, more than any other aspect of military service, sundered the soldier from his former life. Although the change in juridical status had far-reaching social implications, the "freedom" it brought was not immediately implemented, while the professional education of the peasant recruit began from the first day of service. The primary purpose of military training was to prepare the army for combat, but it also served to instill social control and transform peasants into soldiers. In 1855 the official journal for soldiers, *Chtenie dlia soldat*, described four stages in the transformation from peasant to soldier: recruit,

recruit-soldier, young soldier, and old soldier.[1] Once a recruit reached his regiment he became a recruit-soldier under the supervision of an old soldier (*diad'ka*). During the next two years he was supposed to be "reborn" by changing his appearance, habits, speech, and thoughts and by mastering military posture and marching.[2] Once he became a "young soldier," his knowledge and duties were equal to those of an old soldier, except for his lack of experience. The young soldier was fully accountable for his actions and punished for any mistakes or infractions. Mistakes tolerated in a recruit-soldier—because of his ignorance—were now punishable.[3] The most valued soldier was the old soldier who had served ten (or at least seven) years. In addition to his status as a staunch defender of his country, the old soldier was a teacher of young recruits—the "foundation of the regiment, the hope of [his] sovereign and fatherland."[4]

Education and Training

Young peasants who began service entered a new world defined by the duties, hierarchy, and discipline of the imperial army. The state viewed the army as a model for the rest of Russian society—a model that embodied the ideals of service, social discipline, bureaucratic rationality, and cultural modernization. Before conscription, the new recruit's primary identity had lain with his family and village. But now (in most cases involuntarily) he would devote the best years of his life to "the faith, tsar, and fatherland." His weapon would be a wife, his knapsack a brother, his commander a father, and the service his stepmother.[5]

The moment local authorities assigned a recruit to a transport party, he became subject to military law and schedules. Instructions to officers accompanying parties of recruits revealed the sudden change. In March 1806 an imperial ukase prescribed gradual stages of training for recruits assigned to the Siberian and Orenburg Cavalry Inspectorate. By 1838 these provisions were standard for all troops.[6] Initially, recruits were to race, then jump across ditches and cross beams. After achieving some success with these exercises, they learned to stand, walk, and march in military fashion and also were introduced to the various turns, paces, deployments, and parade formations. Next, recruits learned to stand and walk with arms; to dismantle, clean, and reassemble weapons; and finally to load, take aim, and shoot at targets from various distances. The law exhorted commanders to teach recruits the manual of arms "without the slightest violence and force." The government recognized that new recruits needed time to adjust to military life and thus defined progressive stages of physical training.

The 1806 ukase openly admitted that induction into military service was both a physical and psychological shock:

> Experiences of the past showed that it was inexpedient to assign recruits to the regiments immediately after their acceptance. For it is completely natural that a person who has engaged only in farming and suddenly has to change his climate, way of life, [and] activities, and becomes separated from his family, is subject to illness or at least depression, which also often leads to fatal consequences. As a contrary example, it is possible to mention the cantonists [i.e., soldiers' sons], who gradually adapt to the soldier's life [and] bear it incomparably better than recruits.[7]

To ease the recruit's adjustment to military life, a law of 1808 established reserve depots (*zapasnye depo*), where recruits would remain at least eight months before joining their regiments.[8] During that time they performed "light service," so that when they reached their units, they would already know "the main rules of military service." Before arrival at a depot, the recruits learned only posture, marching in step, and turns. But their introduction to military discipline began immediately. Roll calls were held twice a day (in the morning and evening), and on Sundays the recruits listened to readings of those military regulations pertaining to privates. In this way they learned "how honored is the calling of a soldier, how obligated each [soldier] is to fulfill [his] oath, and which crime subjects [them] to which punishment."[9] By imposing strict military discipline on recruits, while at the same time limiting their regular service duties, the government hoped to prepare them for military life without overtaxing their physical strength.

The recruitment regulation of 1831 defined more precisely the initial training and socialization of recruits.[10] By this time recruits proceeded directly from their native provinces to active or reserve regiments, where their early training lasted about six months. Training began immediately on rest days during the march. The accompanying officer conducted a morning and evening roll call, after which prayers were read. After the morning roll call, the recruits learned military posture and how to keep step and turn. They also listened to articles read from the military criminal laws. Other activities designated for rest days included shaving brows and beards, bathing, washing linen, and repairing clothes and shoes. Finally, on holidays the officer was supposed to accompany the recruits to mass if there was a church nearby.

Subsequent legislation continued to stress the need for a gradual approach.[11] An 1834 order of the war minister ruled that recruits who had been in the service less than six months should appear at inspections without weapons and other equipment and were expected to know only correct posture and the military step.[12] But according to the war minister, commanders everywhere were ignoring the need to train recruits in stages.[13] From childhood, young peasants learned to fear the long term of service and the deprivations of military life. Recruits entertained no positive expectations of life in the army, but rather began service with suspicion and hostility. The recruit's initial training was therefore crucial. As the state and military elite recognized, his attitude toward the service and his future development as a soldier depended on his earliest experiences.[14]

Overall responsibility for the soldiers' education lay with the company commander, though dispersion through quartering usually required delegation of this task to noncommissioned officers or even experienced soldiers. The main components of a soldier's education included hygiene and dress, the maintenance of weapons and equipment, religion, discipline, and most important, military drill (including marksmanship). The purpose of this education was to efface village habits and "the peasant spirit" and to create a new military man.[15]

When a recruit reached his assigned regiment, he was placed under the supervision of an older experienced soldier (*diad'ka*, "uncle"), who introduced him to the rigors of military life. The *diad'ka* taught him to dress correctly and care for his equipment and explained the meaning of commands. As a kind of surrogate parent, the *diad'ka* was supposed to treat his charge with patience, affection, and tolerance.[16] He was expected to exert a moral influence on the young recruit, exhorting him to conduct himself in an orderly manner and to give himself "a good military appearance, not to be lazy, to be bold and quick." In a word, the *diad'ka*—whose mission reflected the traditional paternalistic values associated with serfdom—was to instruct the recruit "so that peasant habits are completely extirpated."[17]

External appearance was a major concern of military education. Because the tsar graciously provided for the soldier's basic physical needs and because the soldier should be grateful for having the glorious opportunity to serve his country, he was expected to be happy, his external appearance "always cheerful and satisfied."[18] A correct military appearance also included posture and bearing. The first thing a recruit learned was to carry himself erect, to walk and turn in martial fashion. The soldier was always supposed to look neat and clean. To that end military regulations held him responsible for the maintenance of his weapons, equipment, and uniforms. These items were essential to the army's combat functions and to the cultivation of a military spirit.

The general backwardness of Russian society and the high rates of illness in the pre-reform army demanded attention to basic hygiene. In 1820 the commander of the Second Army's Main Headquarters ordered that each company of the special training battalion for the preparation of non-commissioned officers should have a bathhouse to promote neatness and to protect the health of the men.[19] The military code of 1838 required soldiers to wash their hands and face every day, shave every third or fourth day, and bathe once a week.[20] Another official encouraged soldiers to keep their bodies clean and change their clothing once a week.[21] Despite these exhortations, there is no evidence that soldiers practiced better hygiene than other lower-class groups. The physical conditions of military life made good hygiene virtually impossible. A vigilant commander in a favorable environment might achieve some progress, but such conditions were an extreme rarity.

Religion formed another important aspect of the soldier's daily life, at least from the government's point of view. The 1796 regulation on infantry service required the singing of matins at daybreak and vespers at 5 o'clock. In addition, soldiers were supposed to attend Mass at least twice a week (on Sundays and Wednesdays) and more often during holidays. Although military duties might sometimes interfere with church attendance, even on these days every soldier was obliged to attend one of the three services. And when the army was stationary, Mass was to be sung every day after the posting of guards.[22] According to the military code of 1838, priests conducted services for the regiments every Sunday and on holidays, throughout Lent, and on days when Mass was sung. All military ranks also were expected to attend confession and receive communion once a year.[23]

Soldiers obviously did not object to religious practices. On the contrary, most regiments maintained special funds for their icons, financed by contributions from the lower ranks. Still, popular religiosity was characterized by indifference and general ignorance of Orthodox canons.[24] Not all commanders saw to it that religious practices were observed. In 1829 Count Dibich felt compelled to order the troops of the Second Army to observe the prescribed Wednesday and Sunday fasts—so that God's favor would not be lost because of failure to observe church laws.[25] A later commentator noted that like the vast majority of Russian peasants, soldiers were basically ignorant of the Orthodox religion, their knowledge and understanding of the faith no better than that of children. Perhaps more revealing, literate soldiers showed little interest in reading the moralistic and patriotic tales contained in official soldiers' journals like *Chtenie dlia soldat*.[26] There was nothing exceptional about the role religion played in the soldiers' education. In the tradition of the *Polizeistaat*, military training served a broader moral purpose, as the authorities sought to mold the character and values of the young men who served.[27]

CHAPTER THREE

All armies—regardless of time and place—consider discipline essential to professional performance and victory in combat. Russian sources described strict subordination and obedience to one's superiors as "the soul of military service."[28] Exhortations to observe regulations and to obey commanders were a constant feature of military life. An 1806 ukase noted that on holidays and Sundays, when companies gathered before the church procession, soldiers heard the military articles: on fear of God, firmness of faith, and loyalty to the sovereign; on respect for senior and junior officers; on obedience by privates; on the importance of sentries; on care of weapons, uniform, and equipment; on duties in quarters and in camp; on punishment for desertion, flight from the field of battle, and other crimes.[29] Similarly, the 1838 military code prescribed that on Sundays soldiers should hear the military criminal laws read aloud "with a clear interpretation of their meaning."[30] Subordination also required that soldiers know the names, titles, and proper forms of address for all members of the imperial family, for their superior commanders, and for the officers and noncommissioned officers of their regiment.[31] In this way they were constantly reminded to whom they owed obedience in the military hierarchy.

To instill discipline, military laws strictly regulated daily routines and schedules. Commanders demanded unfailing adherence to prescribed schedules and punished tardiness. Generally, noncommissioned officers were responsible for presenting their men at the designated time and place.[32] Roll was called every morning and evening, and soldiers were forbidden to leave their quarters during the night.[33] The 1838 military code also regulated the soldiers' free time: after sunset they could not walk around town and were forbidden to enter brothels, restaurants, cafes, and taverns. They were allowed to engage in outside work for wages only with the knowledge of their company or squadron commander, and they then could sell "freely" the products of their labor.[34] The important point here, though, is that the law sought to regulate in some manner every minute of a soldier's day. To prevent laziness and idleness, which could lead to "incurable illness and vices," soldiers were supposed to be occupied constantly.[35]

In professional terms, the most important part of the soldier's education was military drill and the use of weapons. The authorities emphasized discipline and precision movements as the attributes needed for adequate parade-ground performance, at this time the crucial measure of military preparedness. The pre-reform army was trained in the linear tactics associated with Frederick the Great—tactics characterized by deployment in closed order into lines, columns, or squares. In the later eighteenth century, the army added skirmishing tactics in extended order to the more traditional and still more widely used closed order formations.[36] In closed order, soldiers were supposed to function like cogs in a machine. Their movements were to be synchronized and mechanical, their responses to signals automatic.[37] (On the battlefield their behavior could be quite different, as survival became the crucial motivation.) Extended order allowed freer movement and required more individual initiative, since it demanded that soldiers use an area's natural cover for protection.[38] A different kind of soldier was needed to perform successfully in extended order. The citizen-soldier of revolutionary France provided the model—hence the Russian military elite's emphasis on remaking peasants into soldiers and the growing discomfort with the serf-soldier. As the nineteenth century progressed, the discrepancy between the traditional social order and the new military tactics became increasingly obvious.

At the beginning of Alexander I's reign, marksmanship became a significant feature of military training.[39] By the reign of Nicholas I, inspectors regularly observed target shooting. According to the 1848 infantry regulation, every company was supposed to have forty-eight soldiers specially trained in marksmanship and extended order.[40] But despite all the attention given to marksmanship in the first half of the nineteenth century, including the introduction of standardized rules after 1819, the inaccuracy of the smooth-bore firearms used by the Russian infantry prevented fully satisfactory results.[41] Some observers also claimed that marksmanship was never given priority or even taught systematically.[42] Inspectors reported improvements in the 1820s, but consistently accurate firepower remained beyond reach.[43] As late as 1855, the time devoted to marksmanship and the results of this training varied even in the elite Guards and Grenadier Corps. In general, the level of achievement was considered unsatisfactory.[44] Thus closed-order tactics remained extremely important, since firing in mass volleys was the only way to make up for the technical deficiencies of the weapons in use at that time.

Although military drills were a daily feature of the soldier's life, the structure and content of training fluctuated seasonally. During the winter when most soldiers were scattered in small groups around different villages, training included individual instruction in marching and the handling of weapons. In good weather, target shooting and marching in small groups was also possible, though in general, Russia's harsh winters greatly interfered with extensive training.[45] In these circumstances, company commanders spent little time actually drilling their men. Responsibility for the soldiers' training thus fell to the noncommissioned officers who were not always prepared for the task. When the troops gathered in larger formations during the spring and summer, company, battalion, and regimental training was possible. Individual instruction continued, but its frequency varied, depending on the soldier's experience and performance.[46]

The legally permitted intensity of drill remained unclear. Officers exercised broad discretionary authority in accordance with the overall performance of their units. Some sources suggested drilling only once a day, others twice. In 1809 the war minister announced that one battalion in the St. Petersburg Garrison drilled twice a day. He reminded commanders that this was forbidden and remarked "that in all the field army battalions in St. Petersburg the lower ranks need less drilling than the officers."[47] By contrast, an 1813 book on military health suggested that at peak times of training, four to six hours a day (two to three hours each in the morning and evening) was not excessively demanding.[48] In 1820 the authorities attributed desertions from the training artillery companies to excessive drill occurring three times a day—the third time by candlelight.[49] Then in 1821 these same authorities reported that the large number of sick soldiers (twenty within a few days) in the Guards Grenadier Regiment resulted from the weather and the "incessant" training held twice a day. According to the soldiers, they had to drill both in the morning and afternoon, so that guard duty was considered rest.[50]

In October 1820, P. D. Kiselev, commander of Main Headquarters of the Second Army, recommended that the early morning be devoted to difficult parade exercises in closed formation, whereas after dinner the soldiers could perform light exercises that included fencing, reading, recruits' training, and marksmanship.[51] Rest was also part of the weekly routine. There was to be no training after dinner on Saturdays and Sundays, except for "the lazy." Although officers could use corporal punishment to exhort deficient soldiers, they were not to inflict more than twenty-five blows with sticks once a day. After three punishments, the company commander himself was to supervise the "lazy" soldier and could order a maximum punishment of fifty blows with sticks. If the soldier still did not improve his behavior, the battalion field officer and then the battalion commander took responsibility for him.[52] Most of the evidence indicates that training usually occurred twice a day. The 1838 military code prescribed that no single type of drill, whether individualized or in groups, should be held more than once a day for three hours maximum.[53] There was, then, some attempt to regulate the intensity of training during the reign of Nicholas I. But the law did not define precisely the nature, duration, or frequency of the training or the permissible means of executing it. Commanders, held responsible for the performance of their men, enjoyed considerable discretion in organizing training, and, as a result, arbitrariness and particularism flourished.[54]

The military functions of the army along with its special economic needs demanded that a variety of skilled personnel man its ranks. A major obstacle to the effective training of the pre-reform army was the low educational level of new recruits. The vast majority were illiterate, and few were trained in any useful crafts (see table 3.1). Troops burdened with large numbers of recruits at any given time had great difficulty preparing them for service.[55] In the absence of troop concentration and modern industry, the soldiers of each regiment had to learn crafts needed for the military economy. The 1838 code stressed that each regiment should have sufficient numbers of tailors and shoemakers, so that the production of uniforms did not interfere with combat training.[56] Without a host of skilled craftsmen, the army simply would have ceased to function. The general backwardness of Russian society forced the army to create its

Table 3.1. Level of Skill among Recruits[a]

Year and Province	Sample Size	Literate	Trained in a Craft
1814			
Voronezh	1,186	2	1
1827–28			
Iaroslavl	282	41	47[b]
Kiev	568	18[c]	30
Kostroma	354	32	53
Kursk	607	10	4
Novgorod	269	5	13[b]
Pskov	251	3	5
Riazan	403	15	4
St. Petersburg	679	96	30
Saratov	429	14	4
Smolensk	395	15	0
Tomsk	116	12	5
Voronezh	551	19	11
1835–36			
Smolensk	1,066	56	14

SOURCE: TsGVIA, f. 395, op. 318, d. 6, 10, 21, 22, 25, 28–30, 33, 37, 43, 45.

[a] Recruits who were both literate and trained in a craft are counted in both categories.

[b] Includes one musician.

[c] Includes eight Jews literate only in Yiddish.

own economic infrastructure, a venture that was costly, inefficient, and most important, deflected valuable time from military training.

The attainment of literacy by the mass of soldiers was less important to the government than artisanal skills. Because of their administrative and instructional duties, noncommissioned officers needed to be literate.[57] Many seem to have achieved some degree of literacy, though precise figures are not yet available. Soldiers' sons who attended special military schools were expected to be literate, and lower ranks in the artillery and engineering troops were also more likely to receive some formal education, because of the more technically advanced subjects they were expected to master.[58] For most soldiers, however, there were few opportunities to obtain any formal education.

The most significant effort to teach literacy began in 1815 under the direction of the future Decembrists M. F. Orlov and S. I. Turgenev. These enlightened officers established a Lancastrian school, which employed the best students as monitors, for Russian troops stationed in France. Subsequently, Lancastrian schools appeared throughout the Second Army, in the Guards Corps, and in branches of the Military Orphanage.[59] The movement came to an end in 1822, following the arrest of V. F. Raevskii, who in the spring of 1821 had become director of the Lancastrian school in the Sixteenth Infantry Division.[60] The education of the lower ranks was a controversial subject. Although Alexander I viewed popular literacy as a tool of moral instruction and state-directed cultural development, other high-level officials regarded it as a threat to the existing social order.[61] For this reason the pre-reform army never committed itself wholeheartedly to the literacy of the lower ranks. Rather, it remained caught between its own desire to improve professional performance—a desire that required better-educated manpower—and its commitment to the traditional social arrangements based on serfdom.[62]

When fully realized, military training produced a professional soldier with a new appearance and speech, new attitudes and expectations, and a new role in society. Removed from his peasant origins, his new identification centered around the regiment and army. The training that was imposed upon soldiers, defined and regulated by the state, clearly separated them from the peasantry. As the education of the lower ranks revealed, they lived in a world distinguished from the traditional village by a much higher degree of direct governmental intervention. In this world the state sought to control both soldier and officer through standardized military training, through the special professional functions and organization of the army, and through the promise of reward and the threat of punishment. As a result, the authorities held soldiers accountable for their behavior in ways that could never be demanded from peasants. Psychologically, socially, and culturally, soldiers constituted a separate *soslovie* characterized by a distinct, albeit state-imposed, way of life.

Training and the Structure of Military Life

Throughout Europe, combat readiness was limited by the very structure of military life, which actually impeded performance. In an original study of military preparedness in the eighteenth-century British army, J. A. Houlding has attributed inadequate training to factors of time and opportunity.[63] Because the army spent most of its time dispersed in billets or on the march and very little time fully concentrated or stationary, there was minimal opportunity for advanced training.[64] Other factors contributing to the "friction of peace"—that is, factors interfering with combat training in peacetime—included the army's police role in fighting smugglers and repressing popular disturbances and its garrison duties.[65] Houlding concludes that the army's role as the guarantor of social peace tended to take precedence over military needs, so that efficient wartime performance was not the predominant role assigned to the standing army.[66]

While Russian society did not share the British hostility toward the standing army, similar factors of time and opportunity played an important role in the quest for adequate training. In towns, fortresses, and garrisons, where military duties included policing and guarding, the burden of nonmilitary service was the most obvious factor interfering with peacetime training.[67] When manpower was short, garrison duties could become especially burdensome. Troops in border regions containing fortresses performed endless guard duty. In the early twenties, P. D. Kiselev reported that one-tenth of the manpower of the Second Army was assigned to guard duties every day.[68]

Conditions in the Smolensk Garrison further illustrate the problem. In June 1828 the assistant commander of Main Headquarters, Count A. I. Chernyshev, demanded that the Smolensk commandant respond to reports of undue harshness in service. According to one memorandum, after the Fifth Infantry Division left Smolensk, the men of the permanent garrison battalion performed guard duty every other day. This reportedly resulted from the large number of posts in the town and from the battalion not being at full strength. In addition, the soldiers were called out to post sentries at five in the morning, when the actual posting did not occur until eleven, "so that they have only a few hours of rest." The Smolensk commandant explained that there were not enough men for three shifts; consequently, postings occurred only on Wednesday and Sunday mornings, and the soldiers began guard duty after dinner. When the number of men further declined, because of official trips and because tailors and shoemakers were needed to outfit recruits, there was sufficient manpower for only two shifts. So the commandant further limited the posting of sentries to Sundays. By the time he wrote his explanation in July, even fewer soldiers were available, and he had ordered simple postings. Even so, on official holidays, the soldiers went from guard duty to church parades and then returned to their posts. Chernyshev accepted these explanations and dropped the inquiry.[69]

Similar problems plagued the Tauride Garrison in 1845–46. Although the battalion was close to full strength, numerous duties and a large number of recruits forced noncommissioned officers and instructors to rotate constantly between guard duty and instruction with practically no time for rest. As a result, the overall supervision of recruits in the barracks was wholly inadequate, and their training lagged.[70]

Since the eighteenth century, in addition to guarding and policing, the army had regularly supplied labor for state works. Soldiers received a lower wage than hired laborers, and so the government preferred to employ troops whenever possible.[71] A close examination of the state works projected for the summer of 1843 indicates the extent to which extraneous military duties interfered with adequate training. The state works included highway and canal building and construction work in fortresses.[72] The logistics of assigning troops to guard duty in towns and fortresses, to state construction projects, and to divisional and corps gatherings for training were very complex. It was important that the troops not waste too much time traveling from one place to another. In addition, the authorities had to locate quarters or camp sites.[73]

The summer activities, lasting from mid-May until mid-September, combined state works, guard duty, and advanced training at the corps or divisional level. Guard duty and state works could be combined with basic training in small groups, but in general these obligations meant that the troops would miss the larger gatherings where reviews and maneuvers were held.[74] In some cases, following large-scale maneuvers, units would proceed to state works from mid-September until the end of November.[75] Although building roads and maintaining fortresses were basic to the army's infrastructure, the use of troops for these tasks deprived them of time sorely needed for advanced training.

Quartering arrangements heightened the need for camp gatherings. For most of the year (usually about eight months) the majority of Russian troops were dispersed in small groups over significant distances. The soldiers lived in peasant homes and were de facto free of military discipline. Training beyond basic individual and platoon exercises was possible only when larger units gathered in the spring and summer.[76] In the early twenties the infantry of the Second Army came together in brigades for six weeks each year. During this time the army held battalion and regimental exercises, and senior commanders reviewed the troops.[77] But P. D. Kiselev did not consider regimental exercises sufficient. Since large-scale camp gatherings and maneuvers provided the only practical military experience in peacetime, divisional and corps exercises were also needed. These taught individual units to maneuver properly en masse and gave commanders a chance to direct concentrations of troops comparable to those they would command in battle.[78] In 1821–23 the Second Army held maneuvers combining several divisions, and in 1823 the emperor approved a proposal to assign each division a permanent location to establish camps.[79] Following his predecessor's lead, Nicholas I made large-scale troop gatherings and maneuvers a regular feature of military life.[80]

The level of troop concentration and the amount of time spent in camp varied. In general, the troops left their winter quarters in April to meet at company, battalion, and regimental levels. These exercises were then followed with brigade, divisional, and/or corps exercises ending in large-scale maneuvers. Then in late August or early September, the troops would return to their winter quarters.[81] According to the 1843 project for summer activities, the Seventeenth Infantry Division (Sixth Infantry Corps) was to gather for ten weeks. The Thirteenth Division would meet for four weeks and then move to a corps camp for another six weeks.[82] Similarly, from mid-April until late May the Grenadier Corps gathered for company and battalion exercises followed by brigade, divisional, or corps camps and maneuvers lasting until September.[83] It was rare for an entire division or corps to gather at one time. Usually, at least some units were absent because of assignment to state works or guard duty.[84] Still, high-level officials regarded maneuvers as the most essential aspect of military training. Although the pressing demand for labor on state works sometimes made attendance at maneuvers irregular, they effectively provided most soldiers with some practical combat training. And because of the dispersed quartering arrangements, their role was especially crucial.

The system of quartering had important implications for military preparation, contributing significantly to the "friction of peace." In 1814, because Vitebsk province was ruined from war and crop failure, the Iamburg Uhlan (light cavalry) Regiment quartered in groups smaller than platoons. As a result, service duties were disregarded, and it became impossible to conduct training exercises.[85] Moreover, in an effort to preserve state uniforms, the soldiers wore peasant dress throughout the winter, except during drills or on official errands.[86] Extended periods in dispersed conditions limited the soldier's involvement in military life, allowing him to revert back to peasant habits.⁸⁷ P. D. Kiselev reported that until 1819 when the Second Army set out to tighten discipline and improve supervision, commanders made few demands on their men after they returned to their winter quarters from summer camp. He further noted that in order to maintain discipline and combat readiness, commanders should see to it that their subordinates observed all the rules of combat service at all times.⁸⁸ Dispersion made sufficient standardized supervision of training extremely difficult, undermining discipline and promoting particularism.

Dispersed quartering also enhanced the role of noncommissioned officers as the backbone of the regiment. During the long winter months, they bore primary responsibility for the soldiers' training. Even among troops concentrated in barracks, the noncommissioned officers were crucial. Unlike officers who spent a few hours a day with their men, the noncommissioned officers lived with the soldiers and were therefore in a position to exercise constant supervision over them.⁸⁹ Their level of skill and attitude toward the men were especially important to the success of military education.⁹⁰ Culturally, most noncommissioned officers were barely distinguishable from privates.⁹¹ Their authority derived from years of practical experience in the details of military life. Often lacking in formal education, they acquired special skills over long years of service.⁹² Still, their level of expertise did not satisfy contemporary observers. Commanders and the military press repeatedly complained that many noncommissioned officers were not equipped to fulfill their duties as moral and technical teachers. They were sometimes accused of excessive severity, though in this regard they probably were following the lead of commanding officers.⁹³ Local differences were also significant. Because regimental and company commanders chose noncommissioned officers, their qualities varied widely, depending upon the individual preferences of their superiors.⁹⁴

A final aspect of military life preventing intensive training resulted from inadequate finances. Out of necessity, every regiment was involved in extensive, time-consuming economic activities. Commanders were impelled to spend a significant amount of time tending to the regiment's economic needs and so could not always supervise carefully the training of their men.⁹⁵ It was also general practice to release groups of soldiers for several months each year to engage in outside work. During this time soldiers were completely freed from military duties. The pressure of subsistence requirements caused the troops to give less attention and energy to their professional military duties.

Quartering arrangements, state works, and economic realities all contributed to the "friction of peace." Clearly, the Russian army suffered from society's general economic and social backwardness. Performance lagged in the absence of an adequate infrastructure for administering and maintaining the troops.[96] But if one examines the pre-reform army in the context of eighteenth-century Europe (where it rightly belongs), this situation is not unusual. The army's physical integrity was always preserved. And it succeeded in promoting Russia's territorial and foreign policy interests. Whatever the social cost for the common soldier, the army generally met the government's basic military needs.[97]

Peacetime Performance and Official Expectations

What did the state expect from the army, and how well did the troops fulfill these expectations? Inspectors' reports identified the government's main peacetime concerns. Following the defeat of Napoleon, Russia's perceived military might seemed unassailable until the Crimean War. This reinforced the normal tendency of officials to stress strength over vulnerability. The complacency and formalism of the pre-reform bureaucracy and the desire to portray institutions in a favorable light affected military as well as civilian administration. The personal involvement of three emperors in the minutiae of military affairs further complicated the situation, since officials might be reluctant to upset the monarch with unfavorable news. More important, inspections were conducted by superior commanders who were disinclined to expose shortcomings, since they themselves were held responsible for the violations of their subordinates.[98] Still, even in the midst of general praise and a certain reluctance to expose weaknesses, the misgivings of high-level officers manage to creep into their reports.

Inspectors were instructed to examine the overall condition of the unit beginning with the appearance of the men.[99] Did they look healthy, cheerful, and satisfied? Were their uniforms and other pieces of personal equipment in good repair? Had they received pay, provisions, and other supplies in full and at the designated times? Did they know the extent and whereabouts of their artel funds, and were the records of these funds in order? Did the soldiers listen to the military articles that were read aloud on Sundays and holidays? Did they suffer excessive or cruel punishments? And finally, did they have any grievances or claims against their superiors? Inspectors were supposed to question soldiers when their commanding officers were not present, and then investigate any complaints.

Inspectors also examined the incidence of death, illness, and desertion. Authorities viewed these data as basic indicators of a regiment's physical condition. Along with retirements and discharges or transfers for disability, they established the unit's numerical strength and, consequently, its fighting capacity. Fighting capacity also depended on the condition of weapons and other munitions, so inspectors checked to see that sufficient amounts of these items were on hand and in good working order. They examined the horses and transport vehicles that were so important to any unit's combat readiness. Perhaps the most crucial barometer of combat readiness was the soldiers' performance of military drills. This usually meant the basic evolutions and maneuvers, handling weapons, and marching in small groups. Increasingly, inspectors also checked marksmanship. Finally, they examined the soldiers' quarters and the regimental infirmary. If the men billeted on civilians, then it was important to ascertain that they were adequately fed and to investigate the complaints of local residents.[100] In a short amount of time inspectors were expected to evaluate the physical, moral, and economic condition of the troops.

Reports on the execution of military drills revealed that performance varied significantly. Authorities usually attributed success or failure to the abilities and zealousness of regimental commanders. Officers and noncommissioned officers were often accused of inefficiency and inadequate knowledge of their service obligations.[101] Inspectors also frequently criticized the soldiers' individual bearing and movements (which provided the foundation for maneuvers in larger formations). The troops were expected to march in step quickly, firmly, and precisely. They were supposed to move with ease and energy and remain perfectly aligned, quiet, and attentive. Their handling of weapons was supposed to be animated and synchronized.[102] As one component in a mass machine, the pre-reform soldier was trained to move and respond mechanically and in total harmony with his comrades. In the linear tactics of the day, a break in battle formation could easily mean defeat and destruction.[103]

The standardization of training, equipment, uniforms, and the order of service was essential if the troops were to function as a synchronized mass machine. But the Russian army could not tackle seriously the problem of standardization until after the Napoleonic Wars. Tsar Paul brought some uniformity to training and service through the military regulations (*ustavy*) of 1796 and through attacks on the independence of local commanders.[104] But his assassination and the ongoing disruptions of war cut short these efforts until the period of relative peace after 1815. The years following the Congress of Vienna witnessed a reconstruction and reordering of military life that was especially visible in the increasingly systematic and extensive bureaucratic regulation characteristic of Nicholas I's government.

At the beginning of Alexander I's reign, comprehensive and precise rules of service still did not exist. Individual regiments kept their own manuals, which they modified at will. There were some regulations on the books, but they were not followed closely. Although army regiments sent officers to St. Petersburg to study the order of service in Guards units, the absence of clearly established written rules resulted in misunderstandings that prevented standardization.[105] Only after 1815 were the authorities able to turn their attention to achieving uniformity in drill, weapons, and the order of service. The troops made significant progress in this area, but complete standardization proved elusive.[106] The government began to issue digests of rules that gave commanders a set of uniform regulations to follow.[107] To promote understanding of the regulations, the army also established special "model troops" (*obraztsovye voiska*) and training units (*uchebnye komandy*), where privates and noncommissioned officers learned correct rules of service and then returned to their regiments to transmit their newly acquired skills.[108] Through more standardized training and procedures, the government hoped to raise professional performance.

Regular inspections promoted the application of increasingly standardized rules.[109] Overall the army made considerable progress toward uniformity in drill. Still, the structure of military life undermined the desire for consistency. Commanders did not apply the standardized regulations uniformly, so that individual preferences tended to determine the nature and quality of the soldiers' training. The dispersal of troops in peacetime made standardization especially difficult, allowing the spirit of particularism to reassert itself. Summer camps and maneuvers were supposed to correct inconsistencies, but not all troops participated in these exercises equally. When officers were not well versed in military drill, mistakes easily became established practice. In addition, scarce economic resources interfered with standardization in weapons and uniforms. Bad equipment and shortages of ammunition also prevented adequate training.[110] No doubt the much-maligned formalism and repetitiveness of military drills were needed to achieve basic uniformity in military practices.[111]

Critics of pre-reform military training denounced the emphasis on preparing for reviews and the inadequate preparation for actual combat. The Decembrist Podzhio derided the army's concern with perfecting ceremonial march, and Pestel stressed the need for practical combat training in the form of regular maneuvers.[112] In a more official vein, Kiselev argued that the pressure placed upon commanders forced them to expend all their resources on improving the external appearance of their units.[113] Foreign observers also detected an excessive devotion to external appearances that harmed the army's ability to perform in battle.[114] Following Russia's defeat in the Crimean War, criticism of military drill became more widespread. Commentators repeatedly noted that commanders devoted most of their energy to preparing for reviews and parades. This emphasis on external appearances and the aesthetics of military drill gave soldiers minimal exposure to actual combat situations.[115]

Russian commanders perhaps did place too much emphasis on ceremonial march and parade-ground performance. But these critics of the repetitiveness and formalism of training exercises were enlightened officers, and it is possible that they were reacting to the increasing depersonalization of modern warfare. Theirs was an aristocratic response to the growing inhumanity and facelessness of battle—a facelessness that manifested itself in the formalistic and mechanistic tactics of the day. John Keegan has noted that after the military innovations of the fifteenth, sixteenth, and seventeenth centuries, killing one's opponent in combat was no longer a gentlemanly affair. Rather, the new emphasis on drill reduced the individual soldier's status to that of an automaton in the order of battle. Gunpowder technology, rigid hierarchies of command, and the wearing of uniforms all reflected and promoted the depersonalization of war, a process completed in the twentieth century.[116] The Russian army's love of drill was not unique. The attention to drill was an essential element in the process of depersonalizing war. Most, if not all, of the drills performed did bear some resemblance to the linear tactics of the day. And the repetition of drills prepared soldiers psychologically for combat. As Keegan argues, for the past two hundred years Western military education has sought "to reduce the conduct of war to a set of rules and a system of procedures" for the purpose of making "orderly and rational what is essentially chaotic and instinctive." Thus military education has focused on rote learning, repetition of standard drills, and use of simulation techniques. According to Keegan, it is precisely the routinization and reductive character of military education that helps to prevent "the onset of fear" and panic in actual combat.[117]

As the government saw it, the Russian army performed satisfactorily until the Crimean War. And it is possible to argue that Russia's humiliating performance in the Crimea had little to do with the quality of the common soldier. Rather, it resulted from logistical difficulties, poor technology, and the army's weak economic infrastructure. Simply stated, the Russian army was poorly armed and poorly supplied.[118] If the formalistic training that soldiers received did not prepare them adequately for combat, this was true of other European armies as well. The Russian soldier's capacity for suffering and his courage and steadfastness in battle were legendary in Europe.[119] Frederick the Great is quoted as saying, "It is easier to kill Russian soldiers than to defeat them."[120] Unfortunately for the Russian army, the courage of its men could not compensate indefinitely for continued economic and technical backwardness.[121]

The Soldier as Loyal Servant

The Russian soldier officially held a special and respected place in society. Distinguished by his "honor and glory," the soldier was supposed to set an example of obedience to authority, discipline, and moral uprightness.[122] The results of military education were ambiguous. Soldiers were clearly a breed apart, permanently separated from their original communities. The difficulty of reintegrating retired soldiers into civilian society attests to their social, cultural, and juridical separateness. The authorities expected soldiers to behave differently from peasants and held them accountable for their conduct in new, often confusing ways. When in 1822 the commander of the Sixth Infantry Corps concluded that desertions by residents and soldiers from the Bessarabian town of Kiliia were related, the local chief of police vehemently denied the possibility. In his view the desertions could not possibly be connected, for "soldiers are not children, but much more educated than peasants."[123] Similarly, in 1832 the governor of Saratov province reported that retired soldiers made better firemen than hired freemen, because they were orderly and disciplined.[124] Military life imposed a rigorous discipline on former peasants and townspeople, and the effects were sometimes lifelong.

While some officials praised the discipline of soldiers, others expressed doubts about their reliability. There is repeated evidence of soldiers fomenting rebellion and discontent among peasants in the 1820s–40s. They reportedly spread rumors about impending reductions in feudal dues, stressing the poverty, hardships, and humiliations of village life.[125] Military regulations also revealed that the authorities regarded soldiers as a reliable police instrument only after long years of service and separation from home. A law of 1832 required that a soldier serve for twenty years before receiving appointment to a garrison battalion or veterans' company in his native province.[126] Similarly, a statute of 1833 forbade the assignment of retired lower ranks to police and fire units in their native towns or districts.[127] The force of local ties and loyalties suggests that national identities and patriotic feelings did not play a significant role in motivating soldiers to perform repressive police duties.

CHAPTER FOUR

The Limits of Bureaucratic Regulation: The Regimental Economy

Throughout history, the relationship between military needs and societal resources has largely determined the material condition of the troops.[1] The Russian army's most serious economic problem was subsistence.[2] For the common soldier and his regiment, subsistence was a pressing concern of daily life. Despite a centralized system of supply, commanders and soldiers were forced to devote excessive time and energy to provisioning, which deflected attention from purely military matters.[3]

Provisioning and Supplies

During the reign of Peter the Great, the government began to assume some responsibility for provisioning and equipping the troops. Legislation defined monthly rations of meal and groats, and the government established magazines to store provisions. New state factories began producing weapons, ammunition, and cloth for uniforms. Peter also created an administrative apparatus to oversee the supply of his troops. The Commissariat *Prikaz* was responsible for pay, clothing, ammunition, and equipment. The Provisioning *Prikaz* provided food and forage or the funds to procure them.[4] Peter's reforms clearly established a role for the central government in supplying the troops.

The army's sources of supply were varied and complex. Most often, the authorities responsible for provisioning concluded contracts with private traders who agreed to deliver a specified amount of grain at a fixed price that was usually below the current market price.[5] The nobility enjoyed special privileges in supplying grain for the army, but their role was insignificant before the Crimean War. Only on rare occasions did the troops receive money to purchase provisions themselves.[6] In wartime, requisitions were common, though civilians could later submit claims for compensation.[7] For the treasury the most desirable means of procurement were donations by nobles and merchants or an "offer" by local residents (if not voluntary, then at the behest of the village or military authorities) to feed without compensation the soldiers they quartered.[8] Despite the existence of a centralized bureaucracy, state supplies were never adequate, and the troops constantly faced shortages of funds and provisions. As a result, procurement remained primarily a local affair with all the variety of Russia's regional divisions.

Quartered among civilians for six to eight months a year, soldiers depended on the surrounding countryside to meet many of their material needs. In 1821–22, for example, a shortage of provisions interrupted grain deliveries to the Second Army. In response the army experimented with a system of provisioning whereby local residents fed their lodgers for eight months a year and in return received a monetary payment.[9] The purpose was to reduce state expenditures by eliminating middlemen and obtaining provisions directly from the primary producer.

The plan affected only troops stationed in Bessarabia, and the results were disappointing. P. D. Kiselev, commander of Main Headquarters of the Second Army, reported complaints by the soldiers of inadequate supplies and conflicts with civilians. Every peasant fed his charge according to his individual means and the customs of the area. Even in agriculturally rich provinces, some peasants could barely feed themselves. Moreover, soldiers accustomed to eating rye bread found themselves in areas where the inhabitants had only corn. And since soldiers knew that their hosts received payment for their upkeep, they were inclined to make excessive demands. For such a system to work, the troops would have to be quartered so that the burden of feeding them was distributed evenly and corresponded to local resources.[10] This was practically impossible, for military considerations often dictated that large numbers of troops be concentrated in impoverished, sparsely populated areas like Bessarabia.

Even if the government itself was not always able to distribute adequate supplies, it still regulated the norms of pay, provisions, clothing, and equipment for the individual soldier and his regiment. For the first half of the nineteenth century, the daily ration of a soldier in the regular army was about two and a half pounds of meal (three pounds of bread) and one-fourth pound of groats. About 1800 every man also received 72 kopecks for meat and 24 kopecks for salt each year, but these amounts were included in the musketeer's yearly pay of 9 rubles, 50 kopecks.[11] According to a law of 1808, the authorities also deducted fees to purchase medicines and support hospitals.[12] The official military history of Nicholas I's reign claimed that under Alexander I, the only soldiers who regularly received meat and liquor were combat ranks in the Guards (thirty-seven pounds of meat per year) and troops in the Crimea and Kherson province (seventy-eight pounds of meat and 156 cups of liquor per year).[13]

In the reign of Nicholas I, the government expanded its obligation to provide supplies in kind. In 1827 troops quartered in barracks near state magazines began to purchase salt from the local authorities at a reduced price of 60 kopecks a pood (one *pud* = thirty-six pounds), one-half pood a year for each soldier and noncommissioned officer.[14] It is also likely that liquor and meat portions became a more regular feature of the soldier's diet. The recruitment regulation of 1831 required residents to provide meat or fish along with bread, kasha, or some other filling food. The accompanying officer also supplied each soldier with one cup of liquor three times a week.[15] The government made some effort to improve the soldier's diet by prescribing meat rations more precisely, though it is unclear whether the law required meat for all soldiers. Legislation from the reign of Nicholas I suggests this was not the case before 1842. Most soldiers received two or three one-half pound meat portions a week (for thirty-seven weeks a year) and two or three cups of liquor.[16] Once a week the regimental commander distributed state monies for the meat and liquor, which the troops acquired locally.[17]

Recognizing that improvements in diet meant stronger soldiers who would be better able to carry out their military duties, in 1849 the government raised the yearly meat allocation to eighty-four pounds (seven pounds a month) and granted half this amount (three and a half pounds a month) to noncombat personnel in field units, to all lower ranks in garrison and worker (*rabochie*) units, and to troops in the regions of military settlement. Combat soldiers in all field troops outside the settled regions of the cavalry were entitled to five half-pound portions of meat each week, except on fast days.[18] The official military history of Nicholas I's reign claimed that in 1826 only about 122,000 soldiers enjoyed meat as a regular part of their diet, whereas by 1850 this number had increased to 1,036,815. Based on the official data, this would have meant that in 1826 approximately 14 percent of the establishment number of regular troops received meat portions, whereas by 1850 the proportion would have jumped to about 95 percent.[19] Given the inadequacies of the military economy and the absence at this time of further corroborating evidence, one should accept these data as no more than a statement of governmental intent and official policy.

Regular supplies of meat would represent a substantial improvement in the diet of the common soldier. In reality, the legislated norms affected only troops living in barracks or gathered for training. Most soldiers spent six to eight months a year quartered among civilians who fed their charges with no regard for military regulations.[20] Troops quartered in poor areas, gathered in camp or in smaller groups (*tesnye kvartiry*), ate "from the common pot" (*iz kotla*) and so were entitled to meat rations.[21] There is no question that some soldiers enjoyed meat as part of their diet. In 1837–38 conscripts on their way to a recruiting station in Orel province were fed beef and fish, vodka, bread, groats, butter, and salt.[22] Similarly, soldiers stationed at the Åland fortifications in 1856 bought meat locally.[23] Because of the quartering system, it is impossible to know how many soldiers actually received meat rations on a regular basis. Even where soldiers ate "from the pot," inadequate allocations may have prevented the procurement of meat.[24] Moreover, in the absence of modern storage facilities, the availability of meat depended on local conditions, which could vary significantly.

Besides pay and provisions, the state provided clothing and equipment for the troops. Some items came ready-made; for others, such as uniforms and boots, the troops received money and materials that regimental craftsmen or the soldiers themselves turned into usable products. Each piece of clothing or equipment was expected to last for a specified period, after which it was replaced.[25] Soldiers wore the same clothing for one to four years.[26] Items like metal instruments, horses, harnesses, and carts were supplied only once at the time of a regiment's formation, after which the troops received a yearly allowance (*remontnaia summa*) for their maintenance and repair. Other necessary equipment—shakos, helmets, knapsacks, belts, and slings—were replaced every four to ten years.[27] Soldiers and their superiors were responsible for maintaining these items, which technically belonged to the state. As one teacher in a cantonist battalion noted, he had to pay for every state article that was lost.[28] The loss or damage of state property even prompted soldiers to desert for fear of punishment. In 1832 one private fled after his horse collapsed, another when his cartridges were stolen, and a third because his horse was injured.[29]

Soldiers' Monies

Once a regiment received its allotted supplies and funds, the regimental commander distributed them through the company or squadron.[30] Although the central authorities treated the regiment as the basic military, administrative, and economic unit, the company was more significant in the daily life of the common soldier. Each company was divided into four platoons (*otdeleniia*) or artels (*arteli*), and each platoon into five *desiatki*.[31] The *desiatka* was a command subunit for quartering, training, and enforcing discipline, and along with the company and artel served as the center of the soldier's daily life.[32] The main purpose of the artel was to control the soldiers' common resources in the interest of economic security. The artel functioned at both the company and platoon levels. The company *artel'shchik* purchased supplies and supervised monies received from the company commander, while the platoon *artel'shchik* actually distributed the provisions and funds to the men.[33] The artel thus served as the unit through which company commanders distributed supplies.

Still, the very existence of the artel implied some degree of popular participation in regulating the company economy.[34] Some sources claim that the lower ranks elected both the company and section *artel'shchiki* for a six-month period.[35] Others go so far as to compare the artel with the village assembly (*mirskaia skhodka*), admitting, however, that any decisions made by the artel required approval by commanders.[36] Memoirs confirm the practice of electing *artel'shchiki*, though P. Nazarov, who served five years as a platoon *raskhodchik* in the 1820s, tried to avoid the responsibility, which he described as "highly dangerous."[37] Despite these reports, it seems highly unlikely that the artel represented a truly autonomous popular institution. The official centennial history of the War Ministry admitted that regardless of legal prescriptions, company commanders usually appointed the *artel'shchik*. According to this source, company commanders controlled the activities of the artel to ensure proper use of the funds for provisions and for the purchase and maintenance of horses and vehicles.[38] Like the noble serf master and the government in general, the company commander exercised tutelage over his subordinates.

The organization of company funds also suggests limited popular control. The 1838 military code identified four types of soldiers' monies (*soldatskie den'gi*): artel, economic, religious, and personal (*sobstvennye*).[39] The purpose of the artel fund was to provide soldiers with a secure financial cushion at the time of retirement. The fund was the property of each soldier, who took his share with him if he left his unit.[40] Artel funds consisted of deductions from the soldiers' pay (up to a third) and munitions money, earnings from outside work, and monetary awards granted by the emperor for training, inspections, parades, and maneuvers. Awards received from the emperor augmented the fund, only if they were not needed for provisions. Commanders also divided half the money earned by soldiers at outside work among the members of the artel, the other half going to the individuals who actually had earned the wages. But if the corps commander decided the money was needed for food, the law allowed him to distribute a third to the economic fund, a third to the artel, and a third to the men who had performed the labor.[41] Finally, the artel included the monies delivered with each recruit.

The structure of the artel approximated the structure of the company. In each company all the individual artel funds comprised a general artel sum that was the direct property of the lower ranks. The general artel sum was divided into four subartels (*kapral'stva*) that served as the basis for calculating the artel monies. An infantry company could keep 180 silver rubles in its artel; additional money was sent to a bank to earn interest. The law treated the artel funds as the property of the lower ranks, clearly stating that they be used for the soldiers' personal needs and not for any extraneous expenditures, such as clothing or the repair of equipment. The artel thus functioned as a financial entity, partly controlled by the soldiers. Still, there were legal restrictions on the soldiers, since the corps commander could reallocate artel funds for provisioning. Moreover, until retirement, when the soldier received his artel funds in hand, he could spend these monies only with the permission of the regimental commander. All company funds were kept in the regimental safe, and the company commander handled deposits and withdrawals in the presence of the *artel'shchik*. The only cash received directly by the lower ranks was their pay and munitions money, but only if their artel fund contained the minimum amount required by law.[42]

Other company resources included a fund for charitable and religious needs (*obraznaia summa*) and an economic fund (*s"estnaia* or *kharchevaia summa*) "for improving the food of the lower ranks." These funds were the collective property of the entire company. When governmental allocations were insufficient or simply not delivered, the company relied on its economic fund to meet its material needs. The fund came from money saved when local inhabitants fed and quartered soldiers without compensation; from monies for meat and liquor rations; from artel and private monies belonging to dead or missing lower ranks (after paying their debts and the cost of burial, as long as no relatives claimed the money); from artel and other monies belonging to deserters; and from awards granted by the emperor for parades, inspections, and maneuvers. Commanders could also augment the fund with deductions from the soldiers' pay and munitions money. Like artel monies, the economic fund was designated only to meet the personal needs of the lower ranks: to supplement their diet or to maintain the clothing and equipment that was considered their property. The economic fund was not to be used to maintain state equipment for which the government allocated special monies.[43]

Both the regiment and company maintained funds to meet religious needs. The company charity and icon fund was supported by the soldiers' voluntary contributions. It was used to paint the company icon, to purchase candles for services, and to pay burial costs for soldiers who did not have sufficient funds in their own artel. The regimental church fund (*tserkovnaia summa*) also consisted of voluntary contributions to support the regimental church.[44] Finally, the personal funds (*sobstvennaia summa*) included any significant amount of independently acquired money belonging to an individual soldier.[45] Many sources do not even mention these funds, so presumably they were rare. In general, the soldiers' monies were designed to enhance the material well-being of the lower ranks at a time when the uncertainties of state supplies and the diversity of local conditions made subsistence a tenuous affair. They did not necessarily provide a reliable solution to subsistence problems, for the extent of the monies varied locally, and individual funds could be quickly depleted (see table 4.1).

The artel and other company funds offered an irresistible enticement for venal commanders. Still, through their artel, soldiers exercised some control over the company economy. Although they enjoyed only limited access to artel monies before retirement, commanders at least theoreti-

Table 4.1. Artel and Economic Sums per Soldier[a]

Year	Artel Sum				Economic Sum			
	1843	1844	1845	1846	1843	1844	1845	1846
Unit								
Guards Corps	8.8	9.7		9.6	2	2		
Grenadier Corps	6.8	6.1		4.4		.98		.52
Sixth Infantry Corps				3.5				
Engineering Troops of Active Army				5.2				
Artillery of Active Army			5.3				3.5	
Georgian Artillery			5.35				2	
Finnish Troops				2.5				
Separate Orenburg Corps				2.9				

SOURCES: TsGVIA, f. 395, op. 101, d. 108, 111, 158, 228, 232, 245, 246; f. Voenno-uchenyi arkhiv, d. 17542, ch. 1–3.

[a] Computations are based on the number of lower ranks actually present or on the service rolls at the time of inspection, whichever is given. In cases of two conflicting figures, I have used the average. Figures are in rubles.

cally had to account for the funds to the satisfaction of their men. Courts-martial records reveal repeated disputes between soldiers and officers over the use of artel funds, soldiers' pay, and munitions money. To prevent irregularities, inspectors regularly checked regimental and company accounts of artel funds.[46] Transactions involving soldiers' monies were supposed to be handled either directly through or in the presence of the *artel'shchik* and other economic officials chosen from the lower ranks.[47] The purpose of this very limited self-administration was not to grant soldiers genuine control over their lives, but rather to legitimize the inevitable hardships and deprivations they would suffer by making it appear that they exercised some control over and, therefore, responsibility for their material condition. For this reason soldiers' assemblies did not exist in the Guards, where relative economic security protected commanders from accusations of corruption. In the army, on the other hand, it was necessary to convince soldiers that the limited means available to them were used in accordance with their decisions.[48] Clearly, the structure and, indeed, the very existence of the artel provided a potential (though not necessarily effective) check on the corruption of commanders and perhaps also of soldiers.[49]

Quartering

According to a law of 1806, regiments gathered only in the spring and summer for training, joining with divisions and corps for six weeks during this period.[50] For the remaining six to eight months of the year, soldiers lived in private homes. A single regiment could be scattered among several villages, making it impossible to preserve the regiment as a unified social unit. An anonymous memorandum written at the close of the 1805 campaign reported that one cavalry regiment was usually quartered in three to four villages and never in less than two.[51] Similarly, in 1827 when the Iamburg Uhlan Regiment was stationed in Tver province, individual squadrons were scattered over three districts (*uezdy*) at an average distance of six to eight days' march (100–110 versts) from regimental headquarters.[52] In 1833 the regiment moved to the town of Bzhetsk, where its squadrons were dispersed in 205 villages and 566 homes throughout the district.[53] As late as 1860, there were sufficient barracks and state buildings to house only about 28 percent of the troops.[54]

Quartering arrangements had significant implications for the soldiers' health, subsistence, and socialization. Most contemporary sources agreed that quartering in scattered villages was detrimental to training and discipline, but beneficial to the soldiers' health.[55] In the absence of modern sanitation, the fresh air of the countryside provided a more hospitable environment than crowded cities. The dampness, filth, and inadequate ventilation of poorly constructed barracks compounded the hazards of urban living and promoted the spread of infectious diseases. In 1845 there was a significant increase in eye infections among recruits and soldiers of the Tauride Garrison Battalion. Once the soldiers were moved from towns to rural villages, the disease began to subside. In January 1846 the tsar agreed that the battalion should continue to send sick and weak recruits to villages near the towns where the unit normally quartered.[56]

Discipline and training clearly suffered as a result of quartering arrangements. When soldiers lived with civilians, their service obligations were minimal. Supervision and training were inevitably limited, and soldiers enjoyed a maximum of "personal freedom." One observer described this time as a needed rest from the difficult summer labors.[57] Others complained that soldiers spent more time with peasants than with their comrades-in-arms, grew accustomed to laziness and inactivity, and lost their martial bearing.[58] As long as the men lived in small scattered groups, supervision of their training was limited.

Quartering arrangements injected an additional element of instability into the already precarious regimental economy. Because the obligation to quarter a soldier usually included feeding him, legally defined rations had little meaning, except when troops lived in barracks or gathered in camp. The regimental economy derived significant benefits when local residents agreed to feed the troops without compensation. Commanders could then sell the regiment's provisions, adding the profit and other unused monies to the artel fund.[59] In most cases local residents received the soldiers' bread rations in return for feeding them.[60] The soldier usually ate whatever his host could spare. Funds for purchasing provisions were meaningless, if local supplies were not available. Where local society was prosperous, the troops' diet was good. But in impoverished areas or in times of crop failure, the troops suffered along with their hosts. In the spring, when peasant supplies were low, the soldier might receive only bread and water. Even in peacetime hunger was a possibility, as was indeed the case for all the lower classes.[61] Cantonist memoirs blamed hunger for widespread theft in their ranks.[62] The soldiers' material well-being depended greatly on local conditions, which varied widely. In the absence of modern communications, soldiers in one district might thrive, while those in an adjacent area went hungry.

Legislation from the reign of Nicholas I reflected the diverse local conditions. In the Caucasus, where the imperial government was struggling to extend its authority, soldiers experienced economic difficulties, because the natives did not recognize the Russian monetary system and always demanded payment in silver. Since the state lacked sufficient silver, soldiers had to change their money with a few "usurers" who arbitrarily fixed the rate of exchange at inordinate percentages. In areas of Daghestan that were recently acquired from Turkey and Persia, local inhabitants refused any contact with Russian troops whenever the slightest disagreement arose concerning payment for provisions. To ease these difficulties, the emperor ordered that troops in the Caucasus receive as much of their pay as possible in silver.[63] The hardships suffered by soldiers in this area revealed a discrepancy between the imperial government's military goals and the resources at its disposal.

Other localized problems resulted from price fluctuations and poverty. Because of high prices in Odessa, troops from the Fifth Infantry Corps were "in extreme difficulty . . . for they not only had spent their economic funds, but even had used significant sums from the regimental and soldiers' artel monies." In response, an imperial ukase of 1847 granted these units additional funds for provisions.[64] Similarly, from October 1849 until April 1850 the lower ranks of the Okhotsk Jager Regiment, stationed in the town of Ostrog, used 78 rubles from their artel to purchase wood for cooking and baking. Due to the absolute poverty of the townspeople, the soldiers ate "from the pot," but the local community also refused to provide wood. The government ordered the community to return the money and to supply wood, for the law prohibited the use of soldiers' funds to buy wood and clothing.[65] Unfortunately for the army, the border regions that required larger concentrations of troops were often the most impoverished and least capable of meeting military needs. Soldiers in Lithuania and Bessarabia experienced unusual hardships.[66] The system of quartering made the soldier dependent on local conditions that varied with the economic, geographical, and cultural diversity of the Russian empire. The dislocation of most troops depended on purely military considerations. Population density and economic prosperity were not necessarily factors. As a result, a significant gap often existed between local resources and the needs of the army.

The diversity of physical conditions helps account for the variety of relations between soldiers and local residents. Evidence presently available shows that relations between the army and its civilian hosts could be either friendly or hostile. Contemporary accounts blamed both soldiers and peasants for the conflicts that arose. Underfed soldiers were accused of stealing from their hosts, while inhospitable peasants were blamed for receiving the troops with suspicion, hostility, and miserliness.[67] The state made some effort to regulate relations between the army and civilians. Military inspectors were supposed to investigate civilian complaints, and commanders received reports from local authorities concerning the behavior of visiting troops.[68] Still, one wonders how effectively the military protected civilian interests.[69]

Regardless of formal regulations, the army took the provisions, transport, and quarters it needed from civilian society.[70] This does not mean that abuses went unnoticed. Officers and soldiers who bullied their civilian hosts were sometimes punished.[71] The sources of conflict were usually economic. Civilians considered the army's demands excessive (which at times they were), while the troops felt that local residents did not feed and house them adequately.[72] Both claims can be documented and both no doubt existed. The military was in a position to take resources by coercion, especially when local residents failed to fulfill their legal obligations. National differences also played a role, for troops were often concentrated in border regions populated by resentful minorities. Additional problems arose when Russian soldiers were dissatisfied with local food to which they were not accustomed.[73] The diverse local conditions made it impossible to create a single system that could function effectively in all areas. Discretionary authority was perforce extensive, and the character of local officals and commanders exerted a decisive influence over military-civilian relations.[74]

It is wrong to portray military-civilian relations as a constant battle. Cooperation was at least as characteristic as conflict. *Russkii invalid*, the official organ of the War Ministry, regularly reported on the harmonious relations that existed between individual military units and their civilian hosts.[75] As mentioned earlier, peasants often fed the troops without compensation. Soldiers also reportedly enjoyed the freedom of living in private homes, while for the peasant household the presence of troops meant additional laborers.[76] An anonymous memorandum received by the tsar in November 1820 suggested that the friendly relations existing between soldiers and peasants threatened the social order. Soldiers who had participated in the Napoleonic Wars reportedly fomented discontent among peasants with descriptions of prosperity abroad and complaints about conditions in Russia.[77] From the state's point of view, the main problem with quartering arrangements was the difficulty of imposing discipline among the troops.

Russia's system of quartering sharply distinguished it from the other military powers of Europe. By the nineteenth century, most troops in Austria, France, and England lived in barracks concentrated in cities. The backwardness of urban development in Russia partly accounts for this difference. A more fundamental problem lay in the chronic gap between governmental policy and available resources, in this instance caused by the large size of the army and the geographical peculiarities of the vast Russian land. In contrast to Prussia, where peasant-soldiers lived and served in their native cantons, Russian soldiers were completely cut off from their families, yet continued to live among civilians. Although the Russian government felt that a peasant became a loyal servant of the state only after removal from his native environment, it could not afford to isolate him in military barracks. The army's relationship to civilian society was one of dependence—a dependence, however, that the central government mediated to the advantage of the troops. The army's inability to house and feed its men without extensive reliance on peasant society created tension between uninvited soldiers and their frequently overburdened hosts. The absence of barracks could also serve as a source of fraternization and integration, giving civilians an understanding of military service and reminding soldiers of their former, perhaps not too distant, peasant past. This direct and continual contact between military and civilian society could only increase awareness and keep memories alive. It could also undermine military discipline and morale, and it is significant that it did not lead to any popular yearning to join the colors. The system of quartering took the soldier out of his military environment, separating him from the regiment that claimed his loyalties and defined his role as a fighter. Despite the lengthy term of service and the recruit's forced break with his family, the line between military and civilian society remained blurred throughout the pre-reform period.

Self-Sufficiency

From a present-day perspective, the difficulties faced by the Russian government in its efforts to feed and clothe its army seem insurmountable. The most obvious economic problem was a chronic shortage of state supplies. Repeatedly, troops either did not receive their allotted funds and supplies or received them late.[78] Even where monies and supplies were available, allocations were not always adequate, and their quality was sometimes dubious.[79] The winter pants worn by soldiers could last the required three-year period only in peacetime conditions, when they were not worn every day.[80] Generally the troops had to supplement state supplies from regimental resources or from gifts by local society.[81]

Economic conditions varied enormously, which made effective centralized planning practically impossible and led to significant fluctuations in the well-being of the troops.[82] Regimental economies differed depending on location, the type of unit, and the character of the commander. Large concentrations of troops in sparsely populated areas presented obvious problems. Often the areas requiring large numbers of troops were precisely those that were most lacking in economic resources.[83] In the pre-reform period Bessarabia and the Caucasus served as painful examples. The lack of adequate roads into these regions also made the transport of supplies from the interior erratic and uncertain.[84] The cavalry experienced special problems because of the need for large numbers of horses.[85] The sedentary life of troops in garrisons and fortresses allowed them to establish stable sources of supplementary income. Gardens provided a significant supplement for Guards units, but were exceptional among the more mobile troops of the regular army.[86] Generally speaking, the more frequently mobilized troops of the empire's western regions were less well off than the more stationary units of interior areas such as western Siberia.[87] Price fluctuations were another annoying cause of economic instability. The cost of provisioning a soldier could vary significantly from region to region and within a single area from year to year.[88] This problem could only intensify the want that resulted from frequent shortages and inadequate tables of allocations.

Conditions in the Second Army during the early 1820s illustrate the constant economic problems. In 1821 one million rubles were withheld from the Army's allocations, but because of crop failures in 1821 and 1822, prices did not decline. In addition, the Second Army was on the march and in concentrated quarters from March 1821 until November 1822. These circumstances resulted in a shortage of funds for provisions during 1822. As late as November of that year, the Army still had not been notified what monies would be available for 1823 and so was unable to conclude contracts for obtaining supplies. The Army also had debts from 1822.[89] It is not known what happened in the interim, but in an effort to reduce state expenditures, in March 1823 the tsar requested that the Second Army obtain provisions locally for a fixed price. P. D. Kiselev, the commander of Main Headquarters, responded that this would be feasible only in Kiev and Podolia provinces, where the population was occupied mainly with farming, but not in Bessarabia or in Kherson, Ekaterinoslav, or Tauride provinces, where local residents earned their living from raising cattle and population density was low. According to Kiselev, if a soldier's state ration was eliminated, it would be impossible to define "positively" what he should receive. Local residents provided food that varied according to the prosperity and customs of the region. Thus in Bessarabia, soldiers who were used to eating rye would have to eat corn.[90] Ambiguity in the definition of a soldier's rations could also lead him to place excessive demands on his civilian hosts. The proposed system would place additional burdens on both soldiers and residents, and the state would still have to obtain provisions for troops gathered in camp or in concentrated quarters. Finally, inequalities among residents in the area occupied by the Second Army presented another obstacle. Many residents could hardly feed themselves, so in order to implement the policy, the dislocation of troops would have to be changed.[91] Kiselev's statements clearly indicate the variety of economic conditions, and given this variety, the impossibility of establishing a single regularized system of supply for the entire army.

The lack of an effective, centralized system of supply and the wide variations in local conditions required that individual units become self-sufficient to a significant degree. When the state was unable to provide provisions and supplies in kind, it allocated money so that the regiment could purchase the goods from private contractors.[92] Besides having to obtain provisions, the regiment also produced its own uniforms. Regiments received cloth and leather from the state, but regimental tailors and bootmakers or the soldiers themselves made the uniforms and footwear.[93] A variety of regimental artisans met other economic needs. Regiments counted among their ranks copyists, barbers, bakers, blacksmiths, carpenters, metal workers, joiners, and painters.[94] The artel was another manifestation of the regiment's economic self-sufficiency.[95] In the absence of adequate state supplies, soldiers' monies made up the difference.

The health of the regimental economy depended significantly on the size of the artel-economic funds, which could be depleted very quickly. In 1810 soldiers from the Keksgol'mskii Musketeer Regiment testified that they had spent their personal and artel funds to purchase new uniforms and boots. Although their old uniforms were decrepit and the legal lifespan had expired, they did not receive replacements from the regiment.[96] Aside from the sale of unused provisions, the other major source of regimental funds was from unofficial outside work (*vol'nye raboty*).[97] Soldiers were released for such work in the fall, following the hard labors of summer maneuvers and reviews.[98] A portion of the money earned at outside work belonged to the collective resources of the unit, rather than to the individual soldier.[99] Consequently, unofficial labor could be a profitable source of income for a military unit and a particularly needed one, considering the inadequacies of governmental supplies.

The relative autonomy exercised by the regiment in its economic affairs allowed a large and diverse realm of unofficial economic activity to exist. There were four basic types of outside work. In one type soldiers performed services directly for the benefit of their superiors. In 1825, for example, twelve St. Petersburg soldiers built a house for their commander. They worked on a daily basis and each received 25 rubles.[100] In a second type, parties of five to ten men worked under contracts concluded by their company commander with an outside party.[101] In a third type, soldiers with special skills, especially artisans, used their free time to produce goods for sale.[102] And in the final type, some stationary regiments were able to organize collective enterprises that benefited both the soldiers and their commander. In 1826 the Preobrazhenskii Regiment operated three vegetable gardens, a bathhouse, and three shops.[103] In 1843 and 1844 the Guards and Grenadier Corps obtained sizable supplies of vegetables from regimental gardens.[104] Reports from 1846 show that the troops of the Moscow Garrison and the Separate Orenburg Corps also planted gardens.[105] There is no question that outside work benefited individual regiments significantly.[106]

Profitable as outside work might be, it also brought disruptions to military life. The possibilities for abuse were enormous. The law permitted soldiers to engage in outside work within prescribed limits. For the state it was important that this work not interfere with the performance of military duties. In addition, the work was supposed to be voluntary and safe, and the soldiers were supposed to be paid. A 1796 ukase confirmed that officers could employ soldiers only "with their agreement, or for wages, but not by force."[107] A law of 1797 noted that since officers in garrison battalions were not entitled to orderlies, they could use privates to perform personal services, though not at the expense of their regular military duties.[108] After the doctor of the St. Petersburg Engineering Unit illegally employed a barber for private needs, an 1803 ukase again forbade the use of soldiers for personal services that removed them from their "real duties."[109] Similarly, in 1817 the tsar ordered the court-martial of an officer who had sent his servant and another private on an unauthorized trip. In addition, the private's regimental commander was arrested for two days for failing to forbid the trip.[110] Once again unofficial work had removed a soldier from his military duties. But as these repeated decrees suggest, the legal restrictions had scant effect.

Laws issued during the reign of Alexander I sought to protect the lives of lower ranks employed at outside labor.[111] Manpower was too precious to risk losing it at tasks unrelated to military service. The main restriction on employing soldiers seems to have been that officers not use them as personal servants, a role the orderlies were supposed to fulfill. The law clearly sought to regulate the commander's right to exploit his men, as opposed to any independent activities pursued by the soldiers themselves. The intent of these laws reveals that some commanding officers shared the patrimonial mentality of the landed gentry. To combat this mentality, the government distinguished between labor performed for the benefit of the army and that performed for the personal gain of the commander.

Despite governmental efforts to regulate outside work, it was essentially an unregulated activity. The "free" work often had a coercive aspect, and abuses were rampant. In 1826 the soldiers of the Preobrazhenskii Regiment—which operated three gardens, three shops, and a bathhouse—complained that if their commander were not so greedy, they would each have up to 200 rubles, rather than 30, in their artel. The soldiers claimed that in addition to keeping most of the profits from these enterprises, he forced them to pay for maintaining the shops and repairing and even using the bathhouse.[112] In 1826 three artillery officers went on trial for employing twenty-four soldiers and eighteen state horses for almost five months. The soldiers transported wood belonging to one officer, for which each received 5 rubles. But they had been promised 25 kopecks a day and also had agreed to work without good food or a daily allocation of liquor.[113] Here soldiers and officers concluded a private agreement in which the soldiers provided wage labor for their superiors. Like the master who released his serfs for seasonal work, the commanding officer controlled the economic activities of his subordinates and was in a position to exploit their labor for personal gain.

Throughout the reign of Nicholas I, officers (and soldiers) continued to abuse the right to engage in outside work. In August 1828 War Minister Chernyshev ordered the Smolensk commandant to investigate allegations that the commander of the local garrison battalion privately exploited town land allocated for vegetable cultivation by soldiers. According to a denunciation received by the authorities, the battalion commander used the land for haymaking and had three privates guarding the grass, so that *there were not enough men to guard the town.*[114] *Similarly, the 1836 report* of the Inspectors' Department indicated that the men of the Ialutorovskii Veterans' Unit complained at an inspection that their commander forced those who had horses to transport wood for him.[115] In both cases commanders allegedly exploited the labor of soldiers for personal profit.

Other cases of abuse involved collusion between soldiers and officers. By the latter part of Nicholas I's reign a very extensive private economy had developed at the Kinburn Artillery Garrison.[116] In August 1850 the fortress commandant reported that the commander of Artillery Half-Company No. 1, Lieutenant Colonel Loman, illegally ran a farm nearby, where he kept up to twenty head of cattle, pigs, and geese, which produced terrible filth harmful to the health of the troops. Loman's farm was not in itself illegal, but the extent of his activities did violate the law. In December 1851 three bombardiers testified that many soldiers willingly worked for Loman. They usually received 75 paper kopecks a day, of which only 25 went to improve the provisioning artel and the rest belonged to them. These and other testimonies showed that Loman enjoyed a harmonious, mutually satisfying relationship with his men. In contrast, other officers complained that when they ordered soldiers to perform service duties, they responded with disrespect, coarseness, and outright disobedience. According to these officers, Loman freed the soldiers from service obligations and training, if they worked for him without pay. While officers hostile to Loman may have exaggerated the disorder and lack of discipline in the Kinburn Garrison, the judicial authorities were certain that Loman's attitude toward unofficial work had begun to interfere with the fulfillment of service duties.

Despite the apparent excesses, conditions in the Southern Artillery Region showed that unofficial work was an essential economic resource used to supplement insufficient state supplies. On March 9, 1846, the Southern Artillery commander informed all garrison commanders that if state funds were not sufficient to produce the soldiers' munitions, commanders should release three privates from each half-company to engage in outside work. Those released should receive a fourth of their earnings. The rest should go to the economic sums, and with the knowledge of the men, be used to purchase the materials needed to make the uniforms and other items of equipment for which they were supposed to receive state funds. The regional commander gave the order on the basis of the 1838 military code (Book 1, Part 3, Article 438), because the Commissariat still issued munitions monies for the artillery according to a table of 1809.[117] Since these sums were no longer adequate, the garrisons had no choice but to free soldiers for outside work. Russia was not unique in this regard: the Austrian army allowed soldiers to perform odd jobs in their free time, also because of economic necessity.[118] Loman's economic activities seem to have been excessive and disruptive to the service, but they could very well have been motivated by a desire to provide for the material needs of his men. At least some of the private work stemmed from the absolute need to supplement insufficient state supplies. As long as this was the case and as long as the government had to rely even partially on outside work to maintain the troops, it would have difficulty regulating private pursuits and curbing abuses in the regimental economy.[119]

Corruption

Economic self-sufficiency placed enormous power in the hands of regimental commanders.[120] With authority came responsibility. The economic authority of local commanders might put them in a position to line their pockets, but they also were held accountable for the welfare of their men and for all regimental funds.[121] The state's concern for the preservation of its vital manpower resources meant that accountability was no mere façade. Regimental commanders also answered for the condition of state equipment. When a commander left his post, he had to pay for any damaged equipment and settle all accounts and claims with his men.[122] In addition, officers regularly went on trial for economic crimes. The exercise of power could be dangerous; the commander's broad discretionary authority invited accusation and abuse. Consequently, the plight of the troops depended greatly on the character of individual commanders.

It has been argued that the regimental commander viewed his unit as an estate and his subordinates as serfs, that the relations between officer and soldier differed little from those between landlord and peasant.[123] The exploitation, corruption, and arbitrary power so visible in the administration of the regimental economy support this view.[124] But like the serf millionaires of pre-reform Russia, the soldier was more than a passive object of exploitation; he could also be a willing participant in unofficial economic pursuits. There is no doubt that abuses existed, that poor noblemen who became officers often used their position for economic gain.[125] But one crucial difference separated serfs and soldiers: through legislation the government sought to regulate the economic activities of a military commander and his subordinates, and in cases of abuse, the soldier did have recourse within the system of military justice.[126]

The issue of corruption is very complex. To attribute it solely to a serf-owner mentality would be simplistic; not just officers, but soldiers, civil officials, and contractors *all* committed economic crimes. Bribery constituted, above all, collaboration to defraud the state of resources or service. As one memoirist who was drafted in 1813 reported, his commanding officer allowed him to spend two extra weeks at home in return for a pound of tea and a sugarloaf (*golova sukharu*).[127] An 1856 report on abuses by officers who led parties of recruits also claimed that the latter obtained leaves in exchange for money. Similarly, officers withheld liquor allotments from the recruits, but in return allowed them to get drunk at their own expense. For this relaxation of discipline, the officer at once made a profit from the vodka and suppressed potential complaints.[128] Soldiers, too, were capable of stealing from the state.[129] In 1837 the commander of the Internal Guard reported that soldiers and military convicts under transport often exchanged or sold their uniforms for goods of inferior quality and upon reaching their destination, claimed that they had received substandard clothing at their former regiment.[130] Clearly, an assessment of corruption and abuse in the regimental economy must also consider the possibility of conscious complicity by the lower ranks.

Certainly, the venality of commanders and economic officials was a major reason for the picture of corruption and lawlessness so commonplace in accounts of both military and civilian administration in tsarist Russia. According to the 1817 annual report of the Military Judicial Department,

Military judicial cases show that some regimental, company, and squadron commanders and officers accompanying recruitment parties (in violation of the law and this has been confirmed repeatedly) for their own profit withhold from the lower ranks their rightful pay, provisions, articles for uniforms and other money; others take their property and artel funds under the guise of a loan and by various tricks; others use the lower ranks ostensibly as hired labor, which is permitted by Military Article 55, but do not pay them for the work they have done and by the most illegal acts [these officers] not only deprive soldiers of property acquired through their labors, but also impair the service in many important respects.

To combat this evil an imperial ukase ruled that if these commanders and officers "dare to withhold for their benefit the pay, provisions, and other items and money legally due the lower ranks; [if they] take their [i.e., the lower ranks'] property, artel funds or do not pay a soldier who has voluntarily hired himself out for the item made or the work done, such [an officer] without exception will be liable to the same punishment as that prescribed for bribery."[131] Military law explicitly forbade officers to pilfer the pay, supplies, and provisions allocated for the lower ranks.

The most common reason for courts-martial of officers was economic abuse. Some commanders stole state monies and supplies outright. In 1810 one garrison officer was convicted of withholding pay and munitions funds, using company monies and supplies for his own needs, and illegally borrowing money from his men.[132] Similarly, an investigation of 1817 revealed that for one year the Second Company of the Forty-third Jager Regiment obtained 3,961.75 bushels of meal and 11 bushels of groats; but the entire company, as well as the inhabitants of the three villages where they quartered, denied receiving any supplies.[133]

An 1836 court-martial revealed a wide array of crimes committed by one Orenburg officer, who also tolerated irregularities by subordinates. For three months he withheld from 107 men about 144 rubles allocated for meat and liquor. For another six months, he withheld five pounds of meal from each 5.75 bushels received. In addition, he granted early leaves to soldiers (presumably pocketing their pay and provisions) and in 1836 failed to supply his unit with state boot soles of the proper size. Because the soldiers' testimony provided the only evidence, the officer's sentence was light: four months' arrest in a guardhouse and permanent retirement from the service.[134] Still, this case provided clear proof of negligence and repeated abuses for personal profit.

Commanders also developed more sophisticated forms of peculation. One device was to buy provisions or supplies of inferior quality, while skimming the profit.[135] A trial of 1810 revealed that the commander of one regiment had bought secondhand uniforms for his men, forcing them to buy new ones with their own artel funds.[136] Similarly, in 1833 old soldiers who distributed bread to cantonists in the Ekaterinoslav Battalion reportedly set aside a portion to sell, so that the cantonists did not always get the prescribed daily ration (one-fourth pound).[137] These and similar methods of profiteering were effective but also risky, inviting complaints of reduced rations and substandard uniforms.[138]

According to official reports, it was more than venality that impelled commanders to misappropriate state funds. In 1856 an inspector investigated forty parties of recruits and attributed corruption among the accompanying officers to economic necessity: only the unmarried officers had sufficient money for the lengthy trips, whereas those with families had doubled expenses and had to supplement their income from the recruits' funds. The officers reportedly connived with local police and hence could falsify the records of expenditures for transport. They also charged the recruits significant sums for hiring vehicles to carry their belongings.[139] Bewildered recruits, only recently uprooted from their customary social network, were perhaps easier to deceive and cheat than seasoned soldiers. But regardless of their vulnerability, the decentralization and irregularity of the army's supply system provided ample opportunities for an officer to engage in fraud and personal profiteering.

It was difficult to eradicate corruption, not simply because the state lacked the will, but because improvisation and, therefore, arbitrariness were essential to the regimental economy.[140] Economic irregularities ultimately derived from the unrealistic demands and inadequate resources of the state. Another factor was the personalized nature of authority relationships, immanent in autocracy and in serfdom, that suffused the command structure of the imperial army. High-level officers discerned clearly the connection between corruption and inadequate resources. In 1822 P. D. Kiselev argued that widespread corruption among regimental commanders resulted from their limited economic benefits and from the absence of state supplies sufficient to maintain their units. The official lifespan of munitions was too long, and the monies allocated for their production and maintenance too meager. Consequently, to improve appearances, some commanders tolerated abuses or diverted soldiers' property for unauthorized purposes.[141]

Military judicial records show that extra-legal measures were sometimes essential to the military economy. An 1800 report on illegal actions against cossack villages noted that commanders of the Caucasus Division seized cossack horses without payment "only because of state needs along the cordon and not for themselves," thereby putting the state interest above the law.[142] The absence of necessary governmental resources forced the authorities to violate official regulations.[143] The government's often worthy plans and intentions far exceeded the material resources at its disposal. This unfortunate situation would continually force the state to approve arbitrary actions, preventing the effective application of regularized rules and procedures.

In September 1822 soldiers from the Second Battalion of the Thirty-second Jager Regiment complained of not receiving funds for cartage in 1818 or for meat and liquor (*portsionnye den'gi*) during eight months of guard duty. In addition, the men of the Second Carabineer Company testified that in 1818–19 they earned 560 rubles, but did not know how this money was spent, and that 800 rubles from their artel was sent to the treasury without their consent. The explanation of the battalion commander revealed the extent of his economic power, as well as deficiencies in the supply system that generated popular grievances. In 1818 a regimental order reallocated funds for transport toward the repair of equipment. The soldiers had received money for meat and liquor for two months of the May trimester, but because the regiment had not received additional funds for the September trimester, the company was holding allocations for the remaining two months.[144] Similarly, the companies had not received provisions for January, because the Kiliia magazine had none; consequently, hostile local residents had to feed the soldiers. Finally, at the order of the corps commander, the battalion commander had put the 800 rubles belonging to the soldiers' artel in a loan bank to earn interest. In the end, the commander-in-chief of the Second Army accepted these explanations and required only that the battalion and company commanders pay the travel expenses of the three investigators.[145] As demonstrated here, soldiers did not control their own artel funds, and when the authorities failed to deliver supplies and monies, economic conflict easily ensued.[146]

The subsistence struggle, so strikingly revealed in the pre-reform regimental economy, reflected the problems of any pre-modern, pre-industrial society. Economic exigencies and the need to survive in a basic material sense repeatedly overshadowed the regiment's professional military functions. The government struggled to mobilize the resources required to maintain its large standing army. Regimental and company commanders struggled to obtain adequate supplies for their men. The common soldier fought to scrape together the most simple necessities in the face of chronic shortages, corrupt or impecunious officers, and the hostility of overburdened civilians. The poverty, the climate, and the very size of the Russian empire made the army's physical upkeep a constant concern. The economic condition of the troops remained highly fluid, the line between abuse and improvisation was permanently blurred. The soldiers' artel provided a measure of security and gave them some limited control over their economic situation. But in general the soldier occupied an especially tenuous position in the already fragile balance of the subsistence economy. The soldier should have enjoyed greater economic security, because theoretically the state provided for his needs. However much a regiment might resemble a private estate, it was still distinguished by a constant governmental presence, if only because commanders were accountable to the central authorities. In reality, the inefficient system of supply made the soldier almost totally dependent on the character and capabilities of individual commanders and local residents. It is no wonder, then, that the "free" status of the soldier (with the remote chance of social mobility it offered) never served as a desirable alternative to the burdens and persecutions of serfdom.

In one sense the soldiers' precarious subsistence undermined state interests by threatening the physical integrity of the army. But in another sense, the semicentralized, semirationalized, highly irregular military economy served well the needs of the autocracy. Since the standing army functioned as such for only four to six months of the year, the government was able at once to control the army politically by centralizing its formal organization and to limit state financing and forestall the rise of a militaristic janissary class by making the institution dependent on mainly local, decentralized, and unregulated economies. It was not just a lack of resources that caused economic instability—though this was a large part of the problem—but also the state's reluctance to assume ultimate responsibility for economic regulation, be it between landlord and peasant, priest and parishioner, or soldier and the billeting community.[147] In effect, the autocracy's "standing army" was actually a quasi-reserve army well suited to the constraints of serfdom and the weak administrative infrastructure.

CHAPTER FIVE

Justice with Order: Autocratic Values and Military Discipline

The administrative history of imperial Russia reveals a continual tension between two Petrine traditions: bureaucratic regulation and unlimited political authority. The result was a combination of administrative arbitrariness and government by laws. Military justice exhibited this same interfacing of bureaucratic regularity and autocratic arbitrariness. Ideally, the government sought to implement in military society the paternalistic values that theoretically defined relations between the "father-tsar" (*tsar-batiushka*) and his obedient subjects.[1] Commanders in the army were seen as "fathers" to their subordinates, who as "children" needed guidance and protection. Even the most progressive officers believed that commanders should control all the economic resources of their units; for the soldiers could not be trusted to look after their own best interests.[2] The tsarist ideal of paternalism combined fatherly concern for the material and moral welfare of the lower ranks with the strictest discipline and punishment. Soldiers owed their superiors unquestioning obedience, and paternal affection was not supposed to degenerate into excessive familiarity. Commanders were expected to punish severely, but not cruelly, any violations of the service order.[3] As father to his men, the commander was supposed to be feared and loved, severe but just. In the image of the biblical God, he was to be both merciful and "awe inspiring."

Reality often fell short of a loving father-child relationship, but courts-martial records show that within limits the state made a genuine effort to act as the impartial arbiter of social relations in military society. Officers no doubt benefited the most from the autocracy's paternalistic pretensions, but there was at times an element of "eglitarianism" in judicial decisions. This "egalitarianism" resulted primarily from the state's efforts to protect its own interests by ensuring that the imperial army functioned smoothly and effectively. Since officers' abuses caused disruptions harmful to the service, commanders repeatedly went on trial for economic crimes and for mistreating their men. Conviction could result in severe punishments that included expulsion from the service and loss of military rank and noble status.[4] The military judicial authorities exhibited a clear tendency to punish men of all ranks who were involved in incidents that undermined the army's ability to fulfill its duties. There is no question that the lower ranks suffered harsher punishments than their superiors and benefited less from acts of imperial mercy. But in a serf society where the rule of law was minimal, any official effort to mediate social relations through bureaucratic regulation was significant, because attempts to delimit discretionary authority implicitly threatened existing social arrangements.

Courts-martial from the reigns of Alexander I and Nicholas I illustrate the ambiguous and contradictory results of military justice. In November 1810, seventy-seven lower ranks from the Keksgol'mskii Musketeer Regiment were convicted of disobedience. The disobedience erupted when the company commander, Colonel Kniazhnin, prepared to punish Sergeant Major Iakovlev and three noncommissioned officers who commanded platoons. At that time the soldiers shouted that Kniazhnin had no right to punish the noncommissioned officers in question and also demanded money for outfitting. The next day the regimental commander, Major General Vel'iaminov, set out to punish one private as the instigator of the disturbance, but the lower ranks declared that he was innocent and refused to permit his punishment. For their disobedience, the emperor sentenced the soldiers to run the gauntlet eight times through one thousand men followed by service in the Danubian Army, where they could participate in actions against the enemy and so atone for their crime "with their own blood."[5]

Although the soldiers clearly were guilty of disobedience, their actions were prompted at least partly by economic grievances. Consequently, the responsible officers also faced trial. Company Commander Kniazhnin had committed several crimes: he withheld money awarded to his men at a parade in 1808 and failed to distribute funds issued to replace worn-out uniforms. In addition, he hit Sergeant Major Iakovlev, which was illegal, because the latter was decorated. With the emperor's approval, Kniazhnin was declared "the cause of the harmful disorder" and expelled from the service.[6] The regimental commander, Major General Vel'iaminov, was also guilty of wrongdoing. He ignored the soldiers' claims in December 1809, trusting Kniazhnin fully and failing to recognize "that perhaps sometimes the men also testified justly."[7] When the lower ranks became unruly, he still did not examine their complaints and as a result they were driven to forbid punishment of one private. But because his crimes were not deliberate and because of his former service and good behavior, Vel'iaminov received an imperial pardon and escaped punishment. Although the government held Vel'iaminov and especially Kniazhnin responsible for provoking the disobedience, this in no way lightened the soldiers' punishment. In general, soldiers suffered significantly harsher punishments than their superiors. Moreover, the authorities often considered violations of the law by commanders justified, whereas soldiers very rarely escaped retribution.[8]

A subsequent case revealed similar patterns in military justice. In June 1832 Private Tokovnik appeared in Tiumen to complain against his commanding officer, Lieutenant Sedikin.[9] Tokovnik claimed that since taking command of the unit in 1827, Sedikin had employed him for various personal services without pay; consequently, Tokovnik claimed, his family had fallen into extreme poverty. Initially, two noncommissioned officers and twenty-two privates supported Tokovnik's claims, but a few months later they denied seeing Sedikin's wife or son abuse anyone. Then in August 1835 one noncommissioned officer and seventeen lower ranks "admitted" that Tokovnik had plenty of time to care for his family. They also testified that if Sedikin sometimes punished Tokovnik, it was because the latter was often drunk and rude.[10] It is unclear why the soldiers changed their testimony. Either they lied initially, seeing a chance to challenge the authority of their commander, or they told the truth and were pressured or bribed to soften their claims.

Whatever actually happened, the soldiers lodged additional claims against Sedikin, complaining that he owed them over 827 rubles for work that included reflooring and painting the unit's barracks. They also accused him of withholding 15 rubles for socks and mittens in 1829. In addition, one noncommissioned officer and two privates demanded payment for cleaning the well in 1829. Another private demanded 25 rubles for boots and shoes he had made for Sedikin, his family, and officials in Tiumen. Finally, one drummer complained that in 1831 he did not receive 20 rubles for painting chairs, making a dress, and building two card tables, a chest of drawers, and various other household items.

Sedikin denied most of these charges. And the Tobol'sk Treasury presented "evidence" (backdated or forged?) that two privates had signed for the money allocated for painting.[11] Although confusing claims and counterclaims complicated the case, the authorities found most of the soldiers' complaints suspect. They had contradicted themselves concerning the plight of Tokovnik's family, and had not presented grievances at official inspections. Documentation from outside institutions such as the Tobol'sk Treasury showed that some of their claims were patently false. It is impossible to determine where the truth lay in this case, for there was good reason to doubt the testimonies of both Sedikin and the lower ranks.

The government clearly did not give the benefit of the doubt to either, but considered both Sedikin and his men guilty of wrongdoing.[12] Sedikin was wrong to order the construction of a gate connecting the kitchen to the soldiers' quarters, so that vodka and other items could be sold to convicts. He was also guilty of forcing the soldiers, some convicts, and other laborers to clean the well and repair the kitchen. Finally, he had employed Private Tokovnik for personal services and owed his men 15 rubles for socks and mittens. With the emperor's approval, Sedikin was expelled from the service; but because of his distinguished record, the government allowed him to remain in the army without a command. He also had to pay his men 15 rubles and cover the cost of the trial (about 224 rubles). For inciting the lower ranks to make largely unfounded claims, the corps commander deprived two noncommissioned officers of their stripes and demoted them to private. For his unauthorized trip to Tiumen and contradictory testimonies, Private Tokovnik was punished fifty blows with sticks. The other soldiers were not punished, since their false and conflicting allegations "stemmed from their ignorance of the investigative order."[13] Finally, the corps commander ordered the Tobol'sk civil governor to send 150 rubles to pay the lower ranks for reflooring their barracks.

Military justice required that the commanding officer be punished for unlawful actions and the responsible lower ranks for violating the service order. When an organization seeks to operate on the basis of bureaucratic rules and procedures, it puts regularity before privilege and implicitly inclines to treat everyone uniformly. The authorities regarded punishments as appropriate or specific to a particular class. Because of their ignorance, soldiers (like peasants and other poll-tax elements) could be "educated" only with corporal punishment. In the case of officers, it can be argued, dismissal from service and loss of privileges was an "equally" severe punishment.

Acts of mercy represented another vital aspect of military justice. Although autocratic mercy primarily affected the social elite, soldiers could also benefit from the tsar's fatherly concern. An ukase of 1810 permitted deserters "who voluntarily appeared from an enemy army" to return without punishment.[14] No doubt motivated by a desire to recover lost manpower, this ukase was still in effect in 1829.[15] Through good service, soldiers could also regain rights and privileges lost as a result of conviction or punishment. In general, soldiers from the poll-tax population who had been subjected to corporal punishment lost the right to retire. But a law of August 1826 discharged soldiers who had lost the right to retire for minor crimes not exceeding the seriousness of a first desertion. If any of these men had mistakenly received the order of St. Anne for twenty years of irreproachable service, they could keep their decorations.[16] Subsequent legislation established permanent rules for restoring rights and privileges. An ukase of 1830 defined soldiers subjected to corporal punishment as "trustworthy" after ten years of unblemished service.[17] The law also permitted them to receive stripes for ten years of irreproachable service. Soldiers who did not suffer corporal punishment were eligible to receive decorations, pensions, and other privileges associated with retirement after five years of irreproachable service.[18] From 1838 even soldiers sent to the Caucasus for participation in the Decembrist revolt could receive the order of St. Anne.[19] Finally, a law of 1840 ruled that soldiers punished by verbal order of a commander for minor infractions omitted from the service record were eligible for decorations, pensions, and retirement benefits.[20] During the reign of Nicholas I, the restoration of rights and privileges lost as a result of punishment gradually became incorporated into military criminal law. While these rules reflected the broad discretionary authority of commanders, they also represented an important step toward defining the legal boundaries of punishment.

Legislation from 1843 extended mercy to persons punished for more serious crimes. Measures to prevent desertion ruled that soldiers punished for two desertions could regain the right to retire after ten years of irreproachable service.[21] More specifically, soldiers who had run the gauntlet only twice could retire after ten years of unblemished service, though for each running of the gauntlet, they had to serve an additional two years. Similarly, soldiers demoted from the Guards and from grenadier units without a trial for misdemeanors could retire after two extra years, if recognized by their commanders for good service. Records from 1850 showed that the rule requiring additional service did not apply if soldiers were guilty of only minor misdemeanors and did not receive corporal punishment.[22]

These laws affected soldiers guilty of relatively minor offenses. But even soldiers convicted of the most serious crimes sometimes became eligible to retire. An imperial order of 1850 granted retirement rights to soldiers who had participated in the Sevastopol mutiny of 1830 and the 1831 disorders among "ploughing soldiers" in Staraia Rusa. Soldiers of the Vyborg Infantry Regiment and the Guards Grenadier Regiment who were convicted of disobedience in 1831 and 1836, respectively, also received the right to retire. There was, however, one important distinction: the years of service before the punishments for these crimes did not count toward retirement.[23] Still, through good conduct and zealous service, these soldiers were able to atone for their offenses and regain former privileges.

In addition to measures allowing soldiers to regain lost rights and privileges, imperial manifestos also pronounced general amnesties. Amnesties occurred in honor of coronations and other special events in 1801, 1826, 1841, and 1855. In commemoration of the tsarevich's wedding, the emperor issued a manifesto on April 16, 1841. All persons under investigation or on trial that day received pardons, except for persons accused of specified crimes: sacrilege, murder, brigandage, robbery, bribery, theft of state property, counterfeiting, forging state papers, disobedience and rudeness toward commanders, and in general all crimes punishable by death, loss of class rights, and hard labor. Criminals sentenced to corporal punishment and hard labor, exile to Siberia, or service in a convicts' company for crimes not included in the pardon were freed from corporal punishment, but not from exile. The pardon also extended to deserters who returned within six months, if in Russia, or within a year, if abroad. Finally, the government would rescind monetary fines that did not exceed 600 silver rubles.[24] The amnesty of 1826 and related explanatory ukases also remained in effect. Consequently, the pardon did not extend to cases where commanders used soldiers for private work without pay or withheld pay, provisions, equipment, and funds.[25] All sentences declared before April 16 also remained in effect. Alexander II's ascension to the throne brought another amnesty.[26] Guided by the pardons of 1826 and 1841, it retained their basic features and also shortened the sentences of offenders sent to hard labor, exile in Siberia, or service in convicts' companies. These manifestos provided the most sweeping form of imperial mercy for military society. More important, they served to tie acts of mercy to the person of the monarch.

Broadly speaking, military justice involved the punishment of anyone, high or low, who violated the service order as determined by the state. In practice, the common soldier bore the brunt of autocratic arbitrariness, for the extensive discretionary authority of commanding officers allowed them to discipline their men with summary corporal punishment. Still, the state regarded commanders with some suspicion and was eager to hold them responsible for the offenses committed by their subordinates. For this reason many cases resulted in the simultaneous though unequal punishment of officers and their men. The practice of punishing all parties to a conflict stemmed from the peculiar legalities of pre-reform military society and embodied two essential ingredients of autocratic rule: the supremacy of the state interest and society's obligation to serve. It also compensated for the sheer ineptness of the judicial order that could not easily establish the facts of a case and sought to discourage such litigiousness in the first place.

Administration and Laws

Military justice in pre-reform Russia was an administrative process based on military criminal laws.[27] In the first half of the nineteenth century, four types of punishment were inflicted on the lower ranks: demotion, transfer, corporal punishment, and hard labor. Corporal punishment, by far the most common, applied to the smallest offenses as well as to more serious crimes such as theft, desertion, and disobedience. For serious crimes, corporal punishment consisted of running the gauntlet. Because this method of punishment required the participation of numerous soldiers, it served a prophylactic purpose as well. For lesser infractions, commanders used sticks (*palki*) and birches (*rozgi*) to punish offenders.[28] Although the law forbade the use of broadswords (*tesaki*) and ramrods (*shompoly*), commanders continued to employ these methods as late as 1844.[29]

Military justice strikingly revealed the immense power of officers over their subordinates. Regimental, brigade, divisional, and corps commanders decided most cases against the lower ranks. With the reign of Catherine the Great, punishments became less brutal, as more humane attitudes began to prevail. Increasingly, the government sought to regulate and limit disciplinary measures. Catherine's 1764 instruction to regimental commanders allowed them to sentence soldiers for crimes punishable by running the gauntlet no more than three times.[30] Paul's military regulation of 1796 restricted the authority of regimental commanders to imposition of "light punishments" for mistakes or bad behavior.[31] In wartime, however, the legal powers of the regimental commander greatly increased, and he could order a soldier executed for shooting out of order or for cowardice in battle.[32] In normal conditions the highest judicial authorities reviewed the most serious cases involving soldiers and all cases involving officers. The War College confirmed sentences against all officers below the rank of colonel that deprived them of rank and demoted them to private.[33] Beginning in 1797 the Military Judicial Department (*General Auditoriat*), established as the highest military court and directly subordinate to the tsar, reviewed cases involving officers, lower ranks of noble origin, and those awarded the cross of St. Anne. It then submitted its opinion for imperial confirmation.[34] In general, the punishment of nobles and officers required the highest confirmation, while the lower ranks were largely at the mercy of their local commanders.

During the reign of Alexander I, judicial decision making became more centralized. A decree of 1802 forbade the court-martial of officers without first informing the tsar.[35] Similarly, beginning in 1802 inspectors of the troops confirmed all sentences against the lower ranks, except for death sentences, which required confirmation by the War College and beginning in 1805 by the Military Judicial Department.[36] After the 1805 reorganization of the troops into brigades, divisions, and corps, a law of 1806 sought to facilitate the judicial process for minor crimes committed by non-noble lower ranks.[37] Brigade commanders decided cases of first desertion and theft not exceeding 20 paper rubles without convening a court and could impose sentences of 500–1,500 blows by running the gauntlet.[38] Cases involving a second desertion, a second petty theft, or theft exceeding 20 rubles required a court decision and confirmation by the divisional commander, who could assign a punishment of no more than three thousand blows. The corps commander decided cases up to the fifth desertion and other serious crimes carrying a sentence of no more than five thousand blows. Finally, the Military Judicial Department confirmed sentences for multiple crimes and for crimes carrying the death penalty or punishments replacing the death penalty, such as hard labor, exile to Siberia, and dishonorable discharge from the army. This department was also supposed to fix the number of blows with lashes when confirming sentences against lower ranks, though a Senate decree of July 1812 noted that it was not doing this.[39] The law of 1806 created a hierarchy of judicial authority corresponding to the army's administrative/tactical divisions and reflecting the government's intention to regulate military justice more closely.

In wartime the commanders-in-chief replaced the Military Judicial Department as the highest judicial authority. In addition, imperial ukases to individual commanders empowered them to impose the death penalty and deprive officers of rank without confirmation by the Military Judicial Department or the emperor.[40] The most important of these wartime measures was the 1812 statute for administering the Active Army.[41] The statute allowed the commander-in-chief to confirm all sentences involving the death penalty and loss of rank and granted corps commanders comparable authority over soldiers and over officers below the rank of colonel.[42] Following the Napoleonic Wars, some recentralization of judicial powers took place, though the commander-in-chief retained his extensive wartime powers. The commanders of separate corps lost some of their wartime powers, but continued to approve sentences against soldiers and against officers below the rank of colonel, unless the punishment involved loss of life or rank.[43]

The division of judicial powers established under Alexander I continued in the reign of Nicholas I. The 1838 military code preserved the judicial powers of commanders-in-chief, brigade, divisional, and separate corps commanders as defined in 1806 and 1815.[44] For troops outside the jurisdiction of the commanders-in-chief and commanders of separate corps and for officers above the rank of colonel, the Military Judicial Department remained the highest military court, often serving as a clearinghouse for sentences that required imperial confirmation. These included cases involving officers and lower ranks subject to loss of nobility; lower ranks deprived of the crosses of St. George or St. Anne, guilty of heresy or of insulting the tsar; cases involving ten or more defendants; and cases where corporal punishment was intended to be exemplary and therefore exceeded the legal norm.[45] The assignment of judicial powers followed the basic administrative divisions in the army. Most cases affecting the lower ranks were not reviewed above the level of corps commander. Consequently, military justice represents an especially important barometer of social relations between soldiers and officers in the pre-reform army.

The legal sources rarely mention the judicial powers of regimental and company commanders, the officers most directly responsible for the soldiers. Catherine the Great's 1764 instruction to regimental commanders empowered them to decide cases against lower ranks, as long as the crime carried a sentence of running the gauntlet no more than three times.[46] In the absence of precise legal definitions, soldiers experienced a wide range of punishments, the severity and frequency of which depended on immediate superiors.[47] Some enlightened commanders took steps to limit the authority of subordinates to impose corporal punishment. In 1774 Colonel Count S. R. Vorontsov forbade company commanders to beat soldiers for mistakes in military exercises. For laziness, lying, slovenliness, and drunkenness, he limited punishments to thirty or forty blows with sticks. Noncommissioned officers could punish privates, sergeants could punish noncommissioned officers, and only company commanders could punish sergeants. In addition, serious crimes involving theft, drunkenness while on guard duty, disobedience, fighting, and coarseness were to be forwarded to regimental headquarters.[48]

Going even further, in 1815 the commander of the Twelfth Infantry Division, Lieutenant General M. S. Vorontsov, forbade all officers except the company commander to inflict corporal punishment on the lower ranks.[49] Company commanders could impose a punishment no greater than forty blows with sticks for minor offenses such as frequent drunkenness, loss of or damage to equipment, unacceptable behavior toward residents who provided quarters, and failure to carry out the orders of superiors. Vorontsov regarded cases of repeated failure to carry out orders accurately or rudeness (*grubost'*) to superiors as disobedience and instructed company commanders to forward these to the regiment. The regimental commander also decided cases of soldiers who had never before experienced corporal punishment. For such a soldier "is much more capable of [those] feelings of ambition that are fitting for a true warrior and son of the fatherland, and it is more likely that he will serve well and be a good example to others."[50] Vorontsov also limited the authority of regimental commanders. Punishments exceeding one hundred blows with sticks and any running of the gauntlet were approved by the brigade commander, who himself could not impose more than one thousand blows.[51] Finally, Vorontsov completely forbade the use of corporal punishment for mistakes in drill.[52]

Despite individual efforts to define the judicial authority of regimental and company commanders, irregularities and arbitrariness remained dominant features of military justice.[53] Neither the law of 1806 nor the 1838 military code mentioned the regimental or company commanders. Presumably, they could punish soldiers for minor infractions like laziness or drunkenness, while any crime equivalent to a first desertion or minor theft and carrying a punishment of running the gauntlet through more than five hundred men came under brigade commanders. This silence in the legislation was broken only around 1850, when the naval criminal code specified that regimental commanders could order a punishment of two hundred blows with birches, and company commanders of one hundred blows.[54] It seems that these officers were permitted to apply the birch as often as they pleased for the slightest infractions, as long as the number of blows did not exceed legal norms. Not just in military life, but throughout the lower levels of Russian society, corporal punishment was the most widespread form of discipline.

At least on paper, the reigns of Alexander I and Nicholas I witnessed an amelioration in the severity of coporal punishment in peacetime.[55] An ukase of 1801 forbade the use of torture to extract confessions, though actual practices lagged behind the legislation.[56] Similarly, in sentences inflicting the knout, a law of 1802 forbade military courts to include the expression "punish mercilessly" (i.e., over fifty blows).[57] In 1825 the commander of Main Headquarters ordered that for crimes carrying a sentence of corporal punishment and exclusion from the military, the gauntlet should replace lashes (*pleti*). As before, use of the knout, which remained only for the most serious crimes, required that the accused first be discharged from the army.[58] Finally, in 1830 commanders-in-chief and corps commanders received an imperial order abolishing punishment with the knout, even upon exclusion from the army, as "inconsistent with the military calling." Instead, the order prescribed a punishment of running the gauntlet through one thousand men six times, exclusion from the military, and hard labor in Siberia. In cases of serious disobedience, a punishment of running the gauntlet through one thousand men more than six times was possible, but required imperial approval.[59]

Having eliminated punishment with the knout, the government of Nicholas I took some tentative steps to reduce sentences. Starting in 1834 the most severe sentence allowed in peacetime without imperial confirmation was running the gauntlet through one thousand men three times and hard labor.[60] Similarly, an imperial order of 1834 defined the sentence for a third desertion and comparable crimes at running the gauntlet through five hundred persons no more than five times. Then new rules issued later that year lowered the limit to three times.[61] The changes in corporal punishment evident in this period reflected the new moral sensibilities emerging in Russia's leading political and intellectual circles—sensibilities that made serfdom and the serf army increasingly unacceptable institutions. Still, Russia, like Austria, lagged behind other European powers. By the nineteenth century, corporal punishment was rare in the French army. Although Prussian military law permitted flogging after proper investigation, and some commanders continued to beat their soldiers, the reforms of 1808 abolished the gauntlet as punishment. England also abolished running the gauntlet by the nineteenth century, though floggings continued until 1881.[62] Russia was not the only country to employ corporal punishment extensively, but other armies were well on their way to eliminating it altogether.

It is also not certain that these improvements were ever implemented in Russia. The 1838 military code restored the 1806 norms in full.[63] It is still possible that the imperial orders of 1834 had some effect. According to one historian, the 1834 order limiting punishments to three thousand blows without imperial confirmation secretly remained in effect.[64] Another secret order from 1839 that affected only the Guards Corps eliminated running the gauntlet as the punishment for a first desertion. Since such punishment required demotion from the elite Guards, first-time deserters who had committed no other crimes were punished with birches.[65] In addition, although military courts were supposed to observe strictly the letter of the law and impose the maximum sentence, the reviewing authorities usually reduced the punishment.[66] Secrecy was characteristic of all reformist activity in the reign of Nicholas I and reflected a fear that magnanimity would undermine authority.

The government formulated norms of punishment very loosely, though for recruits the law was more precise. An ukase of 1808 prescribed the gauntlet with five hundred men for a first desertion or first theft not exceeding 20 paper (6 silver) rubles. The commander of a recruitment depot could reduce this to punishment with sticks, depending on circumstances. For a second desertion, a second petty theft, or a theft exceeding 20 rubles, the offender had to run the gauntlet through five hundred men two or three times. For repeated desertions and thefts (but no more than five), the law specified a punishment of running the gauntlet up to five times; in these cases the depot commander was supposed to get the approval of his superior, the chief commander of reserve recruits.[67] The recruitment regulation of 1831 was even more precise and slightly eased the norms of punishment. Recruits guilty of a first desertion and a first petty theft not exceeding 20 paper rubles while en route to their assigned units did not face a court-martial. Rather, the accompanying officer assigned a punishment of up to one hundred blows with birches. Moreover, if a runaway recruit returned to his party voluntarily, he did not suffer any punishment. Once a recruit reached his unit, the punishment for a first desertion or petty theft was running the gauntlet once through five hundred men. For a second desertion or petty theft and for any crime more serious than the first desertion or petty theft, recruits went to trial. Finally, accompanying officers could punish recruits and soldiers in their party up to fifty blows with birches for fighting, drunkenness, and playing cards. Clearly, for petty crimes committed only once, the law assigned lighter punishments for recruits than for soldiers.[68]

Developments in military justice also revealed some concern for preserving the health of the soldiers. An order of 1801 required the presence of a regimental doctor at the execution of corporal punishments to ensure that the convict would survive. If the doctor thought otherwise, he was to stop the punishment and take the soldier to the hospital.[69] By 1853 military courts that submitted decisions to the higher authorities for confirmation were supposed to include a medical certificate indicating whether the convict could undergo the legally prescribed punishment without endangering his life.[70] The government did not feel that corporal punishment should lead to death, and even for crimes carrying a death sentence, executions were extremely rare. Still, beatings did sometimes result in death, and the responsible officers were not always punished.[71] Nevertheless, the concern for preserving the life of the accused combined with the more lenient legal norms suggests a more humane attitude toward military discipline. It also indicates that the regime was not terribly worried about social control in the army. Given the relative lack of fear about mutiny, the manpower-conscious state took steps to protect its soldiers from the maiming and death that could so easily result from corporal punishment.

Transfers were another disciplinary measure, usually taken after corporal punishment, that constituted either demotion or an attempt to isolate troublemakers. Traditionally, the authorities sent serious offenders to serve in the garrisons.[72] After 1817 transfers probably did not affect many soldiers from the regular line army. Complaints from the commanders of the Separate Caucasus, Finnish, Orenburg, and Siberian Corps concerning deserters and criminals sent to their units noted that these "depraved" soldiers not only corrupted good and young recruits, but also deserted repeatedly. Consequently, the tsar forbade the army to transfer soldiers to these garrisons for a fourth desertion, instructing officials to send only the truly hopeless cases to work in mines and fortresses.[73] According to the military code, troublesome soldiers in the army should stay with their units, unless they were so utterly depraved that they were sent to convicts' companies.[74] Despite attempts to limit transfers, the garrisons continued to contain large numbers of convicted soldiers.[75] The transfer of convicted soldiers to the garrisons of the Internal Guard resulted in a high crime rate throughout the reign of Nicholas I. From the government's point of view, these transfers served to isolate troublemakers from the main body of combat troops, while preserving them as a source of manpower.

A convicted or troublesome soldier, if not sent to a garrison or convicts' company, could also be transferred to another unit. For soldiers in elite units, this meant demotion to the regular army.[76] The records of the Inspectors' Department from 1820 contain lists of privates and other lower ranks sent from the Guards Corps in St. Petersburg to the artillery and from the First Carabineer Regiment and various grenadier regiments to the army.[77] These soldiers had committed the usual violations, such as theft, desertion, unauthorized absences, and drunkenness. Finally, according to the 1838 military code, "lower ranks of bad behavior are intolerable only in guards, cuirassier, grenadier, and carabineer regiments and in pioneer battalions."[78] These rules on punishment and transfers vividly reflected the distinction between elite troops and the regular army.

Sometimes the authorities dispersed an entire group of troublesome soldiers to different regiments. This happened in 1851, when forty-three men from the Arkhangel'sk Garrison were sent to various battalions "far from their homeland."[79] According to authorities, these men associated with "depraved people" and had participated in thefts, robbery, murders, and the sale of stolen goods. As with the removal of an unpopular commander, the dispersal of difficult soldiers could bring order to a volatile unit. Undesirable soldiers were also sent to fight in the Caucasus. This practice caused the government considerable concern, for the chance to fight for the fatherland was supposed to be an honor. Thus in 1847 Nicholas I ordered officials to stop sending soldiers punished for "degrading" acts like theft and desertion to the Caucasus Corps; for assignment to this corps "should not be considered a punishment, but a special grace that provides the possibility of serving out one's term [of service] in action against the enemy."[80] Despite the tsar's warrior ideal, the practice of appointing soldiers to the Caucasus as punishment suggests that the men themselves did not necessarily regard combat duty as a glorious and cherished opportunity.

Military criminal laws reveal the officer's extensive power over the soldier. Regulations permitted corporal punishment for even the slightest infractions. The only legal limitations were related to the seriousness of the crime and the severity of the punishment. Courts convened in cases of repeated or serious crimes, and a court decision required confirmation at least above the level of brigade commander. In contrast, regimental and company commanders could order punishments for minor infractions as frequently as they liked. Because of loose legal definitions, the harshness of military discipline depended significantly on the character of individual officers, who enjoyed broad discretionary power in meting out punishments. In his daily existence, the soldier was at the mercy of his immediate superiors, so that military justice embodied the social relationship between officer and soldier, between ruler and ruled in military society. As with training and the regimental economy, the state was only a partial regulator. Governmental control over officers was surely greater than over landlords; but the "omnipotent" autocracy made a conscious decision—reflected in imprecise legal norms—to assign local commanders extensive disciplinary powers. This resulted partly from an inadequate administrative apparatus for investigating and deciding judicial cases. However, it also suggests that the government did not discern any serious threat to social control and hence did not see a need to impose effective regulation.

Crime and Punishment in Military Society

The judicial records preserved in central archives primarily concern trials for serious crimes and sentences requiring confirmation by commanders-in-chief, the Military Judicial Department, or the tsar. Hence most breaches of discipline and minor infractions by soldiers remain undocumented.[81] Consequently, the historian must rely upon exceptional cases of deviance in order to understand social relations, norms, and expectations in the pre-reform army. In 1836 the Military Judicial Department began to issue annual reports containing general statistics on crime in the army. Although the data are limited to the reign of Nicholas I, they still provide a context for examining problems of deviance. True to their bureaucratic purpose, the data give only the number of men under formal investigation or on trial (*pod sudom*) for a particular crime in a given year. Since judicial investigations sometimes took years, these data tell us nothing about the number of crimes actually committed each year. They also provide no information about crimes that did not result in a formal investigation or trial. Although their analytical value is limited, they do identify the types of crimes most characteristic of particular groups and indicate which offenses the government considered most serious.[82]

The crime rate in the lower ranks was not great, but significantly, among those of non-noble origin, desertion and theft were by far the most widespread offenses (see tables 2.3–2.4, 5.1–5.6). Theft stemmed from the economic hardships and deprivations of military service. Desertion was a more complex issue, involving popular attitudes toward service and responses to the harsh realities of military life. Along with suicide, disobedience, and rebellion, desertion was a key index of discontent and even despair among the lower ranks.

Desertion was a common problem among the European armies of this period. In Russia the rate of desertion was not especially high, but the general concern about manpower made any loss a serious matter.[83] First desertions, assuming the culprit was even caught, did not necessarily require a court-martial, so that many cases probably remain undocumented. But in cases important enough to demand intervention by the central authorities, the government's concern and impotence are clearly visible. Although most soldiers did not desert, there was little the government could do to control those who did, except to hold commanding officers responsible.

Legislation suggests that desertions were more frequent in the borderlands. In these areas the government fought desertion with the threat of severe wartime punishments.[84] Local residents who assisted deserters faced fines and exile.[85] Desertions were also more likely among troops on the march—troops bound by time schedules and more difficult to supervise. A soldier could flee, and his unit would not have the time or the means to pursue him. He might also be left behind in a hospital and either accidentally or intentionally not return to his unit.[86] As with many cases of popular action, a heightened sense of possibility was crucial to the decision to desert. And the chances of success were certainly greater in areas where one could take refuge across a foreign border.

Desertion reflected the difficulties faced by the state, as it struggled

JUSTICE WITH ORDER

Table 5.1. Rate of Desertion[a]

Year	Regular Army	Guards Corps	Grenadier Corps	Sixth Infantry Corps[c]	Separate Orenburg Corps
1808	1.2				
1827	.50				
1835	9,974[b]				
1836	.79				
1837	.83				
1838	.49	.2			
1839		.3			
1840		.2			
1841		.14	.43	1	
1842		.11	.43	.8	
1843		.11	.3	.4	
1844		.1	.3	.4	1
1845		.1	.22	.4	.7
1847	.61				
1848	.62				
1849	.4				
1850	.4				
1851	.3				

SOURCES: TsGVIA, f. 395, op. 325, d. 19–22, 31–34; op. 101, d. 111, 115, 228; f. Voenno-uchenyi arkiv, d. 17542, ch. 1–3; *Imperatorskie ukazy i prikazy voennogo ministerstva za 1809*.

[a] For the regular army, computations are based on the number of lower ranks on the service rolls January 1 of the year indicated. For the remaining units, computations are based on the number of lower ranks on the rolls or present at the time of inspection, whichever is given.

[b] This is the absolute figure, which seems unusually high. For other years the absolute figures are: 1808—4,067; 1827—5,106; 1836—6,563; 1837—6,824; 1838—4,199; 1847—5,656; 1848—5,891; 1849—3,765; 1850—3,570; 1851—3,109.

[c] Data run from July to July.

against popular resistance to service. In the absence of effective local administration, the government was forced to rely on officers to control desertion, just as it relied on landlords to administer their peasants. But whereas the lord had absolute power over his serfs, the officer was subject to central regulation. Held responsible for the condition and behavior of his men, he was subject accordingly to rewards and punishments. The military regulation of 1796 imposed fines for each deserter on all com-

CHAPTER FIVE

Table 5.2. Crime among Lower Ranks of Non-Noble Origin[a]

Year	Total Number of Accused Lower Ranks	Economic Crimes (%)[b]	Desertion (%)[c]
1836	11,740	3,385 (28.8)	5,423 (46.2)
1837	10,560	3,241 (30.7)	5,174 (49)
1838	11,595	3,723 (32)	5,386 (46.5)
1839	10,419	2,302 (22)	6,089 (58.4)
1840	10,550	2,179 (21)	6,506 (61.7)
1841	10,715	1,907 (17.8)	7,098 (66.2)
1842	9,453	1,725 (18.2)	6,107 (64.6)
1843	9,077	1,851 (20.4)	5,459 (60)
1844	8,097	1,928 (23.8)	5,236 (64.7)
1845	8,020	1,865 (23.3)	4,501 (56)
1846	8,708	2,008 (23)	4,920 (56.5)
1847	8,763	1,962 (22.4)	4,839 (55)
1848	8,212	1,968 (24)	4,490 (55)
1850	9,960	2,259 (23)	5,339 (54)
1853	9,548	2,512 (26)	4,685 (49)
1854	9,017	2,226 (25)	4,749 (53)
1855	9,497	1,964 (20.7)	5,393 (56.8)
Total	163,931	39,005 (23.7)	93,393 (55.7)

SOURCE: TsGVIA, f. 801, op. 60, d. 35–49.

[a] Some lower ranks tried for multiple crimes could have been counted in more than one category. The sources do not indicate how such cases were recorded.
[b] Includes theft, robbery, fraud, loss of state property, conscious damage to weapons and munitions, crimes in administering and storing military property, smuggling contraband, bootlegging, and cutting state forests.
[c] Includes desertion, unauthorized absences, and leaving the fatherland.

pany officers and regimental commanders.[87] Legislation from the 1840s specified permissible rates of desertion and held regimental, battalion, and company commanders responsible. If desertions exceeded legal limits, commanders faced arrest and even loss of command. If no desertions occurred for one or two years, they received decorations or a year's additional pay.[88]

Subsequent legislation took account of variations in the probability of desertion. Beginning in 1844 commanders in the Guards Corps received awards, only if there were no desertions for three years, rather than two.[89]

Table 5.3. Types of Crimes Committed by Non-Noble Lower Ranks (as a percentage of accused non-noble lower ranks)

Year	Economic	Desertion	Rebellion and Mutiny	Disobedience	Failure to Fulfill Duties	Dueling, Fighting, and Disorderly Conduct	Drunkenness	Rape	Murder or Attempted Murder
1836	29	46	1	1.3	4.6	1.6	2.1	.2	1.4
1837	31	49	.05	2.2	4.1	1.5	2.5	.2	1.7
1838	32	46	.1	1	3.6	1.7	2.7	.1	2
1839	22	58	.01	1.5	.75	.8	2.8	.1	2
1840	21	62	.23	1.1	.5	.6	2.6	.3	2
1841	18	66	.04	1.1	.45	1	1.8	.2	2
1842	18	65	1	1.7	.83	.7	2.3	.2	2.7
1843	20	60	0	2.2	1	.7	2.2	.2	2
1844	24	65	0	1.8	1.4	.9	2	.2	2.8
1845	23	56	0	1.3	.9	.8	3	.1	2
1846	23	56	0	1.1	1.6	1.4	2.7	.3	2
1847	22	55	.01	1.2	1.7	1	4	.3	2
1848	24	55	.02	1.8	1.6	1.2	3	.2	2
1850	23	54	0	1.6	2.1	1.2	4.2	.5	2
1853	26	49	0	1.9	2.3	2	6	.4	2
1854	25	53	0	1.6	1.6	1.3	5.4	.4	2.4
1855	21	57	0	1.8	1.7	2.4	5	.2	2

SOURCE: TsGVIA, f. 801, op. 60, d. 35–49.

Table 5.4. Crime among Lower Ranks of Noble Origin[a]

Year	Total Number of Accused Lower Ranks	Economic[b]	Desertion	Disobedience	Rebellion	Drunkenness	Dueling, Fighting, and Disorderly Conduct	Murder
1836	116	7 (6)	42 (36)	12 (10)	36 (31)	5	2	0
1837	77	13 (17)	29 (38)	11 (14)	0	4	1	3
1838	51	7 (14)	24 (47)	9 (18)	0	2	1	2
1839	55	9 (16)	29 (53)	8 (14)	0	3	1	0
1840	64	13 (20)	30 (47)	4	5	1	2	2
1841	77	15 (19)	33 (43)	13 (17)	1	4	1	1
1842	48	9 (19)	17 (35)	11 (23)	0	3	1	0
1843	43	4 (9)	26 (60)	4	0	2	0	0
1844	43	6 (14)	15 (35)	10 (23)	0	0	0	0
1845	32	8 (25)	18 (56)	0	0	3	0	0
1846	45	7 (15)	20 (44)	5	0	2	0	1
1847	36	9 (25)	16 (44)	3	0	0	1	0
1848	53	9 (17)	17 (32)	5	0	1	3	3
1850	58	13 (22)	21 (36)	13 (22)	0	0	0	2
1853	70	12 (17)	18 (26)	9 (13)	0	7 (10)		0
1854	65	44 (68)	19 (29)	5	0	7 (11)	2	2
1855	77	17 (22)	27 (35)	6	0	2	3	1

SOURCE: TsGVIA, f. 801, op. 60, d. 29–49.

[a] Figure in parentheses gives the percentage of accused lower ranks.

[b] Economic crimes include crimes in administering military property, theft and loss of state property, sale and deliberate damage of weapons and munitions, robbery, theft and fraud, and use of soldiers for private work without pay.

Table 5.5. Crime Rate
(Ratios of Accused Officers and Lower Ranks)

Year	Officers	Lower Ranks
1835	1:203	1:86
1836	1:143	1:94
1837	1:223	1:100
1838	1:251	1:92
1839	1:287	1:103
1840	1:253	1:100
1841	1:174	1:104
1842	1:203	1:112
1843	1:203	1:120
1844	1:262	1:137
1845	1:295	1:143
1846	1:265	1:128
1847	1:231	1:133
1848	1:223	1:139
1849	1:183	1:47
1850	1:207	1:118
1826–50	1:118	no data
1855	1:95	1:222

SOURCES: TsGVIA, f. 801, op. 60, d. 36–40, 42, 45; Chernyshev, *Istoricheskoe obozrenie*, p. 153; Bogdanovich, *Istoricheskii ocherk*, 2:32–33.

Similarly, regimental commanders faced three days' arrest if the number of desertions in a year equaled fifty in the infantry or twenty-four in the cavalry. For the Guards Corps, the law reduced the permissible numbers to fifteen from infantry and six from cavalry regiments.[90] Recognizing the large number of convicted soldiers in the Separate Caucasus, Siberian, and Orenburg Corps and in the Internal Guard Corps, the government reduced the standards required for reward and raised the acceptable level of desertion.[91] Rules of 1846 raised by one in most troops the number of years without desertions required for officers to receive rewards.[92] As these regulations reveal, desertion was less frequent among elite troops like the Guards, but more common in border regions, among recruits, and among soldiers in the less desirable units whose members included significant numbers of convicted soldiers.[93]

Compared with desertion and theft, other important crimes committed by non-noble lower ranks seem only incidental. Rebellion and mutiny account for only 244 of 163,931 non-noble lower ranks investigated or tried between 1836 and 1855. Disobedience—which was close to revolt,

Table 5.6. Crime among Officers[a]

Year	Total Number of Accused Officers	Economic[b]	Negligence	Abuse of Power	Disobedience	Desertion[c]	Dueling, Fighting, and Disorderly Conduct
1836	170	65 (38)	27 (16)	14 (8)	9 (5)	11 (6)	15 (9)
1837	127	28 (22)	27 (21)	7 (5)	13 (10)	6 (5)	10 (8)
1838	113	36 (32)	23 (20)	10 (9)	8 (7)	2	10 (9)
1839	102	27 (26)	13 (13)	7 (7)	13 (13)	6 (6)	12 (12)
1840	121	23 (19)	18 (15)	18 (15)	18 (15)	11 (9)	10 (8)
1841	183	45 (25)	33 (18)	12 (6)	9 (5)	18 (10)	21 (11)
1842	154	29 (19)	29 (19)	9 (6)	35 (23)	7 (4)	13 (8)
1843	143	28 (20)	34 (24)	10 (7)	13 (9)	12 (8)	12 (8)
1844	110	25 (23)	11 (10)	9 (8)	15 (14)	4	9 (8)
1845	95	19 (20)	18 (19)	3	13 (14)	11 (12)	10 (10)
1846	116	25 (21)	18 (15)	9 (8)	13 (11)	15 (13)	7 (6)
1847	117	17 (14)	24 (20)	6 (5)	9 (8)	31 (26)	9 (8)
1848	137	18 (13)	28 (20)	9 (7)	8 (6)	23 (17)	13 (9)
1850	161	43 (27)	25 (15)	15 (9)	8 (5)	14 (9)	12 (7)
1853	194	38 (20)	35 (18)	11 (6)	25 (13)	18 (9)	34 (17)
1854	217	171 (79)	183 (84)	13 (6)	12 (5)	18 (8)	32 (15)
1855	238	38 (16)	68 (29)	16 (7)	14 (6)	22 (9)	18 (8)

SOURCE: TsGVIA, f. 801, op. 60, d. 35–49.

[a] Some officers tried for multiple crimes could have been counted in more than one category. The sources do not indicate how such cases were recorded. Figure in parentheses gives the percentage of accused officers.

[b] Includes bribery and extortion, use of lower ranks for private work without pay, crimes in administering military property, theft and loss of state property, sale and conscious damaging of weapons and munitions, robbery, theft and fraud, bootlegging, and cutting state forests.

[c] Includes desertion, unauthorized absences, and leaving the fatherland.

at least as passive noncompliance—was more widespread and accounts for 2,503 of those investigated or tried. The failure to fulfill service duties was also a noteworthy category, but the social significance of this offense is uncertain. Many lapses in this area could have resulted from incompetence and would not necessarily represent deliberate acts or expressions of discontent. Disorderly conduct and drunkenness, which represent obvious violations of military discipline, also appear negligible in the crime statistics. The figures are deceiving, however, since most offenses of this type would have been punished summarily at the company or regimental level. Only repeat offenders or violations associated with more serious crimes would have been formally investigated or tried by a court. Finally, violent crimes like rape, murder, and attempted murder appear relatively infrequent, though one must wonder how many cases of rape went unreported (see table 5.3).

Crime patterns among noble lower ranks were similar to those among non-nobles. Desertion and theft remained the most frequent offenses, though there was a higher incidence of disobedience among this group (see table 5.4). One can imagine that the frustrations experienced by nobles who were forced to suffer the humiliations of service in the ranks might lead them to commit offenses that most obviously expressed discontent with their lot. Unlike soldiers from the poll-tax population, nobles were less inclined to accept passively an affront to honor or dignity.

Even among officers, desertion and disobedience were not unheard-of crimes.[94] Drunkenness, dueling, and disorderly conduct were also significant. Abuse of power claimed a fair share of tried officers, but in general the most common crimes among officers were neglect of duty and economic violations (see table 5.6). Economic abuses and cruel treatment by officers were the two most frequently identified causes of social conflict in the pre-reform army, but unfortunately, the available data do not allow precise measure of these violations. Many offenses went undetected, and the data presented here surely underestimate their frequency. Moreover, "cruelty" (physical maltreatment) is not mentioned in any of the categories of crimes. Although cruelty could have been subsumed in a category such as "abuse of power," its absence probably reflects the government's ambivalence toward questions of discipline and order, especially the fine line between justified severity and outright cruelty. The categories of economic crimes also do not touch directly upon the condition of the lower ranks.[95] Rather, they are concerned primarily with state and military property. If some economic crimes are not identified as such, the sources still cite various economic offenses as among the most common committed by officers. This fact corresponds closely to the importance of economic claims in soldiers' complaints against superiors and in their explanations of disobedience. Still, the failure to identify crimes involving economic abuses and cruelty as directly impacting upon the lower ranks is indicative of the inequities of military justice. The autocracy presented itself as the impartial mediator of social conflict, but the system of military justice that it devised reflected not the formal legalisms of a modern bureaucratic society, but the traditional norms of a serf society with its privileged landowning elite and its exploited peasantry.

In order to understand the full meaning of military justice for the common soldier, it is important to determine actual norms of punishment. This is an extremely difficult task, for the norms of punishment and the judicial powers of commanders were never precisely defined for the entire army. This resulted in considerable variation and arbitrariness in the meting out of punishments.[96] Even those legislative limits that existed were not always enforced, especially at the local level, where the number of blows with birches depended on the character of the commander and his attitude toward the offender.[97] Judicial sources from the reigns of Alexander I and Nicholas I report a wide variety of punishments ordered by regimental commanders for minor crimes like drunkenness, tardiness, improper dress, mistakes in drill, negligence, and unauthorized absence.[98] Formal court decisions also varied significantly, depending on the circumstances of the case and the opinions of individuals at every level of confirmation.[99] Although there was greater uniformity in the sentences meted out in court proceedings, comparable crimes in the same regiment in the same month of the same year were not necessarily judged in the same manner.[100]

To establish norms of punishment in the pre-reform army is at best a tenuous undertaking. Still, an impressionistic examination of some sentences actually carried out reveals that confirmed punishments never exceeded the legal maximum, and in a significant number of cases fell below it. It is important to remember, however, that these practices did not result from any precise legal definitions or strict judicial procedures. Rather, they stemmed from common notions of justice shared by a few powerful men who reviewed sentences at the highest level. In the regiments below, variations were more pronounced. Legal limits were very loosely defined, leaving a broad range for discretionary judgments by individual commanders. There seems to have been some amelioration of punishments in the reigns of Alexander I and Nicholas I, but nothing conclusive can be said without further research. Punishments for a first desertion were especially varied, and it is not clear why some first-time deserters were tried by a formal court while others were not. The existence of accompanying crimes or the intentions of the deserter could explain the differences. Did he, for example, desert to the enemy or was he simply absent without leave for a period exceeding three days? Such distinctions were important in judicial decisions, but in the absence of comprehensive statistics, it is only possible to examine these factors on an individual case-by-case basis.[101] Several reasons for the variations in sentencing emerge. Most important was the autocracy's commitment to "justice" and discipline, as opposed to the firm application of laws. Second was the absence of precise legal norms of punishment. And third was the broad discretionary authority accorded individual commanders in all areas of military life. Despite the severity and vagueness of legal norms, judicial practices still reveal an effort to administer the army on the basis of laws and regulations, without, of course, sacrificing order and "true justice."[102]

By modern-day standards and even by the standards of contemporary Europe, Russian military discipline was harsh. But in the Russian context, soldiers did at least have legal rights that they could sometimes use effectively to protect themselves from abusive commanders. This does not mean that soldiers avoided pilfering and beatings at the hands of cruel officers. It does mean that in their dealings with superiors, they were participants in a system of justice, whatever its limitations and inequities. Unlike serfs, soldiers possessed a civic identity and could seek redress for their grievances through formal channels of authority. The reality of the soldier's experience was, of course, ambiguous and contradictory, but by assigning former serfs formal rights and by setting legal limits on punishments, the system of military justice implicitly threatened traditional social arrangements.

CHAPTER SIX

Soldiers in Service: Expectations and Realities

Unlike peasant-serfs, soldiers did possess legal rights and a civic identity. Judicial investigations, courts-martial, and periodic inspections by superiors provided them with formal channels for presenting complaints. In acts of disobedience and desertion, at inspections and trials, soldiers expressed their aspirations and expectations. If they did not in fact truly expect their commanders to behave in accordance with official regulations, they at least understood that accusations of abusive treatment would gain for them a sympathetic hearing at the upper levels of the military hierarchy, and so could be used to justify their own malfeasance. In practice, the soldiers' right to complain against superiors was strictly limited. But it did exist in a very real way. It did result in the prosecution and conviction of abusive officers. And it did mean that soldiers sometimes received redress for their grievances.

The Soldiers' "Right" to Complain

When superior officers conducted official inspections, they were supposed to question the lower ranks about their commanders.[1] Officers repeatedly went on trial as a result of soldiers' complaints—complaints that usually consisted of economic claims or accusations of cruel and unjust treatment. More often than not, however, inspections passed without incident, for there were considerable constraints on the soldiers' right to petition.

The expression of grievances was a risky venture. The authorities were never wholly comfortable with the soldiers' right to complain, which in their eyes could easily degenerate into disobedience, and so implicitly threatened discipline.[2] A heightened sense of possibility was key in stimulating the expression of grievances. Soldiers developed this sense when a commander suffered loss of authority in connection with an investigation or trial and when they themselves were guilty of infractions and sought to justify their actions.[3] Soldiers sometimes initiated petitions, but usually their claims resulted from direct questioning in the context of a formal judicial process. Whatever the stimulus, these claims reflected the aspirations and expectations of the common soldier.

Some commanders encouraged their men to express their grievances and needs directly.[4] But it seems likely that the constraints on expressing grievances exceeded the inducements. Soldiers faced decisive punishment when authorities found their claims unjustified. In 1816 the men of Light Company No. 34 submitted complaints against their commander.[5] Guilty of various economic abuses, the officer was arrested and temporarily removed from his command. But then one sergeant major, four noncommissioned officers, and seven privates were tried as the instigators of "illegal designs" for "submitting a petition in agreement with other ranks, for signing for the others, for hiding these complaints and secret meetings from the company commander." The sergeant major was especially guilty, for he "should have been the first to report on these intentions and repeated meetings concerning the presenting of a petition. But on the contrary, he himself read the written petition before the entire company." The soldiers were also guilty of failing to report the "shortcomings and persecutions" either through their officers or at official inspections. In December 1816 they were convicted of "illegal designs in submitting a petition."[6] Voicing grievances in a collective manner or out of order was dangerous, even when an officer was himself guilty of wrongdoing.[7] Despite the serious economic abuses committed, the soldiers faced punishment both because they had bypassed their commanding officers by submitting a petition to a higher authority and because some complaints, obviously imprecise, were judged "untruthful."

The vast judicial and economic powers of officers repeatedly allowed them to ignore complaints and intimidate soldiers into silence. Sometimes soldiers were too frightened of punishment even to submit claims.[8] When a group of infantry soldiers demanded pay for work performed for their company commander, he accused one noncommissioned officer of inciting the company to rebel and punished him with 150 blows with sticks. The soldier then complained to the battalion commander, who punished him with another 100 blows, and to the regimental commander who also wanted to punish him. In 1827 the company had a new commander who reportedly owed the men 1,500 rubles, but they were afraid to ask for it.[9] Similarly, in 1829 the men of a veterans' unit reported to their commander that they had not received an allotted fifteen rubles. He treated their complaints as rebellion, so that they were too frightened to file additional claims.[10]

In other cases soldiers were tricked into silence. In 1855 the commander of a transport guard unit was found guilty of squandering 358 rubles that belonged to the lower ranks. The soldiers did not report this, because he gave them a small sum of money just before an inspection and promised that they would receive the rest as soon as he could get change. After the inspection, he simply repossessed the money he had already given them.[11] Considering the general weakness of Russian administration, the number of similar cases that went undetected could have been enormous.

Reports on the condition of recruitment parties also suggest that formal inspections had scant effect and failed to provide the lower ranks with a secure forum for voicing grievances. To prevent complaints, one ensign planted disguised guards to report on the recruits' conversations, and after they were questioned at an inspection, he beat them and forced them to carry packs in the heat while wearing sheepskin coats and buttoned greatcoats. In this manner, he "brought them to their knees."[12] Well-meaning officers were aware of these abuses, and in 1856 one inspector of transport parties critically evaluated the effectiveness of inspections:

> Formal inspections often do not achieve their aim, because recruits know that the officer and senior noncommissioned officer will accompany them for the entire trip and justly are afraid to speak. They fear revenge, which I am convinced occurs. An accompanying officer prevents complaints with threats and usually has selected recruits, whom he pampers and who stand at the front and shout louder than all the others: "We are satisfied with everything, and each receive three liquor portions a week." These favorites are chosen from the hired substitutes and are called "elbow-rests" (*podlokotniki*) by the recruits.[13]

The army's own structure of command made inspections an inadequate means of supervision. In most cases, commanders inspected their own subordinates for whose actions they could be held accountable.[14] Officers also used threats, chicanery, and actual punishment to prevent the lower ranks from expressing grievances. Many claims emerged only after soldiers realized that a commander was under suspicion, a fact reflecting the effectiveness of this suppression. The soldiers also must have known that "unfounded" or inappropriately expressed complaints could be dangerous. On the other hand, the very fact that officers resorted to intimidation and repression revealed their own fear and awareness of just how seriously the higher authorities regarded soldiers' grievances.

Social Conflict

The two most important sources of conflict between soldiers and their commanders were economic conditions and corporal punishment. Economic grievances stemming from abuses by officers were among the most common expressed by the lower ranks. Judicial sources repeatedly reveal that soldiers were keenly aware of their right to receive support and of the commanding officer's obligation to secure it, though often they were confused about the extent of this support. Economic claims submitted by soldiers at inspections or during investigations and trials also show that soldiers expected satisfaction to be forthcoming.

In 1800 Captain von Shitz of the Dinaburg Garrison Regiment went on trial for withholding pay and artel funds from his men.[15] The soldiers claimed that they were owed 43 rubles in pay and that von Shitz used a large sum from their artel for his own personal needs. Von Shitz explained that he did not issue pay because he was unable to change assignats, and so had informed the men that the money was in the general company fund. He further testified that with the company's agreement, he used funds from the artel to pay senior and noncommissioned officers.[16] In addition, he borrowed 150 rubles from the company fund, but returned the money.[17] Since von Shitz's company was always in good condition, he was acquitted. The soldiers' complaints stemmed from misunderstanding or distrust. Perhaps they did not understand why von Shitz failed to pay them, after he requested company funds to pay their superiors. Or perhaps out of suspicion, they simply did not believe his explanations. More significant, the soldiers had definite notions of the economic benefits to which they were entitled.

In a similar case, one battalion of the Thirty-second Jager Regiment complained of not receiving money for cartage. They also claimed that for eight months they did not receive funds for provisions, and in addition, the provisions supplied by local inhabitants were unsatisfactory. The Second Carabineer Company testified that in 1818 and 1819 they earned 560 rubles, but knew nothing of the whereabouts of these funds. They also claimed that someone had taken 800 rubles from their artel without their agreement. Despite this chance to articulate grievances, the soldiers received no satisfaction. The authorities had investigated conditions in the regiment following twenty desertions in one month, but accepted the explanations of the battalion commander.[18] It is impossible to determine whether the soldiers' claims were justified. They expressed their grievances during a special investigation, which perhaps prompted them to exaggerate. One also wonders whether primarily illiterate soldiers could keep a precise account of company finances. Whatever the facts, the claims and counterclaims reflected the extensive economic power commanding officers exercised over their men. More important, they revealed the tension characteristic of economic relations in military society. The soldiers' concern for the security of the artel funds and the money they personally earned was especially striking and suggested a basic distrust of their commander's intentions.[19] Sensitive to their economic rights, the soldiers had well-defined expectations of material support—expectations justified by military law and by the actual practices of military justice.

Some officers convicted of economic crimes were punished severely. In June 1800 two cavalry officers were found guilty of misusing company and soldiers' funds. With Paul's approval, they were stripped of rank and noble status and sent to Siberia as settlers.[20] Similarly, in 1810 one garrison officer was convicted of withholding supplies, punishing two men with sticks when they requested provisions, losing state and soldiers' monies amounting to over 256 rubles, and falsifying records. For these crimes he was sentenced to loss of rank and noble status, demotion to the ranks, and a fine equal to the amount he had lost or stolen.[21]

A final example of harsh penalties for economic crimes occurred in June 1855, when Lieutenant Timofeev was found guilty of numerous illegal acts: squandering money and provisions that belonged to soldiers and convicts, failing to pay his men for chopping wood, and refusing to provide one soldier's wife with provisions for her two sons. By the time Timofeev was sentenced, he had paid most of the money owed. Still, the tsar approved a punishment demoting him to private with loss of officers' rights and privileges.[22]

If some soldiers harbored suspicions about the honesty of their commanding officer, others exhibited a patient understanding of the difficulties he might face in fulfilling economic obligations. In 1829 a military court found Captain Tishchenko guilty of withholding munitions money from 146 men. Tishchenko testified that the money "was used because of absolute necessity for various unforeseen needs that arose in the squadron." He provided no evidence to support his claims, and in his testimony could not even recall the specific "needs" that had arisen. Still, the soldiers unanimously declared that Tishchenko was a good squadron commander and because of his "inadequate condition," they did not wish to press claims.[23] Although the possibility of bribes or threats cannot be ruled out, the soldiers appeared to express an understanding of unexpected economic exigencies and of the need to improvise and reallocate resources. Their sympathy for Tishchenko clearly reflected the personalized nature of conflict and loyalties in pre-reform military society.

Inexperienced recruits may have suffered more from economic abuses and also been more prone to misunderstanding. In 1800 a group of 94 recruits complained of not receiving full pay for three months (3 rubles).[24] The local military governor responded that initially each recruit had received 45 kopecks, but since they spent this sum in two days, he ordered that the remaining money be put in their artel, which was then entrusted to three noncommissioned officers. Subsequently, the recruits' commanders decided to use the artel funds to purchase fish and butter for fast days, beef for holidays, and candles for evenings. Moreover, because the recruits were quartered in a state building, it was necessary to buy utensils for storage and cooking. The authorities could thus account for the entire sum of 285 rubles and concluded that the recruits' claims were unfounded. Still, their reaction was understandable, especially since they each received 45 kopecks the first day. They no doubt felt they were entitled to see the money in hand and did not understand that military supervision demanded otherwise. After all, as civilians, they had (except for the payment of taxes and quitrent) been free within the context of an independent household economy to spend their money as they saw fit, and not as their social superiors dictated. Yet the officers were not guilty of any wrongdoing, for they spent the money appropriately to meet the legitimate needs of their charges.[25]

The development of private economic activities also stimulated social conflict. Just as soldiers understood that they were entitled to their full pay, supplies and provisions, they also expected to be paid for any private work. In 1800 Colonel Mart'ianov was found guilty of employing soldiers without pay for his own personal work—work that interfered with the performance of their service duties.[26] Although he had paid the men 150 rubles, they claimed another 664 rubles. Accepting the claims, the authorities instructed Mart'ianov to pay that sum.[27]

That same year 250 Tatars complained that they suffered "persecutions, insults, and bribes" while carting wood, hay, and other materials needed for the construction of their commander's house. In addition, they did not receive state provisions.[28] The case of Second Lieutenant Siziakov shows just how exploitative private work could become. In 1817 the Oranienbaum Veterans' Unit accused him of collecting bribes from each soldier released for private work. They also claimed that he forced them to cut and cart wood from the local town forest, using axes and sleighs purchased at their own expense. Although Siziakov sold this wood to local officials (who confirmed purchases for 1807 and 1814), the veterans received no pay for their labors. When the unit was disbanded in 1818, several veterans presented additional claims concerning inadequate payment for private work.[29]

It is important to note that relations between soldiers and their superiors were not inherently conflictual. As the case of Second Lieutenant Siziakov suggests, private work could take on the worst attributes and abuses of serfdom. But it also could serve to bond soldiers to a particular commander in a mutually beneficial economic relationship. This was the case in 1850 at the Kinburn Artillery Garrison, where the soldiers of Half-Company No. 1 became unruly following extraordinary roll calls on two consecutive nights. On the second occasion, they marched off to their garrison commander, Lieutenant Colonel Loman, for an explanation. Loman denied any knowledge of the reason for the extra roll calls, and at his request the men returned to their barracks. When questioned subsequently by the duty officer, they again became disobedient, and Loman was sent to pacify them.[30] They agreed to return to their duties, but as a result of this incident, eight soldiers were court-martialed, and Loman was dismissed from the service.[31] The trial in December 1851 revealed that the lower ranks were heavily involved with Loman in private economic activities. Their special affection for him thus had an economic basis. It is significant that when the soldiers felt persecuted, they appealed to Loman and at his urging, they immediately returned to order. This behavior suggests a close personal relationship between Loman and his men. Other officers supported this view, reporting that Loman freed soldiers from their service duties to engage in private work and complaining that his close relations with the men undermined their authority.[32] It seems that through lax discipline and the pursuit of mutual economic gain, Loman developed a warm, harmonious relationship with his men. They expressed their personal identification with him in repeated proclamations during the investigation and trial "that they serve only the commander of the garrison, Lieutenant Colonel Loman."[33] At Kinburn, the reality of a beloved commander concerned with the economic welfare of his men clashed with the army's professional need for the strictest discipline.

Along with economic claims, cruel treatment was a frequent complaint leveled at commanders. This could mean excessive or unjustified punishments, as well as unwarranted demands such as extremely long hours of training. Both economic abuses and cruel punishment were potentially explosive issues in the relationship between soldiers and officers. Soldiers deserted, were disobedient, and rebelled on grounds of abusive treatment, while officers faced loss of rank and noble status and expulsion from the service for cruelty toward their subordinates.[34] As early as the reign of Catherine the Great, a few elite members of military society had urged moderation on the part of commanders.[35] In his 1774 instructions to company commanders, Count S. R. Vorontsov expressed the paternalistic ideal that enlightened officials tried to realize in military society: a company commander "should conduct himself like a father with [his] children, admonishing the dishonorable [and] correcting them with advice. [He should] punish the unworthy with charity, single out and love the others, see that evil will be punished and meticulousness and virtue rewarded."[36] Vorontsov also urged special caution during military training, a time when officers became impatient with dull-witted soldiers and often resorted to unnecessary beatings and abuse.[37]

Throughout the first half of the nineteenth century, the government expressed concern about the problem of cruelty. Still, the official message delivered to soldiers and their superiors was ambiguous and contradictory. Judicial decisions and official pronouncements repeatedly voiced disapproval of abusive treatment. In a rescript of 1804, the tsar himself criticized widespread cruelty and forbade excessively severe punishments for minor infractions of the service order.[38] In this rescript Alexander I explained the essence of military discipline: to punish individuals guilty of wrongdoing and to teach the innocent who committed violations out of ignorance.[39] Some "moral crimes" forbidden by all laws demanded strict punishment. These included robbery, theft, fraud, disobedience to a commander, false steps while on guard duty, neglect of weapons and uniforms, unauthorized absence, fear before the enemy, and other equally pernicious crimes. In contrast, minor infractions that were clearly unintentional required a pedagogical approach: these included mistakes in handling weapons, marching, and wording reports. For "through frequent reckless punishments, a soldier is deprived of his health and strength." Moreover, "the continual expectation of blows from a stick, especially in a hurried person, upsets his attention," interferes with his ability to learn, and makes him more prone to error.[40] Troubled by reports of cruel treatment, Alexander I described the conditions prompting his rescript:

> It has come to my attention that in many regiments during training and drills, soldiers and recruits are punished with a severity that is only appropriate for instances of serious crimes. This method [of punishment], which has been so harmful for the service [and is] so opposed to common sense, is of course applied either out of misun-

derstanding about what should constitute military discipline or out of the innate proclivity of some for cruelty. The former is unforgivable in any officer, and the latter, revealing evil characteristics of the soul, destroys in him the very dignity of a man. Unquestionably, discipline among the troops should not be weakened at all, and punishment for offenses should be executed without fail; but mistakes that are unintentional or result from want of habit (especially if it is something the violator was ignorant of before) should not be equated with crimes that subject the guilty to severe punishment.[41]

Despite his express disapproval of severe punishment, the tsar failed to define the limits of acceptable treatment. Indeed, throughout this period the government frowned upon gratuitous cruelty, but in keeping with the character of autocratic authority, left its definition vague and, therefore, arbitrary.[42] Repeated official exhortations that officers exercise restraint in punishing their men show that Alexander's rescript had scant effect.[43] Cruelty remained a problem, despite the efforts of some enlightened commanders.

Following the Napoleonic Wars, highly placed military leaders again raised the issue of cruel treatment. As commander of the Twelfth Infantry Division, Count M. S. Vorontsov encouraged officers to use disciplinary means other than corporal punishment, forbidding its use outright for mistakes in military drill.[44] In 1818 the commander-in-chief of the First Army, General Sacen, ordered inspectors to ascertain whether the punishments inflicted on soldiers were cruel.[45] Before the Decembrist uprising, the Second Army served as a showcase for enlightened attitudes toward corporal punishment. As officers in the Second Army, the future Decembrists M. F. Orlov, V. F. Raevskii, and P. I. Pestel worked to prosecute abuses and soften punishments.[46] Orlov urged his subordinates in the Sixteenth Infantry Division to treat their men "with fatherly solicitation," reminding them "that soldiers are people, just as we are, that they can feel and think and have virtues . . . , and that it is possible to rouse them to great and glorious deeds without sticks and beatings."[47] Heeding the spirit of Orlov's words, A. G. Nepenin abolished corporal punishment in the Thirty-second Jager Regiment (where Raevskii served as a company commander).[48]

While some officers obviously took official exhortations to heart and even adopted measures that exceeded governmental intentions, others continued to abuse their men. Pronouncements made by the commander of Main Headquarters of the Second Army, Major General P. D. Kiselev, revealed the seriousness of the problem. Espousing the need for legal limits on the use of corporal punishment, in 1820 Kiselev attributed desertions, deaths, immorality, and the evasion and fear of service to "despotic punishments":

> Formerly the severe punishment of soldiers served as cause for bragging ... but mores have changed and now, to the honor of Russian officers, cruelty does not elicit praise. This is not to suggest that this evil does not exist at all: it persists, but in a more hidden and double manner—on the one hand, [it results] from the cruelty and morals of commanders, and on the other hand, from their failure to supervise aides. [Consequently], in a regiment all [commanding elements] from the lance corporal to the commander beat and kill people.[49]

In an order to corps commanders, Kiselev placed some very modest limits on the use of corporal punishment, blaming an increase in desertions on the failure of some officers to treat soldiers "with the gentleness needed to improve their performance. These officers, out of ignorance of their duties toward subordinates, destroy the courage, zealousness, and ambition that are appropriate for a soldier and also the willingness to endure service, which entails such difficulty."[50] Kiselev then ordered commanders to avoid "cruelty" for minor escapades, negligence, intoxication, slowness in learning military drills, and everything that did not constitute a crime. Rather, as far as possible, they should use "moral means" to correct the depraved and negligent, "distinction for the zealous and shame for the lazy." He also forbade the use of swords, ramrods, and blows of the hand. Sticks were permissible when all other means "for arousing a lazy soldier" failed, but for minor crimes commanders should not inflict hundreds of blows. Finally, no officer or noncommissioned officer should impose corporal punishment without an order from the company commander. Despite his genuine concern, Kiselev still did not set precise limits on the severity of punishments; on the contrary, careful not to overstep the bounds of his authority, he simply urged moderation, caution, and good judgment on the part of commanding officers. In 1822 the commander-in-chief of the Second Army, Count Wittgenstein, extended these provisions and actually forbade corporal punishment for mistakes in training.[51] For as Kiselev noted two years later, commanders were unable to distinguish mistakes from crimes.[52] Whatever the concrete results, there is no doubt that enlightened officers made significant efforts to limit the abuses associated with corporal punishment.

The overall message emanating from above was still ambiguous and contradictory. There existed an official belief that soldiers did not trust "weak commanders." Rather, they revered severity (*strogost'*) as long as it was just.[53] The authorities frowned upon excessive familiarity between soldiers and commanders: military discipline (and social propriety) required a respectful distance. The government and many officers feared that intimacy with the lower ranks undermined discipline. Thus one of the charges against V. F. Raevskii at his court-martial was inappropriate fraternization with his men.[54] The authorities had difficulty distinguishing Raevskii's familiarity with his subordinates from his more democratic ideas and subversive intentions. Both were deemed pernicious to order and stability.

Judicial cases involving accusations of cruel treatment also reveal the government's contradictory position. Formally, corporal punishment was not supposed to result in death. Even before the 1801 law requiring the presence of a doctor to ensure that soldiers could survive their sentences, official policy opposed physical abuse that led to death. Thus in 1800 Second Lieutenant Sviatikhin was convicted of excessively punishing his orderly with birches and rope. According to the doctor on duty, the orderly contracted a fever and died as a result of these punishments. Although the court concluded that the orderly was lazy and derelict in fulfilling his duties, they also felt that Sviatikhin should have used other means to reform him.[55]

The government's opposition to cruel punishment continued in the reign of Nicholas I. In 1855 Major Pavlov was found guilty of numerous violations resulting in the deaths of eight soldiers. He beat decorated soldiers who were legally exempt from corporal punishment and forced them to wear full parade uniform for up to twelve hours during guard duty and drill.[56] The evidence presented to the court showed unquestionably that Pavlov and his subordinates displayed a consistent pattern of abusive treatment and excessive punishments.[57] Pavlov tried to justify his actions by claiming that his men were undisciplined and morally dissolute. The authorities had no doubts about his guilt, and the emperor approved a punishment of five months' arrest in the casemate and expulsion from the service without privileges.[58]

Subsequent events soon revealed the government's inconsistency on the issue of cruel treatment. In January 1856 the emperor reduced Pavlov's term of arrest to two months and permitted him to remain in the service without the right to command a separate unit. Then in November 1857 he was appointed Tsebel'dinsk police officer, and in 1861 Alexander II ruled that his sentence should not prevent him from receiving service awards and other privileges, except for the order of St. Vladimir and decorations for irreproachable service.[59] The government was concerned about mistreatment, yet failed to enforce this concern with the unequivocal punishment of officers who abused their men. Rather, autocratic mercy for noble servitors took precedence over justice for the common soldier.

Other cases show that even where death occurred, the government did not always find evidence of cruelty. In January 1852 Captain Eliseev went to trial for cruelly punishing Private Voichulionis. In April 1851 Eliseev received orders to punish Voichulionis with three hundred blows with birches for wandering about at night in peasant clothing. Voichulionis was also under suspicion for stealing four skeins of thread valued at 20 silver rubles.[60] After the punishment, Voichulionis was sent to the city hospital, where he died the next day. The doctor on duty concluded that he had died of pneumonia caused by the flogging.

At his trial Captain Eliseev denied that he had any reason to punish Voichulionis cruelly. The private was not even from his unit, so he neither knew him nor was responsible for his behavior. He gave Voichulionis the specified number of blows and did not order blows on unauthorized parts of the body (though when Voichulionis moved, a few birches might have hit his back and upper leg). After two hundred blows the feldsher examined the victim and decided he could receive the remaining one hundred blows without danger. Moreover, after the punishment Voichulionis rose and walked to the hospital.

Unable to determine the cause of death, the authorities sent the case to the Military Medical Academic Committee for analysis. The committee found that Voichulionis had died from an apoplectic rush of blood to the brain. Because of a previous punishment of five hundred blows by running the gauntlet, Voichulionis suffered from an organic disorder of the left lung and spleen. So while the latest punishment did not directly cause his death, it probably hastened it, because of a predisposition to apoplectic seizure (that the responsible officials could not foresee given the absence of medical data). Consequently, the Military Judicial Department found Eliseev innocent, but concluded that the commander of the veterans' company was wrong to order the punishment. Since Voichulionis was suspected of theft and had been punished for crimes twice previously, he should have gone to trial. Obviously, the authorities did not think corporal punishment for minor crimes should result in death. When it did, the responsible officers faced trial and disgrace. Yet the authorities somewhat hypocritically accepted that corporal punishment caused damage to internal organs and therefore might hasten death.

In cases where death did not occur, cruel punishment was a more complicated issue, and the burden of proof rested with the claimants. At a regimental inspection in 1799, an elite dragoon (mounted infantry) squadron complained against Field Captain Lachin.[61] The dragoons claimed that Lachin beat them excessively (a claim they subsequently modified), subjected them to physical exhaustion, and on one occasion, in preparation for a regimental posting of guards, held training after sunset. Lachin denied any wrongdoing, but did admit that on the day in question, training had ended after sunset. He also admitted giving one dragoon two blows with birches for rudeness and slovenliness.

The Military Judicial Department concluded that the accusations of cruel treatment were unfounded. Even if two punishments (three or four blows with sticks) denied by Lachin had taken place, they were not considered "excessive." The credibility of the witnesses clearly swayed the court. In contrast to Lachin, who had an unblemished service record, the petitioners included "many men of bad conduct who bring out vices not only in themselves, but also in others."[62] It is difficult to evaluate the testimony of the lower ranks. It is possible that they were lying, that in the past they really had suffered excessive beatings from Lachin, or that they had complained about the punishments only because the training took place at an unauthorized time, when they were accustomed to some leisure. But because of past disciplinary problems in the unit, the authorities did not give them the benefit of the doubt. From a legal standpoint, the outcome of this case depended entirely upon discretionary judgments. It is also clear that the soldiers' perceptions of what constituted cruelty might conflict with official definitions.[63]

Possible conflicts between popular and official notions of cruelty are vividly revealed in an investigation of 1818, during which the soldiers of the Astrakhan Grenadier Regiment submitted complaints against their former commander, Major Kridner. The commander of Main Headquarters of the First Army, General Adjutant Baron Dibich, found some of the claims justified: many decorated soldiers were subjected to corporal punishment, which, while not excessive, did violate legal prohibitions. A few men also testified that they received five hundred blows with sticks and 100–150 blows with broadswords. But according to Dibich, these claims were exaggerated; for each time he questioned the men, they increased the reported number of blows.[64] The majority of complaints concerned punishments of twenty-five to fifty blows with sticks for neglect of duty—punishments that rarely occurred more than once a month.[65] In Dibich's view, the reported punishments were relatively frequent and severe, but they usually did not exceed legal norms. Furthermore, because the performance of the regiment (which was noted for its "spirit of laziness and insubordination") lagged behind that of others, strict measures were justified. Although the corps commander already had removed Kridner from his post for inappropriate orders revealing contempt for the soldiers, Dibich concluded that Kridner's guilt consisted "solely of excessive zealousness in the immediate reform of the regiment and the inability to use better means for that purpose."[66] Dibich thus accepted severity when discipline was weak.

According to Dibich, one could see "to what degree any real understanding of the duties and obligations of a soldier had been lost in the Astrakhan Grenadier Regiment, and how necessary it was to apply the most severe measures to bring this regiment to the appropriate organization." He attributed the soldiers' perception of cruel punishment to their elite status: among the grenadiers "there are more dissatisfied lower ranks than in other regiments of the Army, because this corps is manned largely by old soldiers from army regiments who, when they join a regiment, are not always treated by their new commanders with the same respect which they had acquired in their former regiments through lengthy service; this breeds in them dissatisfaction that results in laziness, insubordination, desertions, and complaints about the severity of their commanders."[67] Dibich did admit that the punishments meted out were severe, and that would explain the soldiers' complaints. But shortcomings in the performance of duties and military exercises clearly justified severity.

What did the lower ranks consider cruel punishment? When asked in 1818 about the reasons for desertion, the soldiers of the Second Fusilier Company answered that Major Kridner treated them harshly, punishing them with broadswords, ramrods, sticks, and birches "for the slightest infractions" and even for nothing.[68] Thus, if Kridner did not like a soldier's appearance, if a soldier drank vodka, regardless of whether he was drunk, or ate an onion—Kridner punished him. He also punished soldiers who held orders of St. Anne and St. George. Soldiers from other companies with larger numbers of deserters voiced the same complaints. In addition, two companies reported that because of Kridner, a noncommissioned officer had strangled himself out of shame. Since he was illiterate, could not remember orders, and had difficulty discharging his duties, Major Kridner always punished him. Finally, the soldiers complained that they did not understand why they were punished and noted that Kridner punished entire platoons for mistakes in training. In contrast, the officers of the regiment argued that only persons who performed poorly faced punishment.

Excerpts from the 1818 regimental book of orders reveal the officially sanctioned norms of punishment.[69] It is possible that the lower ranks found these norms unacceptable, that they actually experienced more severe punishments, or that out of general discontent or a heightened sense of possibility stimulated by the investigation, they did indeed exaggerate the severity of their commander. According to the regimental record, on April 4 Kridner ordered thirty blows with birches for three noncommissioned officers and two privates who were not dressed correctly. On April 15 the major ordered eight men from each company to appear at the regimental chancery to bleach linen for summer trousers. Noncommissioned officers were to accompany these workers and would be punished if they were late. Violations of the dress code and tardiness were legitimate grounds for corporal punishment.

Mistakes in military exercises also justified severity. On May 11 Kridner ordered the Third Fusilier Company to undergo training the next day for four hours after dinner. The brigade commander was unhappy, because they marched "like peasants, exhibiting laziness and negligence." Kridner also instructed the company commander to use birches and sticks in an effort to apply "strict measures to extirpate laziness and negligence in the men." He was convinced the company could perform better, and since this was not the first time they had exhibited laziness, he ordered each cavalier to clean rifles for two hours, while soldiers who were not cavaliers received seventy-five blows with birches. The Seventh Fusilier Company also displeased Kridner, so that despite a holiday, they were to practice platoon training for three hours in the morning and three hours after dinner. Here too the company commander was to employ sticks and birches. Finally, all officers were to inform their companies that since "gentle treatment of the lower ranks did not promise to bring them to the degree of precision and knowledge demanded by superior commanders," it was necessary "to put them on the right footing with strict measures and punishment for the slightest negligence." Thus Kridner ordered company commanders to punish laziness in training with sticks and birches and threatened them with punishment if their men did not improve. Commanders like Kridner equated mistakes or sloppiness in military exercises with laziness, and beatings were the preferred solution.

Military discipline also required the exact fulfillment of duties. On May 4 inspections revealed problems with the new summer trousers. Kridner ordered "severe" punishment for the responsible tailors. On May 7–8, Field Captain Krymaium failed to supervise adequately the guards at the town gates or "to inspire" the noncommissioned officers on duty to do so. The men were dirty and ignorant of their duties. (They failed to salute the brigade commander appropriately.) Krymaium also did not deliver the morning report on May 8 and failed to attend the posting of sentries. In addition, a disheveled orderly appeared before the brigade commander on May 7. For these violations Kridner gave Krymaium a "severe reprimand" and recommended that the noncommissioned officer on duty receive 200–300 blows with birches, an indication of the latter's responsibility to enforce military performance on the spot. On May 16 Kridner threatened to punish sergeants major whose companies were late for city guard duty with fifty blows with birches. Similarly, on May 18 three sergeants major who were supposed to bring fifty men to a training ground were promised seventy-five blows with birches if their men were late. On

June 6 Kridner demoted a noncommissioned officer to private for negligence in service, repeated drunkenness, and appearing at the evening report intoxicated. In addition, he faced a punishment of four hundred blows with birches and was to be stripped of his stripes before the regiment. Finally, on June 7 a copyist who wrote an unreadable report got one hundred blows with birches. The lower ranks faced corporal punishment for mistakes in training or while on guard duty, for dirty munitions and clothes, for bad work, and for tardiness and loss of state property—all infractions that the authorities regarded as laziness and negligence in service.

In a report of July 14, Major Kridner accounted for his disciplinary measures.[70] When he took command of the regiment, it was in complete disarray. The Tula chief of police repeatedly complained that drunken soldiers wandered about at night, abusing civilians and stealing. The major further explained that he had "only one month to provide trousers for the entire regiment," but the tailors habitually ruined things and had to remake each item several times. Kridner was certain that these problems resulted "from laziness and formal negligence," so he ordered the punishment of tailors "who sewed lazily." Finally, "extreme necessity" forced him to order noncommissioned officers to carry sticks and birches at training. The men were so lazy and stubborn that other methods had no effect. And even formal punishments did not eliminate movement and conversations in formation. During punishments before the battalion, soldiers continued to talk and fidget with their clothes. Experience showed that when sticks were not used, the men exhibited laziness and negligence, refusing to listen to their superiors. Then as soon as the sticks appeared, they became a little frightened and showed more efficiency and obedience. Only the guilty were punished, and no one received more than thirty blows with birches. Without threats, Kridner argued, it was rare for a company to drill with enthusiasm.

Dibich's investigation cleared Major Kridner of any wrongdoing, but the outcome and details of the case remain ambiguous. Laziness was a sticky issue, and officers tended to use the term when the real problem might be incompetence or ignorance—a problem addressed by Alexander I in his 1804 rescript. It is possible that the grenadiers were reacting to a new commander whose demands and standards were higher than those to which they were accustomed in the regular line army. It is also possible that the promotion of experienced soldiers to elite units—where, as individuals, they did not enjoy the same status—affected their performance. The high value they enjoyed in an army regiment might be lost in an elite unit, so perhaps they did become less inclined to exert themselves. The personal nature of relations between soldiers and officers was also important. To Kridner his subordinates were just soldiers. In their former units, long years of service might have produced a degree of understanding and respect between the men and their commanders that Kridner violated, but that they continued to expect. Whatever the underlying causes, Kridner inflicted no illegal punishments, assuming those recorded were truthful. More important, the soldiers did not necessarily accept the legal norms of punishment.

Although the military authorities took decided action against commanders who physically abused their men, official policy on this issue was never consistent. This resulted from the government's contradictory motives and from the failure to define precisely the limits of legal authority. Enlightened officials who shared the eighteenth-century concern for order and symmetry realized that abuses by officers undermined military discipline by compromising their moral legitimacy in the eyes of subordinates.[71] But as the 1810 trial of Major Shchigolev showed, inadequate supervision from superiors coupled with the broad discretionary powers of individual commanders allowed drunken, violent, and arbitrary officers to inflict cruel punishments on numerous occasions.[72] The problem went beyond administrative deficiencies, though this too was an important factor. In the debates of the reform era, there was an underlying concern that the elimination of corporal punishment would undermine military discipline.[73] Similarly, the judicial decisions of the pre-reform era reveal a reluctance (or inability) to define cruelty in a precise manner. Rather, the definition remained ambiguous and dependent on circumstances. What was cruel in one situation was justified severity in another. The losers in this arrangement were, of course, the lower ranks, who were "free" to develop their own understanding of what constituted cruel or unjustified punishment.

Soldiers Attitudes toward Service

Aside from folklore and formal petitions, the sources reveal four ways in which soldiers expressed dissatisfaction with their lives: suicide, desertion, disobedience, and outright rebellion. In these acts of defiance and despair, illiterate soldiers articulated their attitudes, aspirations, and expectations. Their proclaimed motives tell us much about social norms and boundaries of legitimate authority in military society. Although the men who resorted to such extreme acts were clearly exceptions, their reactions to specific situations reveal a well-developed understanding of their rights, a strong sense of justice, and definite notions about the treatment they considered acceptable.

Suicide represented the ultimate act of despair or resistance. Cruel and arbitrary punishments were a major cause of suicide among soldiers.[74] Thus, Private Nikanov accidentally shot and killed a lance corporal while trying to take his own life.[75] On May 21–22, 1820, Nikanov (at that time a noncommissioned officer) was twice punished with sticks and rods (*fukteli*), allegedly for tardiness and for playing cards with a convict.[76] He complained to his company commander and three days later was demoted to private for drunkenness. He could not understand why his superiors treated him with such severity and was so utterly exhausted that he could not perform his duties. Nikanov lost all hope of continuing service "due to the unjust acts committed against him" and resolved to kill himself. The Kherson commandant concluded that Nikanov was driven to suicide by "the injustice which he felt in body and soul" and by his superiors' failure to respond to his complaints or report them to the regimental commander. The tsar reviewed the case and ordered that Nikanov attend confession and that the ensign who had beat him be tried. In addition, the company commander faced arrest for a week and the battalion commander for three days.[77]

Desertion was another important barometer of popular attitudes toward service. Although desertion was not a mass phenomenon, it was one of the most frequent crimes committed by the soldiers. An analysis of the reasons for flight reveals much about the fears and expectations of the lower ranks. Desertion represented a bold refusal to accept existing conditions, though it is difficult to determine whether it was a spontaneous or premeditated act. Some soldiers openly admitted their desire to escape the service. Others, in an effort to justify their behavior, gave more elaborate explanations, which even if invented reflected an awareness of official sympathies.

In cases of desertion, the authorities often suspected abuses by officers. In May 1800 Colonel Dreniakin was tried for the large number of desertions from his infantry unit.[78] He testified that the desertions had occurred before he took command and attributed them to the "depraved behavior" of these men, most of whom had been assigned to the regiment as vagrants and deserters. In addition, he noted that the soldiers voiced no complaints at inspections in 1799. The court found Dreniakin innocent, since official information showed that seventy-seven of the seventy-eight desertions occurred before Dreniakin took charge. The authorities also accepted Dreniakin's view that the desertions resulted from the soldiers' own ill will. Still, he had to furnish evidence that the men had not been mistreated. The government rarely excused desertion, but did assume that it might be unjustifiably provoked. Officers had to account for their charges by explaining their own administrative failures and putative excess demands. This accountability must have been trying for a real blue-blooded squire and could underlie the frustration that manifested in cruelty.

An 1822 report to the commander-in-chief of the Second Army also exhibited the official assumption that abuses might provoke desertion.[79] During December 1820, twenty men deserted from the Second Battalion of the Thirty-second Jager Regiment located in Bessarabia. An investigation concluded that there were no persecutions to account for the desertions: no "excessive severity by the commander" and no training that "exceeded human strength." The soldiers did have some economic grievances, but the investigator considered them unfounded and unrelated to the desertions. Rather, "most of those who deserted were of depraved behavior.... [They] had been convicted for desertion and other misdemeanors, and several have relations abroad." The battalion commander also described them as lazy, careless, slovenly, and inclined to drunkenness and theft. Although the government held the soldiers responsible, the battalion and company commanders were still guilty of negligence in supervising their men and were fined the cost of the investigation (846 rubles).

Desertion among recruits also aroused similar suspicions of abuse by officers. When two recruits deserted from a party escorted by Lieutenant Papsuev in 1800, the emperor ordered an investigation.[80] The recruits had no complaints against Papsuev, who blamed the desertions on the "peasant empty-headedness" of the men. In a similar case, Captain Biretov was tried after six men deserted from a party of 120.[81] After questioning the recruits, who had no complaints against Biretov, the governor general of Riga concluded that three morally depraved recruits (one had been sent to the army as a vagrant and two for theft) incited another three men to desert. In both these cases the authorities found the officers innocent of abuses, but still held them responsible for inadequate supervision, fining them two weeks' pay for each deserter. The government consistently held commanders responsible for desertions among their subordinates, even when abuses had not occurred.

A few enlightened officers drew an unequivocal connection between commanders' abuses and desertion. According to Count M. S. Vorontsov, fear of punishment caused both desertion and suicide.[82] Following inquiries into flight from the training artillery companies, an inspector's report of 1820 noted that in one battery, exercises took place three times a day, the third time by candlelight.[83] During these exercises the sergeant major and company commander frequently inflicted punishments. This together with the drunkenness "that often follows from the dissatisfaction of people of this type, produced desertions." Similarly, in an 1820 memorandum on corporal punishment, Major General Kiselev argued that "the loss of men from desertion and death, lack of morality, evasion of service and fear of it often originate from arbitrary punishments."[84] Kiselev repeated this argument in an 1824 report, when he attributed desertion and suicide in the Second Army to cruel and arbitrary punishments.[85]

While commander of the Sixteenth Infantry Division, M. F. Orlov offered three reasons for desertion: inadequate provisions, excessive severity and cruelty in imposing discipline, and the failure of commanders to treat their men with fatherly solicitation, so that they acquired a sense of duty to the fatherland and the service.[86] Other observers blamed desertions on excessively long training, the use of alcoholic beverages, and the system of conscription with its extremely long term of service, which tore young men from their families and kept them in the army until they were physically exhausted or disabled.[87]

In normal circumstances, where the rate of desertion did not exceed acceptable limits, the authorities tended to blame the morality of the soldiers. This is apparent in a series of inspectors' reports from 1845 to 1846. The main reasons given for desertion included drunkenness, laziness, negligence in service, bad morality, depraved behavior, and fear of punishment.[88] In cases where the number of desertions seemed high, the state's first impulse was to investigate possible abuses by commanding officers. When none emerged, the authorities accepted the officers' explanations. Officers generally tried to clear themselves by questioning the character of deserters or blaming the influence of morally suspect persons. The government also attributed desertions to pernicious influences: an 1841 law thus sought to limit the number of vagrants sent to the regular army, for they "spoil the morality of the lower ranks and increase the number of deserters among them." [89]

The authorities did not dare suggest that desertion might represent a popular form of resistance to military service. Rather, it stemmed from abuses, depravity, or administrative negligence. These explanations were not completely unreasonable. There were abusive and incompetent officers, and among the soldiers there were repeated offenders who were more likely to commit crimes.[90] In their own testimonies, deserters expressed more complicated motivations. Most simply sought to evade service and openly admitted it, an indication of the degree to which desertion represented the conscious renunciation of state-imposed service duties. In June 1800 at the behest of two fellow soldiers, one private fled across the Prussian border, seeking a better life.[91] In 1832 four privates similarly fled, intending to avoid service or return home.[92] A fifth private who began service with an elite cuirassier regiment, but was demoted to an uhlan regiment for drunkenness, also deserted with the intention of returning home. In this case it was perhaps the disappointment of demotion that led to flight.[93]

Desertion was one possible response to difficulties in the service. In 1835 one infantry private was tried for a third desertion. Although he had committed theft immediately before deserting, he attributed his flight to ignorance of military drills and service duties, which he found onerous "because of his old age and stupidity."[94] In 1841 a border guard named Loginov tried to escape to Turkey. When caught, he accused his superior of taking money and bread from the men, though subsequently he admitted that he did not flee in response to abuses. Rather, he had accused his commander out of resentment, because the latter often berated him for not having the required equipment.[95] Here embarrassment and hostility toward superiors underlay the decision to flee.

Some seasoned soldiers gave more imaginative reasons for deserting: one private deserted in 1832 "because of drunkenness."[96] Drunkenness was a frequent explanation for desertion and one that was comfortable for the government, since it did not imply the conscious rejection of service duties.[97] Occasionally, soldiers gave reasons for deserting that saved them from punishment. Thus in 1832 a private fled because he did not want to serve in transport, but sought to continue active service. The authorities returned him to an infantry regiment without punishment.[98] In a case from 1842, Nicholas I pardoned a private who deserted to visit his dying mother.[99] Desertion did not always signify a desire to escape the service.

Punishment and the fear of it were other important reasons given for deserting. In June 1831 one uhlan was sent to obtain a cart for his regiment. During the night his horse broke loose and cut its chest. Fearing punishment, he fled to Austria in hopes of evading service forever.[100] Similarly, a second private fled after his horse collapsed and a third when his cartridges were stolen. Both sought to escape punishment, since the law held soldiers responsible for military property and equipment.[101] Other desertions to escape punishment originated with drunkenness. Thus a Don cossack who spent the night at a tavern with three comrades awoke to find them gone; fearing punishment, he fled to Austria.[102] Similarly, following a drinking bout, one barber who became separated from his unit fled to Austria to avoid punishment.[103] Fear of punishment made it difficult to resist desertion, particularly when a foreign border was near.

Actual punishments also caused desertion. Soldiers used official sentiments concerning cruelty to their advantage. In November 1810 Private Tutorin appeared at the Moscow police station, where he declared that he had deserted "out of his own stupidity, while drunk."[104] During interrogation he claimed that he had fled to report the frequent persecutions and beatings he suffered at the hands of a noncommissioned officer. The divisional commander conducted an investigation, but found no evidence to support Tutorin's claims. During his trial, Tutorin admitted that he had been drunk and fled for fear of punishment. He also testified that he did not suffer any cruelties, but had denounced the noncommissioned officer to justify his absence. This was a rare case, for the defendant openly admitted lying to excuse his actions. He knew that the authorities would respond to his accusations of unjust punishment, so while he could never expect to exonerate himself fully, he might at least ease the punishment by showing just cause.

During the reign of Nicholas I, soldiers repeatedly tried to justify desertion as a response to harsh treatment. In 1832 one private fled to Austria, because "they beat me during training."[105] Similarly, in 1849 Private Sheniavskii explained two desertions as responses to the cruelty of a noncommissioned officer who beat him during training. Subsequently, he admitted that he deserted because "service seemed burdensome."[106] As a young noble from the Polish kingdom (whose status was not officially recognized), Sheniavskii was no doubt distressed by the rigors of military service. Like other soldiers, he instinctively sought to justify his behavior with accusations of unfair treatment.

An important case from 1850 revealed the soldiers' persistent belief in tsarist justice.[107] In June 1849 eleven lower ranks fled into the Kirghiz steppe. They gave a variety of reasons for deserting. Three testified that they fled "in a drunken state without any aim, wishing to enjoy freedom." Others sought to escape the reproaches of their superiors. One complained that his commanders repeatedly threatened to punish him during inspections and drills. A sergeant major also treated him cruelly, but fearing the company commander, he did not express any grievances. Another private testified that the company commander punished him during inspection and drill and then demoted him from lance corporal's assistant. So "unable to bear this shameful disgrace," he fled. Four other privates also complained of unjustified beatings by the sergeant major, who was frequently drunk. Although the soldiers complained to a superior, he either took no action or else punished the men who spoke out. Another private claimed that he repeatedly suffered unjustified punishments from a company commander during training and state works. Finally, one Polish private who claimed noble status deserted because after ten years of service, he had not been promoted and repeatedly was refused retirement. He accused the company commander of twice punishing him unjustly and of treating him not as a noble, but as a "depraved person."[108]

The officers responded that the punishments inflicted were just and the soldiers in question inclined toward drunkenness and sloth. The state accepted their explanations, perhaps because nine of the defendants had records of previous misconduct. In addition, they had taken state property when they deserted. Since this case concerned behavior—which was so much more difficult to fix and verify than monies and supplies—the credibility of the witnesses was especially important. Although the authorities sentenced the company commanders to fifteen days' arrest in the guardhouse, they did not find them guilty of abusing their men. Rather, they were punished for the high rates of desertion from their companies. The soldiers suffered sentences of 1,000–3,000 blows by running the gauntlet followed by service in convicts' companies. Once again soldiers had sought to justify an inexcusable offense with claims of cruel treatment. The numbers involved suggest that claims of cruelty reflected the real sentiments of the defendants. But even if their statements were a clever ploy, they still provide an index of social norms and popular beliefs. At the very least, the soldiers hoped to gain the sympathy of the authorities.

Disobedience and Rebellion

The circumstances prompting disobedience and rebellion show that the soldier had definite notions of his rights and obligations and his relationship to superiors and their responsibilities toward him. The circumstances surrounding acts of disobedience and rebellion are especially important to understanding the attitudes and expectations of the lower ranks. In these acts soldiers released all their pent-up grievances that had long been repressed. Disobedience was also a spontaneous action fraught with danger, a response to particular events, perceptions, and conditions. The combination of spontaneity and the release of unexpressed discontent suggests that acts of disobedience accurately revealed the soldiers' innermost feelings.

The most important cases of disobedience involved collective actions. The judicial record indicates that soldiers expected two things from their commanders: fair treatment and material support. These expectations were completely consistent with official military regulations. The most frequent cause of disobedience was cruel or unjustified punishment. In 1797 five noncommissioned officers and nine grenadiers went to trial for "rebellion and formal uprising" against their company commander. The incident began when Captain Pisanskii prepared to punish a sergeant major for delivering a defective daily report. The grenadiers responded that they could no longer bear his "wrongful beatings" and intended to complain. The company then illegally went into formation and marched off, without an order, to the colonel's quarters. After hearing the grenadiers' complaints, the colonel removed Pisanskii from his command and arrested him.[109]

In the final judicial report confirmed by Paul, the authorities concluded that there was insufficient evidence of cruel beatings and that the soldiers' complaints were largely false. Pisanskii had punished the men for drunkenness and mistakes in training—actions permitted by the law. In June 1798 the tsar ordered that the main instigators of the disobedience be punished with the knout and sent to Siberia.[110] The court had identified the sergeant major and five noncommissioned officers as instigators. The sergeant major had falsely accused Pisanskii of cruel punishment and of withholding provisions and cloth. The five noncommissioned officers had failed to stop the company from submitting its complaint and had refused to obey Pisanskii's order to punish the sergeant major with sticks. Despite the statements of their superiors, the lower ranks obviously felt they had been abused.

In a similar case from 1810, eighty-nine musketeers went on trial for disobedience against their battalion commander, Colonel Kniazhnin.[111] After finding the men on guard duty "dirty and slovenly," Kniazhnin struck a decorated sergeant major on the cheeks and then prepared to punish him and three other noncommissioned officers with sticks. At that moment, seventy-seven soldiers shouted: "Your Honor, please do not punish them, but give us our state munitions." To avoid trouble Kniazhnin withdrew and reported to the regimental commander. When the latter wanted to punish one private as "more guilty than the others," the lower ranks shouted: "We will not permit Your Excellency to punish Petrov, for he is not guilty." And another private dragged away Petrov. This direct interference with the orders of the battalion and regimental commanders clearly constituted disobedience.

A host of economic grievances underlay the soldiers' disobedience. They believed that Kniazhnin wanted to punish the sergeant major and noncommissioned officers, who were not guilty, because the soldiers wore short boots. The company commander had ordered them to buy long ones, but they had already spent their personal and artel funds to buy munitions, for they had not received money that was due for new outfits. Their new uniforms lay in the depot, used only for general postings. Apparently, these economic complaints were justified, for Kniazhnin tried to persuade the company to forget the incident by promising to reimburse them 1,000 rubles. The company refused. Conscious of their rights and imbued with their own sense of justice, they requested an official inspection. Because their superiors had failed to fulfill their prescribed obligations, the soldiers believed that the intended punishment was unjustified.

In 1831 loyalty to comrades again prompted disobedience by the soldiers of a grenadier company. Two lance corporals complained that their company commander beat them unjustly for incorrect positioning while on duty. The lance corporals were transferred to another company, and when their comrades heard of this, they took action. They sent the sergeant major to inform the battalion commander that they could no longer serve with Captain Okerman. The regimental commander rescinded his order to transfer the lance corporals, and the battalion commander notified the divisional commander that it was necessary to transfer Okerman. An investigation followed, and the lower ranks declared that they had requested Okerman's removal because of his excessive severity. Once again soldiers responded to an impending punishment, unjustified in their eyes, by articulating suppressed grievances.[112]

A subsequent investigation revealed that Okerman punished the soldiers with swords, sticks, and sometimes even sabers. In addition, he burdened them with training by candlelight in winter and inspected their outfitting on holidays. Okerman had definitely committed abuses; but because his company was always in good condition and because the soldiers' dissatisfaction "arose only from his use, out of zealousness for the service," of inappropriate means, he was arrested for two months and transferred to the Active Army. He also could not command a company before receiving recognition for "outstanding service." The soldiers, too, were guilty of a crime, and the corps commander demoted eighty-seven grenadiers to musketeer companies, where the instigators were to be identified and brought to trial. There was a fine line between the spontaneous articulation of justified grievances and the unacceptable offense of disobedience.

Collective disobedience also arose when a group of soldiers were singled out for unusually strict supervision. In 1850, following complaints about frequent thefts and reports that soldiers were occupied more with private work than with service, the Kinburn commandant ordered two unexpected checks of Half-Company No. 1.[113] Although on both occasions men were found missing, the half-company complained to their garrison commander, Lieutenant Colonel Loman. They resented the fact that only their unit was checked and wondered whether they were under suspicion for some offense. Loman sent the soldiers back to their barracks, where two other officers questioned them. Again one soldier responded, "Why is only our company under suspicion?" And two others shouted, "What kind of persecution is this? They check our half-company once again, but we do know the reason." When the officers ordered them to be silent, the men repeated these questions even louder, and as a result three "instigators" were arrested.[114] The garrison commandant subsequently instructed one officer to arrest all the instigators, but when he ordered a few men to step forward, voices were heard saying, "Let's all go." At that point he identified four men, who were put under arrest.[115]

It is important to note that the soldiers prosecuted in this case were not the lowliest privates. Their strong reaction to coming under suspicion may have resulted from their higher social standing, which perhaps made them more sensitive to breaches of administrative procedure. They also feared the consequences of coming under suspicion: they might lose their position or face a painful punishment. Economic interests were also at stake. The trial revealed heavy involvement in private business, which the soldiers may have wanted to hide. The repeated absences from the barracks provided clear evidence of misdeed, yet the men responded spontaneously to a perceived violation of disciplinary norms and expected routines. In the conditions of lax discipline and extensive private business prevailing at the Kinburn Garrison, the men reacted strongly to the reimposition of strict controls represented by the surprise roll calls.

Failure to fulfill economic obligations also caused popular unrest. In 1857 twenty-one soldiers from the Åland fortifications went on trial for "obvious disobedience" against their commander, Ensign Shchetinin.[116] On September 28, 1856, Shchetinin informed his men that provisions were low, and they would have to send to Åbo for supplies. The men agreed to provide for themselves with state funds until provisions arrived and received money for food through October 8. From October 7 to 14, the men bought beef to eat (a half pound daily). The beef was supposed to last until October 21, but according to the defendants, half the meat was spoiled. In addition, they received funds for meal and potatoes.

The situation began to deteriorate on October 14, when the supplies did not arrive as expected. The lower ranks received money for the fourteenth, but when they requested additional funds on the fifteenth, Shchetinin told them to wait until the noncommissioned officer returned. He had no more funds and even had added his own money to the last handout. The men worked obediently on the fifteenth and sixteenth, but then on the seventeenth one noncommissioned officer informed Shchetinin that the men of Company No. 4 wanted money. Consequently, Shchetinin distributed money for the fifteenth and sixteenth out of his own pocket and then went to ask the men of Company No. 4 whether they had bread. They unanimously explained that they already owed local residents money for the past two days and had nothing to eat. Shchetinin felt that their hosts could wait until supplies arrived, but the company began to shout: "Please [give us] money; we have nothing to eat." Men from the other companies also began to demand money, but Shchetinin was certain they had provisions and ordered the men to work. A few soldiers from the Fifth, Sixth, and Seventh companies obeyed, but eighteen men from Company No. 4 marched off to their quarters. Shchetinin then gave them more of his own money for the seventeenth. Meanwhile, the men of Companies No. 5, 6, and 7 refused to go to work, saying: "If one company did not go, why are we going? Hardly so that they [alone] will be guilty." On the seventeenth, only Company No. 7 and a few men from Company No. 6 finally went to work; the rest returned to their quarters. Soon after this incident provisions arrived, and Shchetinin took steps to restore his authority. On the eighteenth, he tried to punish three instigators. One bombardier resisted, stepping forward only after the third command. Then the rest of Company No. 4 declared that they would not permit any punishments, "for they did not steal anything." As one gunner put it, "the tsar did not order us to starve." With that the entire company walked off. Seeing that the men were united, Shchetinin punished no one, but initiated a judicial process.

The authorities questioned the motivations of Company No. 4 on two grounds. There was considerable evidence from the testimonies of other soldiers that the men had sufficient food, including bread, potatoes, beef, and pork. However, when Shchetinin inspected these units, he had not visited Company No. 4, which was quartered at some distance. It is possible, then, that the company did not have such supplies. The Military Judicial Department concluded that the lack of funds did not justify disobedience, especially since it resulted from circumstances beyond Shchetinin's control. Moreover, the soldiers could acquire bread on credit from local inhabitants. The authorities repeatedly made this assumption, for when state supplies were unavailable, the military obtained goods locally. But it is not certain that local residents provided adequate food for the soldiers. If Shchetinin was so sure the men had bread, why did he immediately give them money at the first sign of unrest? All this suggests the very real possibility that the men of Company No. 4 were indeed short of food.

Whatever the realities of the food situation, the incident illuminates both the expectations of the soldiers and their relations with each other. The events of 1856 clearly revealed the company as the basic social unit. The men of each company tended to act as a group, and the authorities identified them as such. This collective identity was rooted in daily life, where companies quartered, trained, served, and ate as a unit. There was also a more general solidarity (or perhaps jealousy) between the companies. Therefore when Company No. 4 refused to work, the other companies followed suit—either because they shared the same feelings or because they did not think they should have to work when others did not. The crime of Company No. 4 consisted of demanding money allotted them by law. They knew their commander was obliged to feed them and so refused to work without their daily allowance. Since they received no money for two days and then on the third day got allowances retroactively, they reasonably might have thought that Shchetinin had funds for the third day as well. They showed little regard for extenuating circumstances and pressed demands to receive their due. When Shchetinin tried to punish the instigators, the other soldiers came to their defense: since they had a right to the money, no one was guilty and no punishment was justified. Regardless of formal legalities, the soldiers' behavior revealed well-defined notions of their rights and their commander's obligations. Shchetinin's failure to fulfill these obligations quickly prompted popular action.[117]

Outright rebellion occurred rarely in the pre-reform army. The conditions prompting rebellion were the same that generated disobedience or even the submission of claims against a commander. The main differences lay in the nature and scope of the actions taken by the men and in the extent and severity of a commander's abuses. The basic grievances included abusive treatment, cruel and unjustified punishments, and failure to provide for economic needs. There is no reason to recount here the well-known events associated with the Semenovskii rebellion of 1820 and the Decembrist uprising of 1825.[118] The men of the Semenovskii regiment objected to the excessive severity of their commander, Colonel Schwarz, who upon taking command of the unit (which under its previous commander had enjoyed a liberal regime), set out to impose the strictest discipline. Schwarz introduced an intensive training regimen and inflicted severe punishments for minor violations of the service order.[119] A military court actually found him guilty of cruelty and negligence, but because of his good record, his only punishment was dismissal from the service.[120]

Even the Decembrist uprising was not truly a popular rebellion against the military system as such. The officers who led the rebellion certainly had a political agenda. But the common soldiers were drawn into action by promises to abolish corporal punishment and shorten the term of service and by their loyalty to Constantine Pavlovich, who was believed to be the legitimate ruler.[121] Although the soldiers did not initiate the rebellion, they responded readily to promises addressing their basic grievances. These were the same grievances that prompted suicide, desertion, and disobedience.

Echoes of the Decembrist uprising also appeared in other units. In August 1826 thirteen artillerymen from the First Army were convicted of "mutiny against the government." According to the corps commander, four officers had incited them to rebel. Although the officers had conscious designs "against the government and legitimate state authority," the court concluded that most of the soldiers "were drawn into the crime . . . only through delusions, which resulted from [promises] to obtain for them a shorter term of service and an increase in pay, to improve their condition, to abolish punishments for mistakes in formation and in the rapid adjustment of arms."[122] While these rebellions lacked a mass character, they did reflect the aspirations of the lower ranks. More important, they suggest the vulnerability of a system, where ordinary grievances could be so easily transformed into major rebellions.

The underlying causes of disobedience and rebellion related to punishments, general treatment, and receipt of provisions and supplies. In addition to the expectations and disappointments of the men, acts of disobedience and rebellion revealed much about the fiber of social relations in military society. Most striking was the social cohesiveness of the company, built upon the soldiers' artel and the central role of the company in subsistence, training, and the organization of daily life. Patterns in relations between soldiers and officers suggest the personalized nature of conflict and loyalties. Complaints against individual officers were often at the root of disobedience. But the very act of disobedience might also indicate precisely the opposite phenomenon. Some cases involved appeal to a higher authority in the person of an officer, but in defiance of another commander. Other illegal actions, including rebellions, stemmed from a willingness to follow superiors and might even reflect obedience to orders. Although the men who resorted to disobedience and rebellion were certainly exceptions, their reactions to specific circumstances indicated a well-developed understanding of their rights, a strong sense of justice, and definite notions of the treatment they expected and considered acceptable.

CONCLUSION

The Semi-Standing Army

Examination of the soldier's daily life makes it difficult to speak of a single Russian army, since experiences and realities were so varied and so changeable. The variety of experiences applied to physical and social aspects of military life. Material factors, particularly the diversity of local conditions and the instability of the pre-industrial subsistence economy, largely account for fluctuations in the soldiers' physical wellbeing (though corrupt or inept officials also played a part). Regardless of any precarious wartime conditions, it seems likely that during the course of a service career, each soldier would find himself in a variety of changing economic circumstances. While soldiers prospered in one area, their comrades in an adjacent area might go hungry. Economic instability and the struggle to survive in the most basic physical sense were constant features of military life.

Confusion in social norms presents a more complicated problem. The most obvious reason for this confusion was the inherently arbitrary nature of autocratic authority, which was transposed onto the discretionary power of commanders. The character and abilities of individual officers had a decisive effect on the social and economic condition of the lower ranks. The state either chose or was forced, because of inadequate economic and administrative resources, to rely extensively on ad hoc measures taken by individual officers and to tolerate flagrant violations of the law—all of which eroded bureaucratic rationality and professional efficiency. The gap between laws and actual behavior could only confuse the soldiers' grounds of legitimacy: they could never know for certain when an officer's violations were justified, especially since their own crimes were never justified. Soldiers in the pre-reform era accepted the contradictions and uncertainties of military service. Still, the protests that occurred revealed expectations and aspirations that potentially threatened social stability. Soldiers not only were aware of their legal rights, but also developed their own notions of what was just and reasonable. The ambiguity of a system built upon central regulation and local arbitrariness constituted a time bomb that would explode by 1905, as the soldiers' acquiescence to abuse and irregularity vanished.[1]

Another source of confusion in social norms was the role that service played in Russian society. For the peasant conscript, service brought formal social mobility in the form of juridical emancipation. But the peasant was never conscious of this "freedom." He stubbornly insisted on viewing service as an onerous burden. The army was then left with the unenviable task of trying to transform an obligation that peasant society regarded as an unmitigated disaster into a glorious and heroic deed. If one considers the conditions of military life, then the peasant attitude seems imminently sensible. Since the soldier's "freedom" could not be implemented for twenty or twenty-five years, it was not likely that he himself would benefit directly (though his children and grandchildren might rise in the social hierarchy). "Freedom" gave the soldier a civic identity and some limited legal rights. But above all it meant that he was now individually accountable and regulated in new ways. The definition of "freedom" reflected the viewpoint of the state, which treated the soldier as a valuable resource that needed protection in order to serve the state interest.

The social contradictions embodied in the soldier's newly acquired "freedom" reflected the competing sources of social norms in military society. First, there were the traditional relations between nobles and peasants that derived from serfdom—relations contained by custom and by the lord's unlimited power over his serfs. Another source of social norms was the state, which actively sought to regulate relations in military society by defining in law the mutual obligations of soldiers and officers, as well as their relationship to the army and government. A final source of social norms resulted from the professional functions of the army. Soldiers and their commanders shared common experiences relating to their special military functions. Pre-reform military society embodied all the contradictions, limitations, and ambiguities of a traditional society attempting to modernize without dismantling its underlying structure. It also showed that dynamic forces for change existed within the old regime.

Even when one examines the generally miserable condition of the lower ranks, a single fact stands out in stark contrast to all the problems and brutalities of life in the pre-reform army: as an institution dedicated to the defense of the Russian empire, the army functioned reasonably well. Despite poor administration and inadequate resources, despite abuses and arbitrariness, and despite the difficulty of achieving uniformity in behavior and training, the pre-reform army served as an effective instrument of military and diplomatic policies. The pre-industrial warfare of this period, with its transitional military technology and tactics, allowed the hybrid, ad hoc military order that suited Russia so well to perform adequately. The army also made optimal use of the uneven social resources at its disposal. Poorly equipped, ill fed, sporadically trained, and physically abused, the Russian soldier stood firm in the face of battle. He also rarely rebelled in an open and massive way. Still, he was not a passive instrument in the hands of the ruling class. For the personalized nature of authority relationships—so characteristic of both autocracy and serfdom—deflected the soldier's discontent away from the army as an institution onto individual commanders. In this way the soldier could assert himself when his rights and expectations were violated without ever having to question the legitimacy of the system or ruler he served.

NOTES

List of Abbreviations

CMRS	*Cahiers du monde russe et soviétique*
FOG	*Forschungen zur osteuropäischen Geschichte*
IV	*Istoricheskii vestnik*
JGO	*Jahrbücher für Geschichte Osteuropas*
OVRO	*Otechestvennaia voina i russkoe obshchestvo* (Moscow, 1911–12)
PSZ	*Polnoe sobranie zakonov*
PVM	*Prikazy voennogo ministra*
RA	*Russkii arkhiv*
RI	*Russkii invalid*
RR	*The Russian Review*
RS	*Russkaia starina*
RV	*Russkii vestnik*
SEER	*The Slavonic and East European Review*
SIRIO	*Sbornik Imperatorskogo Rossiiskogo istoricheskogo obshchestva*
SR	*The Slavic Review*
SVM	*Stoletie voennogo ministerstva* (St. Petersburg, 1902–14)
SVP	*Svod voennykh postanovlenii*
SZ	*Svod zakonov Rossiiskoi imperii*
TsGAOR	Tsentral'nyi gosudarstvennyi arkhiv oktiabr'skoi revoliutsii, Moscow
TsGIA	Tsentral'nyi gosudarstvennyi istoricheskii arkhiv, Leningrad
TsGVIA	Tsentral'nyi gosudarstvennyi voenno-istoricheskii arkhiv, Moscow
VMZ	*Voenno-meditsinskii zhurnal*
VS	*Voennyi sbornik*
VZ	*Voennyi zhurnal*

Introduction

1. André Corvisier has tied the development of standing armies to the growing power of the centralized state. See his *Armies and Societies in Europe, 1494–1789*, trans. Abigail T. Siddall (Bloomington: Indiana University Press, 1979), and *L'armée française de la fin du XVIIe siècle au ministère du Choiseul: Le Soldat*, 2 vols. (Paris: Presses Universitaires de France, 1964).

2. The term "lower ranks" (*nizhnie chiny*) refers to privates and noncommissioned officers. Because the sources do not always distinguish these groups, I have used the term when it is important to emphasize that both categories are being considered. Otherwise I have used "soldiers" to denote the mass of troops.

3. See Marc Raeff, *The Well-Ordered Police State: Social and Institutional Change through Law in the Germanies and Russia, 1600–1800* (New Haven: Yale University Press, 1983).

4. John L. H. Keep, "From the Pistol to the Pen: The Military Memoir as a Source on the Social History of Pre-Reform Russia," *CMRS* 21, no. 3–4 (July–December 1980): 315, note 5.

5. *PVM*, 22.I.1854, no. 9.

6. Even soldiers' folklore is often official. Only a trained folklorist is competent to distinguish official folklore (found in journals like *Chtenie dlia soldat*) from genuine popular folklore. See L. N. Pushkarev, "Soldatskaia pesnia—istochnik po istorii voennogo byta russkoi reguliarnoi armii XVIII-pervoi poloviny XIX v.," *Voprosy voennoi istorii* (Moscow, 1965), pp. 422–32.

One. "Conscription"

1. Quoted in "Rekrut," 6, *Chtenie dlia soldat* (1856): 99.

2. L. G. Beskrovnyi, *Russkaia armiia i flot v XVIII veke* (Moscow, 1958), p. 297, and idem, *Russkaia armiia i flot v XIX veke* (Moscow, 1973), pp. 71–80.

3. According to John S. Curtiss, in 1850 the Russian army numbered 859,000, the French army 570,000, the Austrian army 350,000, and the Prussian army 200,000. See John S. Curtiss, *The Russian Army under Nicholas I, 1825–1855* (Durham, N.C.: Duke University Press, 1965), p. 108.

4. A. N. Radishchev, *A Journey from St. Petersburg to Moscow*, ed. Roderick Page Thaler, trans. Leo Wiener (Cambridge, Mass.: Harvard University Press, 1958), pp. 201–202.

5. M. M. Speransky, *O voennykh poseleniiakh* (St. Petersburg, 1825), pp. 4–6.

6. *Arkhiv Grafov Mordvinovykh*, 10 vols. (St. Petersburg, 1901–1903), 4: 39–40.

7. TsGVIA, f. 801, op. 61, d. 77, ll. 465–80.

8. *PSZ* (I) 25: 18481.

9. I. I. Prokhodtsov, *Riazanskaia guberniia v 1812 godu*, 2 vols. (Riazan, 1913), 1: 96–145.

10. *PSZ* (II) 3: 2362, and 15: 13322.

11. *PSZ* (II) 6: 4911. On measures to combat flight among Jews, see *PSZ* (II) 26: 25667.

12. *PSZ* (II) 20: 19060. TsGVIA, f. 395, op. 206, otd. 4, d. 4, ll. 1–1ob.

13. I am grateful to Professor Walter Pintner for sharing this file with me. See TsGVIA, f. Voenno-uchenyi arkhiv, d. 18027.

14. TsGVIA, f. 395, op. 206, otd. 4, d. 4 (1848).

15. *SZ* (1842), t. 4, kn. 1, r. 1, gl. 1, st. 9, 13.

16. Speransky, *O voennykh poseleniiakh*, p. 4.

17. *PSZ* (I) 17: 12748, and 31: 24251.

18. *PSZ* (I) 25: 18388; 28: 21442; 30: 23286, 23759; and 32: 25479.

19. *PSZ* (I) 32: 25021, 25479; 33: 25845, 25981; 34: 26899; (II) 2: 1502, 1545; 3: 1725, 1790.
20. *PSZ* (I) 30: 23759; 32: 25479.
21. TsGIA, f. 1286, op. 3, d. 329.
22. *PSZ* (II) 3: 2543.
23. *PSZ* (II) 6: 4677. "Free farmers" were a category of state peasants consisting of former serfs who had purchased "emancipation" on the basis of the law of 20.II.1803. Jerome Blum, *Lord and Peasant in Russia* (Princeton, N.J.: Princeton University Press, 1971), pp. 540–41.
24. See *PSZ* (I) 30: 23759; 32: 25479; (II) 6: 4677; 22: 21673.
25. *PSZ* (II) 7: 5572.
26. TsGIA, f. 1262, op. 1, d. 6.
27. TsGIA, f. 1262, op. 1, d. 39, ll. 12–14.
28. TsGIA, f. 1262, op. 1, d. 131, l. 1 (1851); d. 145.
29. TsGIA, f. 1262, op. 1, d. 72, ll. 1–4, 12–12ob.
30. Ibid.
31. *PSZ* (II) 3: 2543.
32. *PSZ* (II) 24: 23049.
33. TsGVIA, f. 395, op. 213, d. 22, ll. 41ob., 78ob.; *PSZ* (II) 30: 29346.
34. TsGIA, f. 1262, op. 1, d. 130, ll. 25–27ob.
35. TsGIA, f. 1262, op. 1, d. 130.
36. TsGIA, f. 1262, op. 1, d. 114, 130. In the years 1840–49, only 414 receipts were issued, which led the State Council to conclude that self-mutilation was decreasing. See TsGIA, f. 1262, op. 1, d. 130, ll. 10–11.
37. TsGIA, f. 1262, op. 1, d. 130, ll. 18ob.–19. For a similar appraisal, see TsGIA, f. 1262, op. 1, d. 183, l. 181.
38. TsGIA, f. 1262, op. 1, d. 131, ll. 1–1ob.
39. *Arkhiv Grafov Mordvinovykh*, 4: 39–50, 8: 271–81. Bemoaning the horror of conscription, in 1808 Privy Councillor Obreskov proposed reducing the term of service to seven years, after which soldiers would return to their families and serf status. See M. I. Bogdanovich, "Ob umen'shenii sroka sluzhby nizhnim chinam. Proekt tainogo sovetnika Obreskova (1808)," *RS* 9 (1874): 245–47. In 1817 the general intendant of the army proposed a twelve-year term of service followed by a return to serf status. *RS* 119 (1904): 715–16.
40. TsGIA, f. 1262, op. 1, d. 183, ll. 88–106.
41. TsGIA, f. 1262, op. 1, d. 72, ll. 1–4.
42. *SZ* (1842), t. 4, kn. 1, r. 1, gl. 1, st. 4.
43. *PVM*, 18.III.1840, no. 23; 10.III.1842, no. 21; and 9.I.1845, no. 7.
44. Recruitment policy was harsher toward Jews, who were drafted at age twelve and provided a proportionately higher number of recruits. *PSZ* (II) 2: 1329, 1330; 3: 2045; 9: 7317; 14: 12513; 15: 13751; 25: 24768; 27: 26177, 16502; 29: 28432, 28733; 30: 28903, 29233, 29828. On Jewish conscription, see Emmanuel Flisfish, *Kantonisty* (Tel Aviv: Effect Publications, 1983), and Michael Stanislawskii, *Tsar Nicholas I and the Jews: The Transformation of Jewish*

Society in Russia, 1825–1855 (Philadelphia: The Jewish Publication Society, 1983), pp. 13–33.

45. Groups exempted on an ethnic basis included various nationalities in Siberia, inhabitants of the Caucasus and Bessarabia, Crimean Tatars, Armenians and Tatars in Astrakhan province, and settlers from Europe (Volga Germans, Serbs, Bulgarians, and Greeks in the Ukraine and Caucasus). Inhabitants in distant regions of Siberia were exempted on a territorial basis. Beskrovnyi, *Russkaia armiia i flot v XIX veke*, p. 70. A. Rediger also estimated that in 1858 six million men (20 percent of the adult male population) were fully exempt or paid a monetary fee. A. Rediger, *Komplektovanie i ustroistvo vooruzhennoi sily*, 3d ed. (St. Petersburg, 1900), p. 86. For a lower estimate of under one million calculated by the Ministry of Interior in 1853, see TsGIA, f. 1262, op. 1, d. 183.

46. *SZ* (1842), t. 4, kn. 1, r. 1, gl. 1, st. 13. Levies of priests' sons persisted to the Crimean War.

47. *PSZ* (I) 21: 15721; (II) 6: 4677. *Arkhiv Gosudarstvennogo Soveta*, 5 vols. (St. Petersburg, 1869–1904), 3: 194. A. Rediger, *Uchebnye zapiski po voennoi administratsii* (St. Petersburg, 1888), pp. 87–88.

48. Beskrovnyi, *Russkaia armiia i flot v XIX veke*, p. 71; *SZ* (1842), t. 4, kn. 1, r. 1, gl. 1, st. 13; *PSZ* (II) 13: 11417; 28: 27727, 27728; 29: 28331.

49. Although a complete district was defined as 1,000 souls, the minimum number of souls required for a district to participate in a levy was 250. A law of 1834 lowered the limit to 200 souls. Separate communities belonging to the same social category and recruiting district could be merged for conscription purposes. *PSZ* (II) 6: 4677; 9: 7535. On private estates, all villages belonging to a particular landlord in a given province were counted toward the formation of a recruiting district. *PSZ* (I) 28: 21906, and (II) 3: 2114.

50. TsGIA, f. 1262, op. 1, d. 27, l. 42–42ob.; d. 183, l. 90–90ob.

51. *PSZ* (II) 6: 4677; 9: 7535.

52. *PSZ* (I) 27: 20496.

53. *PSZ* (I) 33: 26279.

54. *PSZ* (I) 25: 18336, 19214.

55. *PSZ* (I) 26: 20019; 30: 23926; and 40: 30320. Beginning in 1828 this provision no longer applied to residents along the Polish border. *PSZ* (II) 3: 2281; 5: 3839. Fearing evasion and resettlement by Jews, in 1829 the Committee of Ministers excluded Jews living within 100 versts of the Prussian border and Baltic Sea from this exemption. The ministers felt that if granted this privilege, Jews would resettle within the 100-verst area. *PSZ* (II) 4: 3297.

56. *PSZ* (I) 37: 28409.

57. *PSZ* (I) 31: 24772; 32: 25172, 25439; 33: 25942; (II) 11: 9443.

58. TsGVIA, f. 11, op. 6, d. 146, l. 6–6ob.

59. *PSZ* (I) 32: 25172.

60. *PSZ* (I) 37: 28409.

61. *PSZ* (I) 37: 28579.

62. *PSZ* (I) 40: 30229.

63. TsGIA, f. 1262, op. 1, d. 27, l. 43–43ob.; *PSZ* (II) 6: 4677.

NOTES TO CHAPTER I

64. *PSZ* (II) 6: 4677.
65. *PSZ* (II) 9: 7535; 30: 2766.
66. *PSZ* (II) 11: 9443.
67. *PSZ* (II) 13: 11417.
68. Ibid.
69. *PSZ* (II) 2: 1330.
70. *PSZ* (II) 6: 4869.
71. PVM, Manifesto of 10.VII.1843; Ukaz Pravitel'stvennomu Senatu from 1.IX.1847; Manifesto of 10.VII.1850; Manifesto of 15.VII.1852; 29.I.1854.
72. These measures affected twenty-two provinces. *PSZ* (II) 5: 3889, 3950, 3990, 4075; 6: 4517, 4971; 22: 21534, 21531.
73. *PSZ* (II) 8: 6361; 15: 13632, 14044; 16: 14729; 20: 19423–25, 19563; 24: 23198. *RI*, 5.VIII.1834, no. 196, pp. 783–84.
74. See *PSZ* (II) 18: 17026; *PVM*, Manifesto of 26.IX.1846; *PSZ* (II) 24: 23463; 25: 24310; 28: 27431.
75. *PSZ* (I) 32: 25198.
76. *PSZ* (I) 32: 25279.
77. *PSZ* (I) 32: 25314.
78. *PSZ* (I) 32: 25417–19, 25421, 25422, 25438; 33: 25955.
79. *PSZ* (II) 3: 1949, 2246–48; 4: 3081, 3103.
80. *PSZ* (II) 6: 4380; 8: 6114.
81. *PSZ* (II) 30: 29828, 29909.
82. *PSZ* (II) 30: 29871.
83. TsGIA, f. 1262, op. 1, d. 183, l. 4.
84. *PSZ* (I) 17: 12748.
85. *PSZ* (I) 29: 22275, 22348; 30: 23263, 23848; 31: 24773; 32: 25438; 33: 25945.
86. There were no height requirements for these young recruits, who were supposed to enter the schools for soldiers' sons. *PSZ* (I) 32: 25021, 25172; 33: 25945.
87. *PSZ* (I) 33: 25942.
88. *PSZ* (II) 2: 1332; 3: 1929, 1950; 4: 2789, 3082.
89. *PSZ* (II) 6: 4296, 4737; *RI*, 19.II.1831, no. 43, pp. 170–71.
90. *PSZ* (II) 6: 4336, 4983.
91. TsGIA, f. 1262, op. 1, d. 27, l. 38; *PSZ* (I) 29: 22275, 22348.
92. *PSZ* (II) 29: 28149.
93. A law of 1849 previously established this provision. See *PSZ* (II) 24: 23172.
94. *PSZ* (II) 29: 28216, 28271; 30: 28893, 28902, 29302, 29363, 29767, 29771.
95. *PSZ* (II) 29: 28709, 28271, 28742; 30: 28893, 29771. The line and lottery systems are described below, pp. 20–24.
96. TsGIA, f. 1262, op. 1, d. 20, l. 32ob.; f. 1286, op. 3, d. 329.
97. TsGIA, f. 1262, op. 1, d. 27, ll. 2–4; TsGVIA, f. 395, op. 213, d. 22, ll. 114ob.–15.

98. TsGIA, f. 1286, op. 3, d. 329.
99. TsGVIA, f. 395, op. 213, d. 22.
100. TsGIA, f. 1262, op. 1, d. 27, ll. 2–4.
101. Ibid.
102. TsGIA, f. 1262, op. 1, d. 20, ll. 18–40ob.
103. TsGIA, f. 1262, op. 1, d. 20, l. 9–9ob.; d. 27, ll. 3ob.–4.

104. In 1841 almost half of the eligible families in Kazan province reportedly did not meet the required standards for height. The problem was most acute among the Chuvash and Cheremis. TsGIA, f. 1262, op. 1, d. 20; d. 27, l. 39–39ob.; d. 72.

105. TsGIA, f. 1262, op. 1, d. 20, l. 10–10ob.; *Arkhiv Gosudarstvennogo Soveta*, 3: 209–10.

106. *PSZ* (I) 33: 25945; TsGIA, f. 1262, op. 1, d. 20, ll. 36–37.
107. TsGIA, f. 1262, op. 1, d. 20, ll. 38ob.–39; d. 72, ll. 5–8ob.
108. TsGIA, f. 1262, op. 1, d. 20, l. 20.
109. *PSZ* (II) 19: 17581; 24: 23172.
110. TsGIA, f. 1262, op. 1, d. 27, l. 34–34ob.
111. TsGVIA, f. 801, op. 61/2, d. 250; f. 395, op. 213, d. 21, ll. 1246–49ob.; d. 22, ll. 161–64ob.
112. *PSZ* (I) 29: 22486.
113. *PSZ* (I) 30: 23503. Cf., *Arkhiv Grafov Mordvinovykh*, 4: 45.

114. *PSZ* (II) 26: 25668; *Arkhiv Gosudarstvennogo Soveta*, 4, vypusk 2, ch. 2, k. 663–65; TsGVIA, f. 395, op. 213, d. 22, l. 20ob.; and Henry Hirschbiel, "The District Captains of the Ministry of State Properties in the Reign of Nicholas I: A Case Study of Russian Officialdom, 1838–1856" (Ph.D. dissertation, New York University, 1978), pp. 203–204.

115. Bribery also hurt the state interest, for communes could bribe officials to accept underaged or physically unsuitable recruits. See V. A. Aleksandrov, *Sel'skaia obshchina v Rossii: XVII–nachalo XIX v.* (Moscow, 1976), p. 285; L. S. Prokof'eva, *Krest'ianskaia obshchina v Rossii vo vtoroi polovine XVIII-pervoi polovine XIX veka* (Leningrad, 1981), pp. 154–55.

116. *PSZ* (I) 30: 22982; *Arkhiv Grafov Mordvinovykh*, 4: 39.
117. TsGVIA, f. 395, op. 213, otd. 4, d. 33, l. 12.

118. P. A. Zaionchkovskii estimated that on the eve of the Great Reforms, hired substitutes constituted 10–20 percent of recruits. See his *Voennye reformy 1860–1870 godov v Rossii* (Moscow, 1952), p. 180. Poor families could also buy substitutes by going into debt. TsGIA, f. 1262, op. 1, d. 27, ll. 10ob.–11. Some communes used the rotational line system to buy recruits collectively. Prokof'eva, *Krest'ianskaia obshchina*, pp. 153–54. For the legislation on substitutes, see *PSZ* (I) 25: 18525; 30: 23926; (II) 6: 4677; 10: 7795; 16: 14175, 14690; 17: 16134; 28: 26951.

119. [Statistik], *Naem rekruta v polovine XIX-go stoletiia v Arkhangel'skoi gubernii* (Arkhangel'sk, 1912), pp. 4–5.

120. According to an agreement between two Stroitel'skoe peasants, the substitute was paid 70 rubles initially and another 30 once he was accepted at the

recruiting station. If he was rejected he would still keep the 70 rubles. Normally, the local community paid the treasury a sum to provide clothing, provisioning, and a small allowance for each recruit. In this case the hiring peasant bore the expense. Ibid.

121. Ibid., pp. 6–7.

122. Ibid., pp. 8–9.

123. TsGIA, f. 1262, op. 1, d. 6, l. 6–6ob. (1836); TsGVIA, f. 801, op. 90, d. 48, ll. 161–78 (1841).

124. TsGVIA, f. 801, op. 90, d. 48, ll. 162ob.–63; Aleksandrov, *Sel'skaia obshchina*, pp. 283–85.

125. TsGVIA, f. 801, op. 90, d. 48, ll. 6–9.

126. Allegedly the traders who conducted this business received up to 700 silver rubles for each substitute. Although the substitutes were paid only 30 to 60 rubles, they were fed and clothed until they were needed as recruits. Local officials also were involved in registering the vagrants and runaways as *odnodvortsy*. TsGIA, f. 1262, op. 1, d. 95, ll. 3–7; 8ob. In Russia proper, the term *odnodvortsy* referred to a group of déclassé Muscovite servitors, who, like the peasantry, were obliged to serve and pay the poll tax, and like the nobility, enjoyed the right to own land and serfs. Thomas Esper, "The Odnodvortsy and the Russian Nobility," *SEER* 45, no. 4 (1967): 124–34.

127. Rediger, *Uchebnye zapiski*, p. 96; idem, *Komplektovanie i ustroistvo*, p. 90.

128. Rediger, *Uchebnye zapiski*, p. 96.

129. Rediger, *Komplektovanie i ustroistvo*, p. 90; TsGVIA, f. 395, op. 208, d. 3, ll. 1–3.

130. TsGVIA, f. 395, op. 208, d. 3, ll. 4–11ob.

131. Ibid., ll. 4–11ob., 31ob.–34.

132. Official laws did not apply to manorial serfs, though actual practices on private estates resembled state laws. *SZ* (1842), t. 4, kn. 1, r. 1, gl. 2, st. 79–146; Rediger, *Komplektovanie i ustroistvo*, pp. 87–88. For a recent description of recruitment practices on a private estate in Tver province, see Rodney D. Bohac, "The Mir and the Military Draft," *SR* 47, no. 4 (Winter 1988): 652–66.

133. *PSZ* (I) 17: 12748; Beskrovnyi, *Russkaia armiia i flot v XVIII veke*, pp. 32, 299–301; idem, *Russkaia armiia i flot v XIX veke*, p. 71; Aleksandrov, *Sel'skaia obshchina*, pp. 242–93; and "Novye nachala voennoi povinnosti v Rossii," *VS* 35, no. 2 (February 1864): 217.

134. Aleksandrov, *Sel'skaia obshchina*, p. 244.

135. *PSZ* (I) 28: 21906.

136. *PSZ* (I) 6: 4677.

137. On the Sheremetev estates, men between the ages of sixteen and sixty-five were counted; see Prokof'eva, *Krest'ianskaia obshchina*, p. 156.

138. Rules issued in 1837 regarded families composed of a grandfather and grandson or an uncle and nephew as having only one laborer. The new rules also stated that persons who were completely blind in both eyes, missing an arm or leg, or paralyzed in both arms or legs did not count as laborers. *PSZ* (II) 12:

10346. Beginning in 1850 paralyzed or immobilized men did not count as laborers until they recovered, as long as a majority of the recruiting district considered the exemption just. *PSZ* (II) 25: 23832. A law of 1854 also excluded the deaf and dumb from the number of laborers. *PSZ* (II) 29: 28843.

139. V. A. Aleksandrov has documented the wide range of peasant practices, but does not explain the divergent and contradictory phenomena. See *Sel'skaia obshchina*, pp. 242–93.

140. Ibid., pp. 254–60.

141. Communes might do this even when it meant paying the recruit's taxes and supporting his indigent family. Ibid., pp. 248, 256; Prokof'eva, *Krest'ianskaia obshchina*, pp. 151–56. Landlords obviously benefited by sending poor peasants to the army and protecting prosperous ones. See "Rekrut," pp. 99–100.

142. Many communes organized the collective purchase of recruits. Landlords encouraged this practice, and in the early eighteenth century some granted temporary exemptions from all dues to peasants who purchased recruits. Landlords also sold exemptions. Aleksandrov, *Sel'skaia obshchina*, pp. 248–54, 260–73, 283–84.

143. Such sentences were not always justified. Ibid., pp. 273–83; Rediger, *Uchebnye zapiski*, p. 86; *RS* 87 (1896): 82; *Arkhiv Gosudarstvennogo Soveta*, 4, vypusk 3, ch. 1, k. 63–67, 71–72. Officials believed that recruits from the vagrant and criminal population were a bad influence on other soldiers, had behavioral problems, and needed rehabilitation before they would be morally fit for service. TsGVIA, f. Voenno-uchenyi arkhiv, d. 17980; TsGAOR, f. 48, op. 1, d. 473, ch. 2, ll. 125ob.–26 (views of P. I. Pestel). On special military units for the rehabilitation of these recruits, see *PVM*, 16.II.1835; 18.III.1840, no. 3; 9.I.1845, no. 7.

144. TsGVIA, f. Voenno-uchenyi arkhiv, d. 17980, l. 1–1ob.; f. 395, op. 206, otd. 4, d. 4, l. 1–1ob. (1848).

145. Prokof'eva, *Krest'ianskaia obshchina*, p. 156; Aleksandrov, *Sel'skaia obshchina*, pp. 248, 254–60.

146. TsGIA, f. 1262, op. 1, d. 16, ll. 33–33ob., 60.

147. TsGIA, f. 1262, op. 1, d. 16, ll. 37–39; TsGVIA, f. 395, op. 213, d. 22, ll. 116ob.–17, 152; Rediger, *Komplektovanie i ustroistvo*, p. 89.

148. TsGVIA, f. 395, op. 206, otd. 4, d. 4, ll. 2ob.–6.

149. *PSZ* (II) 13: 11417; I. M. Druzhinin, *Gosudarstvennye krest'iane i reforma P. D. Kiseleva*, 2 vols. (Moscow and Leningrad, 1946 and 1958), 2: 164–68; Hirschbiel, "The District Captains," pp. 200–14; Beskrovnyi, *Russkaia armiia i flot v XIX veke*, p. 75; and Rediger, *Komplektovanie i ustroistvo*, p. 81. Peasants on private estates previously used lotteries as part of the line system. See Prokof'eva, *Krest'ianskaia obshchina*, pp. 153–54.

150. *PSZ* (II) 29: 28331; Hirschbiel, "The District Captains," p. 152. This does not include the Baltic provinces of Livland, Estland, and Kurland. Although in 1854 the lottery system also became law in these areas, the Crimean War delayed implementation. *PSZ* (II) 29: 28332, 28567; 30: 29306.

151. *PSZ* (II) 28: 27727–28. The new system also did not affect Jews.

NOTES TO CHAPTER 2

152. Hirschbiel, "The District Captains," p. 215.

153. See TsGIA, f. 1262, op. 1, d. 183, ll. 168–83.

154. Rediger, *Komplektovanie i ustroistvo*, p. 81; Druzhinin, *Gosudarstvennye krest'iane*, 2: 166–68; Hirschbiel, "The District Captains," pp. 203–204, 218–25; and TsGVIA, f. 395, op. 213, d. 22, ll. 47ob.–48, 79–79ob., 114ob.–17, 147–54ob.

155. Hirschbiel, "The District Captains," p. 224; TsGVIA, f. 395, op. 213, d. 21, l. 46; d. 22, ll. 114ob.–15.

156. From 1716 until 1810, each regiment was attached to a territory (*okrug*) from which it acquired recruits; see Beskrovnyi, *Russkaia armiia i flot v XVIII veke*, p. 32; idem, *Russkaia armiia i flot v XIX veke*, p. 71; *PSZ* (I) 30: 23297; (II) 6: 4677.

157. *PSZ* (I) 17: 12748; 30: 23082, 23275, 23297, 23961; 31: 24381; 32: 25179, 25209; 33: 26301; TsGIA, f. 1284, op. 17, d. 19, l. 48–48ob.; TsGVIA, f. 395, op. 213, d. 21, ll. 107–108.

158. *PSZ* (II) 6: 4677; TsGVIA, f. 395, op. 206, otd. 4, d. 84, ll. 4ob.–5 (1848).

159. On the cost of conscription to civilian society, see TsGIA, f. 1281, op. 11, d. 104b, ll. 64–65 (1829); f. 1409, op. 2, d. 6214 (1838), 6271 (1839).

160. *PSZ* (I) 29: 22282; (II) 3: 2362; 6: 4677, appendix 6; 18: 16920; 21: 20182; 25: 23831; 27: 26880.

161. TsGIA, f. 1262, op. 1, d. 27, l. 34–34ob. An 1850 memorandum from the Inspectors' Department reported that out of 20,712,756 men fulfilling conscription obligations in kind, only 6,900,000 were physically suitable. See TsGIA, f. 1262, op. 1, d. 183, l. 4.

162. TsGIA, f. 1262, op. 1, d. 183, ll. 178ob.–79.

163. Speransky, *O voennykh poseleniiakh*, pp. 2–3.

164. Ibid., pp. 29–31.

165. Soldiers on indefinite leave remained subject to training and call-up for five years.

166. "Russkoe voennoe obozrenie," *VS* 57 (1867): 30. The secondary sources suggest a direct connection between the absence of reserves and the military reforms of the 1870s. See P. A. Zaionchkovskii, *Voennye reformy*; P. A. Zaionchkovskii, ed., *Dnevnik D. A. Miliutina*, 4 vols. (Moscow, 1947–50), 1: 17; and Curtiss, *The Russian Army under Nicholas I*, pp. 110–11. Other historians attribute the decision to emancipate to the need for military reform. See Alfred J. Rieber, ed., *The Politics of Autocracy* (Paris: Mouton, 1966), and Dietrich Beyrau, "Von der Niederlage zur Agrarreform: Leibeigenschaft und Militärverfassung in Russland nach 1855," *JGO* 23 (1975): 191–212.

Two. "Military Society and the State"

1. Preservation of the troops also meant fewer levies, which benefited all society. See N. Glinoetskii, "Voennaia statistika i soldatskii byt," *VS* no. 2 (1858): 446.

NOTES TO CHAPTER 2

2. See A. N. Leont'ev, *Soldatskaia knizhka*, 2d ed., 2 vols. (St. Petersburg, 1866), 2: 270.

3. Fedor Zatler, *Uchast' ranenykh i bol'nykh vo vremia voiny*, 2d ed. (St. Petersburg, 1868), pp. 79–94; Speransky, *O voennykh poseleniiakh*, pp. 2–5; TsGVIA, f. 395, op. 208, d. 35, ll. 1–3ob., 7–9ob. On the relationship between good morale and physical health, see *Arkhiv Grafov Mordvinovykh*, 4: 41; Plaskin, "Prakticheskie zamechaniia o pritvornykh nedugakh rekrut," *VMZ* 100, no. 12 (December 1867): 12–13; TsGVIA, f. Voenno-uchenyi arkhiv, d. 17147, ch. 1–3, ll. 1–3.

4. See the discussion of an epidemic eye disease that hit the troops of the Black Sea line in 1845. The epidemic created a serious manpower shortage that threatened to undermine the physical integrity and performance of the troops. TsGVIA, f. 395, op. 100, d. 120.

5. TsGVIA, f. 395, op. 248, d. 17, ll. 28–31.

6. TsGVIA, f. Voenno-uchenyi arkhiv, d. 17147, ch. 1–3, ll. 103–104ob.

7. TsGVIA, f. Voenno-uchenyi arkhiv, d. 793, l. 14; f. 395, op. 100, d. 120, ll. 20–28, 49–55, 84–84ob.; P. Brant, "Kazarmennoe raspolozhenie voisk i vliianie ego na zdorov'e nizhnikh chinov," *VS* 30, no. 3 (March 1863): 77–99.

8. Military doctors whose reports appear in *Voenno-meditsinskii zhurnal* repeatedly stressed the role of climatic conditions in the appearance and spread of disease. See Bulgakov, "Obzor boleznei poiavliavshchikhsia v voiskakh IV pekhotnogo korpusa s 1-go noiabria 1848 po 1-e noiabria 1849 goda," *VMZ* 55, no. 1 (1850): 3–4; TsGVIA, f. 395, op. 100, d. 120, ll. 3–6ob., 17–18ob., 22.

9. "Vypiska iz dela ob obrevizovanii voenno-sirotskikh otdelenii s 1823 po 1826 god," *SVM*, vol. 4, pt. 1, bk. 1, sec. 2, appendix 18, pp. 68–69; TsGVIA, f. 405, op. 9, d. 344, ll. 25–31; Akim Charukovskii, *Voenno-pokhodnaia meditsina*, 5 parts (St. Petersburg, 1836), 1: 10–11, 155; *VMZ* 1, no. 3 (1823): 456; Brant, "Kazarmennoe raspolozhenie," pp. 81–82.

10. TsGVIA, f. Voenno-uchenyi arkhiv, d. 17147, ch. 1–3, l. 100. In 1840 cantonists in Tobol'sk reportedly bathed once a week (TsGVIA, f. 405, op. 9, d. 344, ll. 25–31). An 1857 publication recommended bathing at least twice a month; see "O tom, chto nuzhno sluzhivomu cheloveku v voennoi sluzhbe," *Chtenie dlia soldat*, no. 3 (1857): 89–90.

11. For examples of educational publications, see I. Enegol'm, *Karmannaia kniga voennoi gigieny, ili zamechaniia o sokhranenii zdorov'ia russkikh soldat* (St. Petersburg, 1813); M. Bogdanovich, "O gigiene (sokhranenii zdorov'ia) russkogo soldata," *VZ*, no. 4 (1855): 1–26; "O tom, chto nuzhno sluzhivomu cheloveku"; Iakov Villie, Glavnyi po armii Meditsinksii Inspektor, "Sposoby dlia sokhraneniia zdorov'ia soldat v voennoe vremia," *VMZ* 12, no. 2–3 (1828): 139–55.

12. TsGVIA, f. 405, op. 9, d. 344. It turned out that the reports of excessive illness were false, but the commander was still required to pay the cost of the investigation. On the cantonists, see pp. 38–39, 166n.

13. The death rate for the first three months of 1842 was 1: 325 compared

with a rate of 1: 430 in other cantonist battalions. TsGVIA, f. 405, op. 9, d. 801, ll. 17–20ob.

14. See Enegol'm, *Karmannaia kniga voennoi gigieny*, pp. 2, 65–67.

15. A. A. Kozhevnikov, "Armiia v 1805–14," *OVRO*, 7 vols. (Moscow, 1911–12), 3: 80.

16. TsGVIA, f. Voenno-uchenyi arkhiv, d. 709.

17. TsGVIA, f. Voenno-uchenyi arkhiv, d. 17184, ch. 1, l. 31ob.; d. 17147, ch. 1–3, l. 105–105ob.

18. TsGVIA, f. Voenno-uchenyi arkhiv, d. 17147, ch. 1–3, l. 105; *SIRIO* (St. Petersburg, 1890–91) 73: 577–78; 78: 98–102.

19. N. Kutuzov, "Sostoianie gosudarstva v 1841 godu. (Zapiska N. Kutuzova, podannaia imperatoru Nikolaiu I)," *RS* 95 (September 1898): 524–25.

20. *SVM*, vol. 8, pt. 1, pp. XL, LXIII–LXIX; *PSZ* (I) 4: 2319.

21. *SVM*, vol. 8, pt. 1, p. LXXXVI.

22. TsGVIA, f. 395, op. 325, d. 2, 5, 7, 10. A. I. Chernyshev, *Istoricheskoe obozrenie voenno-sukhoputnogo upravleniia s 1825 po 1850 god* (St. Petersburg, 1850), p. 83.

23. Chernyshev, *Istoricheskoe obozrenie*, p. 84.

24. Ibid., p. 90.

25. *PVM*, 29.VIII.1837, no. 98; 22.X.1837, no. 105; 16.IV.1846, no. 67.

26. *PVM*, 5.IV.1850, no. 28.

27. L. Il'ianshevich, "Statisticheskoe issledovanie smertnosti v nashei armii," *VS* 29, no. 2 (February 1863): 362–64, 369, 399, 407.

28. Statistical data for the period 1826 to 1850 are found in Chernyshev, *Istoricheskoe obozrenie*, pp. 95–99; *SVM*, vol. 8, pt. 1, pp. 147–55. When examining data on disease, it is important to be aware that many diagnoses were incorrect. I am grateful to Professor Mary K. Matossian of the University of Maryland for alerting me to this problem. According to Professor Matossian, internally manifested diseases such as fevers were less likely to be diagnosed correctly, than diseases that manifested external symptoms, such as syphilis, tuberculosis, cholera, and smallpox. See also A. Shil'tov, "O nashikh voennykh gospitaliakh s nauchnoi tochki zreniia i prichinakh grudnykh stradanii voiska," *VMZ* 101, no. 4 (April 1868): 35–36.

29. See the 1856 memorandum of General Adjutant Glinka 2 to Alexander II, printed in *SVM*, vol. 1, appendix 10.

30. Dietrich Beyrau, *Militär und Gesellschaft im vorrevolutionären Russland* (Cologne: Bohlau Verlag, 1984), pp. 161–62, and the literature cited herein; Gunther E. Rothenberg, *The Art of Warfare in the Age of Napoleon* (Bloomington: Indiana University Press, 1978), pp. 236–38.

31. *VMZ* 76, no. 6 (1859): 95.

32. Gregory L. Freeze, "The *Soslovie* (Estate) Paradigm and Russian Social History," *The American Historical Review* 91, no. 1 (February 1986): 11–36.

33. *SVP* (1838), ch. 2, kn. 1.

34. *SVP* (1838), ch. 2, kn. 1, st. 291–97; Beskrovnyi, *Russkaia armiia i flot v*

XIX veke, p. 75. In 1829 and 1831, Nicholas I granted early retirement to some soldiers. *PSZ* (II) 4: 3177; 6: 4990.

35. *Arkhiv Gosudarstvennogo Soveta* (St. Petersburg, 1878) 3: 194.

36. *PVM*, 28.II.1834, no. 23; *PSZ* (II) 8: 6397; 9: 6796, 6864, 7147, 7373–74, 7486, 7506, 7540; 16: 14418.

37. TsGAOR, f. 672, op. 1, d. 80.

38. *PSZ* (II) 16: 14442; *PVM*, 6.XI.1842, no. 137. Ukrainian cossacks and military colonists were eligible for indefinite leave after fifteen years of service and for retirement after twenty. *PVM*, 10.XII.1846, no. 185; 6.III.1851, no. 27; 1.V.1852, no. 48.

39. *PVM*, 25.I.1842, no. 8; *PSZ* (II) 17: 15237.

40. Soldiers on indefinite leave were not entitled to land allotments in state villages. TsGAOR, f. 1155, op. 1, d. 185a, ll. 5ob.–6; Kutuzov, "Sostoianie gosudarstva v 1841 godu," pp. 525–27; "Russkoe voennoe obozrenie," *VS* 57 (1867): 28–29.

41. Filimonov, *Postepennoe razvitie meropriiatii po mobilizatsii russkoi kadrovoi armii v XIX stoletii* (St. Petersburg, 1908), pp. 9–12.

42. Zaionchkovskii, *Voennye reformy*, pp. 18–19.

43. Speransky, *O voennykh poseleniiakh*, pp. 5–6. Survival to retirement or indefinite leave was not likely, which explains the popular view of conscription as a death sentence. TsGAOR, f. 48, op. 1, ch. 2, ll. 125–27ob. For a statistical estimate, see "O smertnosti v gvardeiskom korpuse," *VS* (1858) 6: 387–89; TsGVIA, f. Voenno-uchenyi arkhiv, d. 682, l. 45–45ob. According to one estimate from 1808, soldiers lived only an average of five or six years in service. See Bogdanovich, "Ob umen'shenii sroka sluzhby," p. 246. A later estimate concluded that about one in three soldiers reached retirement. Glinoetskii, "Voennaia statistika," pp. 448–49.

44. Very little is known about the status of retired soldiers who returned to their native villages; Aleksandrov, *Sel'skaia obshchina*, pp. 290–92, and idem, *Obychnoe pravo*, pp. 242–43.

45. Aleksandrov, *Obychnoe pravo*, pp. 242–43; Kutuzov, "Sostoianie gosudarstva v 1841 godu," pp. 525–27; M. A. Rakhmatullin, "Soldaty v krest'ianskom dvizhenii 20–kh godov XIX v.," *Voprosy voennoi istorii* (Moscow, 1969), pp. 351–58; *PVM*, 31.III.1834.

46. "Russkoe voennoe obozrenie," *VS* 57 (1867): 28–29; TsGVIA, f. Voenno-uchenyi arkhiv, d. 19188, ll. 176ob.–77.

47. In 1829 there were 83,797 retired soldiers in Russia. See *RI*, 23.III.1831, pp. 278–79.

48. *RI*, 9.XI.1829, p. 1138.

49. Civil service positions included employment in fire and police units, in the customs mounted patrol, as tellers (*schetchiki*), jurors (*prisiazhnye*), couriers, postmen, inspectors, prison and forest wardens, and guards. *RS* 113 (1903): 130.

50. TsGIA, f. 1284, op. 17, d. 54, l. 10–10ob.

51. Soldiers too weak or ill to support themselves were assigned to veterans' companies without the obligation to serve or placed in institutions maintained by

local welfare boards (*prikazy obshchestvennogo prizreniia*). *RI*, 9.XI.1829, p. 1138.

52. In the town of Rybinsk (Iaroslavl province) retired soldiers and those on indefinite leave reportedly earned about 15 rubles a year as shoemakers, tailors, and joiners. TsGVIA, f. Voenno-uchenyi arkhiv, d. 19188, ll. 176ob.–77; TsGIA, f. 1287, op. 8, d. 65, l. 38–38ob.

53. The government was considering new legislation to cope with the problems. TsGAOR, f. 1155, op. 1, d. 185a, 186.

54. For an 1842 report of favorable conditions for retired soldiers in Rybinsk, see TsGIA, f. 1287, op. 39, d. 36, ll. 240–43.

55. Elise Kimerling [Wirtschafter], "Soldiers' Children, 1719–1856: A Study of Social Engineering in Imperial Russia," *Forschungen zur osteuropäischen Geschichte* 30 (1982): 61–136.

56. P. Brant, "Zhenatye nizhnie chiny," *VS*, no. 12 (1860): 359–60, 376.

57. Ibid., p. 359.

58. Aleksandrov, *Sel'skaia obshchina*, pp. 289–90, 296–98; idem, *Obychnoe pravo*, pp. 213–14.

59. *PSZ* (II) 16: 14278; 27: 25883.

60. TsGVIA, f. 11, op. 7, d. 25, ll. 2ob., 15ob.–16.

61. John L. H. Keep, "Catherine's Veterans," *SEER* 59, no. 3 (July 1981): 291, note 24.

62. *SVP* (1838), ch. 3, kn. 1, st. 47.

63. *SVP* (1838), ch. 2, kn. 1, st. 1793–94.

64. Brant, "Zhenatye nizhnie chiny," p. 359.

65. David Ransel, "Abandonment and Fosterage of Unwanted Children: The Women of the Foundling System," in David Ransel, ed., *The Family in Imperial Russia* (Urbana-Champaign: University of Illinois Press, 1978), pp. 189–217; idem, *Mothers of Misery: Child Abandonment in Russia* (Princeton, N.J.: Princeton University Press, 1988).

66. *PSZ* (I) 29: 28474; 37: 28714; 38: 29059, 29301.

67. D. A. Miliutin, *Karmannaia spravochnaia kniga dlia russkikh ofitserov* (St. Petersburg, 1856), p. 612. In the Tula Infantry Regiment No. 72, only soldiers who had served at least ten years could marry; F. D. Sosedko, *Istoriia 72-go pekhotnogo Tul'skogo polka, 1769–1901* (Warsaw, 1901), p. 234. Marriage rates were supposedly higher among sergeants major, feldshers, and artisans. Brant, "Zhenatye nizhnie chiny," pp. 363–64.

68. Brant, "Zhenatye nizhnie chiny," p. 363.

69. *Arkhiv Gosudarstvennogo Soveta* 4, vypusk 2, ch. 2, k. 1955.

70. *PSZ* (II) 29: 28474.

71. *PSZ* (I) 38: 29301; (II) 1: 764.

72. *PSZ* (II) 1: 764; Brant, "Zhenatye nizhnie chiny," pp. 360–61.

73. Laws of 1821 and 1829 forbade soldiers and their wives to acquire immovable property. Laws from 1837–39 allowed only those serving in Siberian line battalions and artillery garrisons, in the Separate Orenburg Corps, and in

Finland to own immovable property. *PSZ* (II) 12: 10355; 13: 10984, 11738; 14: 12445, 12600.

74. TsGVIA, f. 801, op. 87/32, d. 9, ch. 1, ll. 23–23ob., 99–103ob.

75. According to one commentator, writing in 1860, the number of soldiers in Guards regiments who had families with them ranged from one in six to one in ten. Of these only one-half to one-third were able to live together in state quarters. Finally, at least half of the married soldiers did not have their wives with them. Brant, "Zhenatye nizhnie chiny," p. 366.

76. Since 1848 soldiers could marry women they impregnated, regardless of whether there were openings. The authorities gave these women passports to live outside the barracks until vacancies occurred. *PSZ* (II) 19: 18489; 23: 22688; TsGVIA, f. 395, op. 325, d. 32, l. 76–76ob. An 1855 law allocated quartering money to the families of Guards soldiers who left for campaigns. Apparently, the soldiers themselves previously had received these funds to house their families. *PSZ* (II) 30: 29926.

77. *SVP* (1838), ch. 4, kn. 4, st. 129.

78. Brant, "Zhenatye nizhnie chiny," pp. 372–73.

79. Ibid., pp. 365–66, 369, 373–76.

80. Ibid., pp. 365–66, 368–69, 373–75.

81. Ibid., pp. 370–72.

82. After 1805 soldiers' children were called cantonists (*kantonisty*). Kimerling [Wirtschafter], "Soldiers' Children," pp. 61–136.

83. Ibid., pp. 99–128.

84. In 1820 there were 82,975 soldiers' sons: 22,779 with the troops; 38,462 in the military schools; and 21,741 living with relatives (TsGVIA, f. 395, op. 325, d. 10, ll. 23–24). By 1832 the total number of cantonists reached 160,105. *RI*, 6.VIII.1833, no. 198, p. 788; Kimerling [Wirtschafter], "Soldiers' Children," pp. 108, 114.

85. Of 29,606 cantonists appointed to service in the years 1824–32, 19,689 received combat assignments. *RI*, 6.VIII.1833, no. 198, p. 788.

86. Data from 1863 for 654 officers promoted from the servile population provide the following *soslovie* breakdown: 365 (56%) from the soldiers' children, 162 (25%) peasants, 84 (13%) townspeople, 19 (3%) from the clergy, and 24 (4%) baptized Jews. "Chislovye dannye o sostave korpusa ofitserov nashei armii po vospitaniiu i sosloviiam," *VS* 34, no. 11 (November 1863): 247.

87. In the years 1836–56 special cantonist units trained 15,634 noncommissioned officers and 6,771 musicians for the army; Bogdanovich, *Istoricheskii ocherk* 1: 191–93. See also TsGAOR, f. 48, op. 1, d. 473, ch. 1, l. 10–10ob.

88. Kimerling [Wirtschafter], "Soldiers' Children," pp. 70–76, 110.

89. TsGAOR, f. 48, op. 1, d. 10, *Russkaia pravda*, l. 132ob.

90. TsGVIA, f. 395, op. 325, d. 10.

91. *PVM*, 1842.

92. *PVM*, 22.VI.1852, no. 70.

93. Keep, "From the Pistol to the Pen," pp. 300–303.

94. L. F. Shepelev, *Otmenennye istoriei—chiny, zvaniia i tituly v Rossiiskoi imperii* (Leningrad, 1977), pp. 25–32.

95. Ibid., p. 33; P. A. Zaionchkovskii, *Pravitel'stvennyi apparat samoderzhavnoi Rossii v XIX v.* (Moscow, 1978).

96. *Sovetskaia voennaia entsiklopediia*, 3: 434. Drummers were considered privates.

97. *Sovetskaia voennaia entsiklopediia*, 3: 317; *SVP* (1838), ch. 3, kn. 1, st. 18–24; *PSZ* (I) 24: 17588; I. Trike, *Pamiatnaia knizhka dlia nizhnikh chinov, napominaiushchaia im o znachenii i dolge russkogo soldata i o glavnykh obiazannostiakh ego v razlichnye periody sluzhby* (St. Petersburg, 1853), pp. 32–36; TsGAOR, f. 48, op. 1, d. 473, ch. 5, ll. 331–33.

98. *PVM*, 5.X.1851, no. 114.

99. "Russkoe voennoe obozrenie," *VS* 30, no. 4 (April 1863): 542–43; TsGVIA, f. 1, op. 1, d. 2062, ll. 39–40; d. 1638; f. 395, op. 286, d. 250, ll. 62–64; TsGAOR, f. 48, op. 1, d. 473, ch. 5, ll. 331–33; "Nachertanie o polevoi egerskoi sluzhbe," *VZ*, no. 5 (1810): 25–26; A. Serebrenitskii, "Postoi voisk v poseleniiakh," *VS* 38, no. 7 (July 1864): 311–14; Dm. Shatilov, "Mysli po povodu unichtozheniia telesnogo nakazaniia v voiskakh," *VS* 33, no. 10 (October 1863): 367–74.

100. Miliutin, *Karmannaia spravochnaia knizhka*, p. 609; "Nachertanie o polevoi egerskoi sluzhbe," pp. 16–17; TsGVIA, f. 16233, op. 1, d. 563.

101. Shepelev, *Otmenennye istoriei*, p. 31.

102. *PSZ* (I) 24: 17534.

103. *Sovetskaia voennaia entsiklopediia*, 3: 434, 8: 266.

104. Ibid., 8: 266.

105. *PSZ* (I) 24: 17588.

106. *SVP* (1838), ch. 3, kn. 1, st. 468; *PVM*, 3.II.1809, no. 19. On the special training troops, see *SVP* (1838), ch. 2, kn. 1, prilozhenie 4, st. 40–42; TsGVIA, f. 1, op. 1, d. 1638, 2062.

107. *SVP* (1838), ch. 2, kn. 1, st. 446, 469.

108. *SVP* (1838), ch. 3, kn. 1, st. 661–65.

109. *PSZ* (I) 24: 17588; *PVM*, 3.II.1809, no. 19.

110. *PVM*, 24.XI.1837, no. 71; *PSZ* (II) 12: 10385.

111. Illiterate noncommissioned officers were almost nonexistent in the engineering troops, significantly more numerous in the artillery, and most common in the cavalry and infantry. Bogdanovich, *Istoricheskii ocherk*, 1: 189–91.

112. Corvisier, *Le Soldat*, 2: 779–84; Gunther E. Rothenberg, *The Army of Francis Joseph* (West Lafayette, Indiana: Purdue University Press, 1976), p. 61.

113. General Denikin was one example. See A. I. Denikin, *The Career of a Tsarist Officer*, trans. Margaret Patoski (Minneapolis: University of Minnesota Press, 1975).

114. *PSZ* (I) 24: 17588

115. *PSZ* (I) 24: 18237.

116. The "volunteers" included sons of men who had reached senior officer rank only upon retiring from military or state service; academicians and gradu-

ates of the school attached to the Academy of Arts who were "free" (*vol'nye i svobodnye*) and graduates of other institutes with comparable privileges; and finally, foreigners possessing documentary proof of their "free status" (*vol'nost'*). PSZ (I) 27: 20542.

117. Ibid.
118. *PSZ* (I) 28: 21357.
119. *PSZ* (I) 29: 22199.
120. *PSZ* (I) 29: 22340.
121. *PSZ* (I) 35: 27269.
122. He attached a list of 225 officers who were "unable to express their thoughts on paper." M., "Neskol'ko mislei otnositel'no proizvodstva v ofitsery nizhnikh chinov," *VS* 30, no. 4 (April 1863): 404; N. Glinoetskii, "Istoricheskii ocherk razvitiia ofitserskikh chinov i sistemy chinoproizvodstva v russkoi armii," *VS* 174, no. 4 (1887): 279.
123. *PSZ* (II) 4: 2874.
124. *SVP* (1838), ch. 2, kn. 1, st. 503; *PSZ* (II) 10: 8337.
125. *SVP* (1838) ch. 2, kn. 1, st. 7–9, 504. The government strictly enforced the literacy requirement for candidates from the poll–tax population who had served twelve years as noncommissioned officers. *PVM*, 30.X.1809.
126. *SVP* (1838), ch. 2, kn. 1, st. 506, 514, 518.
127. *SVP* (1838), ch. 2, kn. 1, st. 527; *PSZ* (II) 6: 4379.
128. *SVP*, vtoroe prodolzhenie, ch. 2, kn. 1, st. 7–8; *PSZ* (II) 15: 13176; 16: 14747; 24: 23448.
129. *PSZ* (II) 16: 14187.
130. *PVM*, 26.III.1843, no. 39; 10.X.1843, no. 114; *PSZ* (II) 20: 19339.
131. M., "Neskol'ko myslei," pp. 403–404.
132. Glinoetskii, "Istoricheskii ocherk razvitiia ofitserskikh chinov," p. 278; Kozhevnikov, "Armiia v 1805–14," 3: 78.
133. Filimonov, *Postepennoe razvitie*, p. 11.
134. *SVP* (1838), ch. 2, kn. 1, st. 435; *PSZ* (II) 6: 4696; 15: 13695, 13867; 18: 16567, 17078, 17155; 19: 17759; "Po voprosu ob unter-ofitserakh," *VS* 95, no. 2 (February 1874): 293–98; *PVM*, 22.I.1843, no. 10; 22.X.1843, no. 125; 21.III.1845, no. 50.
135. P. Brant, "Proizvodstvo nizhnikh chinov v ofitsery," *VS* 31, no. 6 (June 1863): 477–80.
136. Ibid., pp. 479–80.
137. This policy also would ensure an adequate supply of experienced noncommissioned officers; "Po voprosu ob unter-ofitserakh," pp. 293–94.
138. "Chislovye dannye o sostave korpusa ofitserov," p. 238.
139. By rank the numbers were: general, 0; colonel, 5; lieutenant colonel, 4; major, 27; captain, 56; staff captain, 164; lieutenant, 182; second lieutenant, 222; ensign, 86. Ibid., pp. 239, 241–42. A higher estimate of the number of officers promoted from the poll-tax population puts the ratio at 9 percent in the infantry and 8 percent in the cavalry; Brant, "Proizvodstvo nizhnikh chinov," p. 475. In 1857 when the number of non-nobles promoted to officer rank was con-

sidered very high, they still comprised only 10 percent of the officer corps. This was attributed to the low educational level of the common people; M., "Neskol'ko myslei," p. 400.

140. M., "Neskol'ko myslei," p. 404; "Chislovye dannye," p. 247.

141. "Chislovye dannye," p. 247. Eighteenth-century French commanders regarded lieutenants from the noncommissioned officers as important guarantors of order and discipline in the regiment, because of their closeness to and understanding of the men. See Corvisier, *Le Soldat* 2: 784–86.

142. "Po voprosu ob unter-ofitserakh," pp. 297–98; "Russkoe voennoe obozrenie," VS 30, no. 4 (April 1863): 540–41.

143. M., "Neskol'ko myslei," p. 404; "Russkoe voennoe obozrenie," VS 30, no. 4 (April 1863): 545.

144. M., "Neskol'ko myslei," p. 404; "Russkoe voennoe obozrenie," VS 30, no. 4 (April 1863): 542–43; P. Mart'ianov, "Eshche neskol'ko slov po povodu predpolozheniia ob otkrytii dostupa nizhnim chinam k proizvodstvu v ofitsery," VS 33, no. 10 (October 1863): 379.

145. *PSZ* (I) 24: 17547, 17908; (II) 1: 197; 4: 2820; 20: 19339; *SVP* (1838), ch. 2, kn. 2, st. 239, 242–43, 249.

146. *PSZ* (I) 29: 22455; (II) 8: 6611; 11: 9373; *SVP* (1838), ch. 2, kn. 1, st. 112, 116–17; kn. 2, st. 240.

147. *PSZ* (I) 24: 17908; 29: 22455; (II) 6: 4828; 8: 6611; *PVM*, 8.X.1836, no. 113; *SVP* (1838), ch. 2, kn. 2, st. 144, 25–58.

148. *PSZ* (I) 26: 19265.

149. *PSZ* (II) 22: 21142.

150. *PSZ* (I) 29: 22455; 30: 23160, 23380; Ukaz E.I.V., 10.XI.1809, in *Imperatorskie ukazy i prikazy voennogo ministerstva za 1809*.

151. *PSZ* (I) 30: 23930.

152. *PSZ* (I) 31: 24228; (II) 7: 5417. An 1833 statute extended this right to commanders-in-chief. *PSZ* (II) 8: 6611; 18: 16847.

153. *PSZ* (II) 8: 6611; 18: 17336; *SVP* (1838), ch. 2, kn. 2, st. 150–51, 261.

154. *PVM*, 22.X.1843, no. 125; *PSZ* (II) 18: 17255; 19: 18408.

155. *PSZ* (I) 40: 30309, 30361; *SVP* (1838), ch. 2, kn. 2, st. 356–58, 365, 373.

156. *PSZ* (I) 31: 24258; (II) 6: 5049; 14: 12653; *SVP* (1838), ch. 2, kn. 2, st. 375.

157. *PVM*, 22.X.1843, no. 125.

158. *PSZ* (II) 18: 17255; 19: 18308; 22: 21142.

159. *PSZ* (I) 30: 23378; *SVP* (1838), ch. 2, kn. 2, st. 418, 428.

160. *PSZ* (I) 30: 24015.

161. *PSZ* (II) 3: 2198.

162. *PSZ* (II) 6: 4283.

163. *SVP* (1838), ch. 2, kn. 2, st. 431; *PSZ* (I) 40: 30361; (II) 1: 109, 582; 2: 1315, 1612; 6: 5028; 24: 23657; 29: 28135.

164. *SVP* (1838), ch. 2, kn. 2, st. 445, 448; *PVM*, 1.VII.1842, no. 70.

165. *SVP* (1838), ch. 2, kn. 2, st. 454; *PVM*, 6.II.1835, no. 18; 24.X.1836, no. 120; 5.V.1837, no. 53; 5.V.1845, no. 75.

166. "Serf millionaires" also implicitly threatened traditional social arrangements, but they remained outside the formal legal order.

167. This issue is raised in the literature on the old regime and the French revolution; see. Leonard Krieger, *Kings and Philosophers 1689–1789* (New York: W. W. Norton, 1970); J. M. Roberts, *The French Revolution* (Oxford: Oxford University Press, 1978).

Three. "From Peasant to Soldier"

1. "Obshchee znachenie soldat," *Chtenie dlia soldat*, no. 6 (1855): 55.
2. Ibid., pp. 56–57.
3. Ibid., p. 57.
4. Ibid., pp. 59–61. The Decembrist P. I. Pestel considered the best soldiers those who had served five to fifteen years: five years were needed to adjust to military life, but after fifteen years strength and enthusiasm began to decline. TsGAOR, f. 48, op. 1, d. 473, ch. 2, l. 127–127ob.
5. L. V. Evdokimov, "Russkii soldat i ego sluzhba v narodnykh vozzreniiakh," *VS*, no. 3 (1916): 135–36.
6. *PSZ* (I) 17: 12748; 29: 22066; *SVP* (1838), ch. 3, kn. 1, st. 644. The law did not provide a timetable, but an undated document from the late eighteenth or early nineteenth century indicates a period of at least nine months during which the use of weapons and the various turns, paces, and maneuvers would not be introduced before the seventh month. TsGVIA, f. Voenno-uchenyi arkhiv, d. 17817, l. 1. According to the 1848 regulation on infantry service, this sort of training began in the third month; *Voinskii ustav o pekhotnoi sluzhbe* (SPb 1848), ch. 1.
7. *PSZ* (I) 30: 23297; TsGVIA, f. Voenno-uchenyi arkhiv, d. 17816; TsGAOR, f. 48, op. 1, d. 473, ch. 1, ll. 10–15ob.
8. *PSZ* (I) 30: 23297; *PVM*, 9.I.1809, no. 5; 29.XII.1809, no. 171.
9. Attendance at church services was also a regular part of the recruits' training. *PSZ* (II) 6: 4677.
10. *PSZ* (II) 6: 4677; *PVM*, 15.XII.1836, no. 133; 22.V.1837, no. 60.
11. B.P., "Vzgliad na postepennoe obrazovanie rekruta i soldata," *VS*, no. 2 (1859): 503–38.
12. *PVM*, 28.VIII.1834, no. 110.
13. *PVM*, 28.VIII.1834, no. 110; *Voinskii ustav o pekhotnoi sluzhbe* (1848), ch. 1.
14. B.P., "Vzgliad na postepennoe obrazovanie," pp. 503–16; *Voinskii ustav o pekhotnoi sluzhbe* (1848), ch. 1, kn. 1, st. 3.
15. "Instruktsiia rotnym komandiram, za podpisaniem polkovnika grafa [S.R.] Vorontsova, 1774 goda ianvaria 17 dnia, v 17 punktakh sostoiashchaia, na 13 listakh," *VS* 82, no. 11 (November 1871): 39. In the stories of N. A. Polevoi, a retired soldier describes his transformation from a backward, ignorant peasant

into an intelligent soldier as a kind of rebirth. See *Rasskazy russkogo soldata* (St. Petersburg, 1852), pp. 68–69, 70–71, 80.

16. B.P., "Vzgliad na postepennoe obrazovanie," pp. 504–505, 513–16; Vorontsov, "Instruktsiia rotnym komandiram," p. 39; Trike, *Pamiatnaia knizhka*, p. 389; "Obshchee znachenie soldat," pp. 56, 66.

17. *SVP* (1838), ch. 3, kn. 1, st. 642. The *diad'ka* was supposed to be a decorated soldier who had served irreproachably for at least ten years. Trike, *Pamiatnaia knizhka*, pp. 37–38. Patriotic literature addressed to soldiers depicted older, experienced, and literate soldiers as a model and inspiration for the young soldiers whom they instructed in the details of military life. See I. Skobelev, *Podarok tovarishcham, ili perepiska russkikh soldat v 1812 godu* (St. Petersburg, 1833).

18. Trike, *Pamiatnaia knizhka*, p. 16; "Nekotorye zametki dlia nizhnikh voinskikh chinov," *Chtenie dlia soldat*, no. 6 (1857): 53; Major General Rusanov, "O soldate," VZ, no. 9 (1810): 71–72; "Obshchee znachenie soldat," p. 58.

19. TsGVIA, f. 16231, op. 1, d. 430, ll. 5–7.

20. *SVP* (1838), ch. 3, kn. 1, st. 372, 375, 379, 407–408, 412, 436–46.

21. Trike, *Pamiatnaia knizhka*, p. 13.

22. *PSZ* (I) 24: 17588.

23. Each regiment also had its own patronal festival. *SVP* (1838), ch. 3, kn. 1, st. 372, 375, 379, 407–408, 412, 436–46.

24. TsGVIA, f. Voenno-uchenyi arkhiv, d. 17184, ch. 4, l. 174–174ob.; B.P., "Vzgliad na postepennoe obrazovanie," pp. 520–21. This phenomenon was characteristic of the lower classes as a whole. Gregory L. Freeze, *The Parish Clergy in Nineteenth-Century Russia: Crisis, Reform, Counter-Reform* (Princeton, N.J.: Princeton University Press, 1983), "Introduction."

25. "Iz prikazov po 2–i armii," VS, no. 2 (February 1905): 156–57.

26. P. Brant, "Gramotnost' i eia razvitie mezhdu nizhnimi chinami," VS 29, no. 2 (February 1863): 444; B.P., "Vzgliad na postepennoe obrazovanie," pp. 520–21. For a religious morality tale with a military theme, see *Voennaia sluzhba spaseniiu dushi ne pomekha ili soldat vozvrativshiisia posle pokhoda na rodinu. Povest'* (St. Petersburg, 1850).

27. On the nature and goals of the *Polizeistaat*, see Marc Raeff, *The Well-Ordered Police State*.

28. Vorontsov, "Instruktsiia rotnym komandiram," p. 33; *SVM*, vol. 4, pt. 1, bk. 2, sec. 2, appendix 14, p. 72; Trike, *Pamiatnaia knizhka*, p. 25; Major General Khatov 1, "O voinskoi distsipline," VZ, no. 3 (1827): 41; Colonel Chernevskii, "O voennoi distsipline," VZ, no. 3 (1856): 46.

29. *PSZ* (I) 29: 22161.

30. *SVP* (1838), ch. 3, kn. 1, st. 372, 375, 379, 407–408, 412; Vorontsov, "Instruktsiia rotnym komandiram," pp. 42–43.

31. Vorontsov, "Instruktsiia rotnym komandiram," pp. 42–43; Trike, *Pamiatnaia knizhka*, pp. 55–62.

32. TsGVIA, f. 36, op. 1, d. 605, ll. 31–37ob.

33. *PSZ* (I) 24: 17590; *SVP* (1838), ch. 3, kn. 1, st. 372, 375, 379, 407–408, 412, 436–46.

34. *SVP* (1838), ch. 3, kn. 1, st. 372, 375, 379, 407–408, 412, 436–46.

35. Desirable leisure activities included singing, playing musical instruments, laughing, talking, reading, and telling funny and cheerful stories. Trike, *Pamiatnaia knizhka*, p. 14.

36. Rothenberg, *The Art of Warfare in the Age of Napoleon*; Beskrovnyi, *Russkaia armiia i flot v XIX veke*, pp. 102–16; A. A. Komarov, "Razvitie takticheskoi mysli v russkoi armii v 60–90–kh godakh XVIII v.," *Vestnik Moskovskogo Universiteta*, Seriia 8, Istoriia, no. 3 (1982): 57–66.

37. John Keegan, *The Face of Battle* (New York: Penguin, 1978), pp. 121–97; P. S. Lebedev, "Preobrazovateli russkoi armii v tsarstvovanie imperatora Pavla Petrovicha, 1796–1801," *RS* 18 (1877): 227–60, 577–608; Glinoetskii, "Voennaia statistika," pp. 443–44; S.N., "O gramotnosti v voiskakh," *VS* 4, no. 7 (1858): 2–3.

38. *Voinskii ustav o pekhotnoi sluzhbe* (1848), ch. 2, otd. 3, gl. 1, st. 1–2; B.P., "Vzgliad na postepennoe obrazovanie," pp. 522–23, 533.

39. Kozhevnikov, "Armiia v 1805–14," 3: 66. *SVM*, vol. 14, pt. 1, appendices, pp. 14–31; N. Dubrovin, "Russkaia zhizn' v nachale XIX veka," *RS* 108 (1901): 465–66; S. S. Volk and P. V. Vinogradov, eds., "Dva prikaza M. F. Orlova po 16–i divizii," *Literaturnoe nasledstvo* 60, no. 1 (Moscow, 1956): 10.

40. *Voinskii ustav o pekhotnoi sluzhbe* (1848), ch. 2, otd. 3, gl. 1, st. 1–2. For the inspectors' reports, see TsGVIA, f. Voenno-uchenyi arkhiv, d. 683, ll. 10ob., 17–17ob.; d. 17542, ch. 2, ll. 26–29; ch. 3, ll. 18ob.–19; f. 395, op. 101, d. 111, l. 137ob.; d. 108, l. 256ob.; d. 120, l. 26ob.; d. 228, ll. 1–1ob., 18; d. 232, l. 73; d. 245, ll. 3–10ob., 28–29, 32, 47–50ob.; d. 246, ll. 4–4ob., 92ob.

41. TsGVIA, f. Voenno-uchenyi arkhiv, d. 793, ll. 14–15; d. 17184, ch. 1, ll. 31–3ob.; ch. 2, l. 71; ch. 4, l. 161ob.; f. 395, op. 101, d. 245, ll. 3–10ob., 28–29; B.P., "Vzgliad na postepennoe obrazovanie," p. 534.

42. "Vzgliad na sostoianie russkikh voisk v minuvshuiu voinu," *VS* 1, no. 1 (1858): 12; S.N., "O gramotnosti v voiskakh," p. 3; P. Alabin, *Chetyre voiny. Pokhodnye zapiski v 1849, 1853, 1854–56 i 1877–78 godakh*, 4 parts (Moscow, 1890), 2: 1–2; Krestovskii, *Istoriia 14–go Ulanskogo Iamburgskogo eia imperatorskogo vysochestva velikoi kniazhny Marii Aleksandrovny polka* (St. Petersburg, 1873), p. 406.

43. Thus in 1843 the Guards Corps, which practiced marksmanship daily during the summer and early fall, characterized as "satisfactory" the results in which one-third to one-fourth of the shots fired hit their target. TsGVIA, f. Voenno-uchenyi arkhiv, d. 17542, ch. 2, ll. 28–29.

44. *RI*, 12.VII.1855, no. 151, p. 721.

45. *PSZ* (I) 29: 2161; *SVP* (1838), ch. 3, kn. 1, st. 630–34, 638, 648–51, 654–60, 677–78.

46. *PSZ* (I) 29: 22161; *SVP* (1838), ch. 3, kn. 1, st. 630–34, 638, 648–51, 654–60, 677–78.

47. Enegol'm, *Karmannaia kniga voennoi gigieny*, p. 57.

48. *Imperatorskie ukazy i prikazy voennogo ministerstva za 1809*; *PVM*, 30.IV.1809, no. 52.

49. TsGVIA, f. Voenno-uchenyi arkhiv, d. 709, l. 2.

50. Ibid., l. 3. Officers sometimes were punished for holding training at unauthorized times. TsGVIA, f. 801, op. 62, d. 720, ll. 43–54; op. 60, d. 11, ll. 449–50.

51. TsGVIA, f. Voenno-uchenyi arkhiv, d. 17184, ch. 1, l. 31ob.; f. 16231, op. 1, d. 430, ll. 5–7.

52. TsGVIA, f. 16231, op. 1, d. 430, ll. 5–7.

53. *SVP* (1838), ch. 2, kn. 1, st. 630–34, 638, 648–51, 654–60, 677–78. Sources from the late 1850s indicate that drills were conducted for about three hours each day. B.P., "Vzgliad na postepennoe obrazovanie," p. 530; "Nekotorye zametki," p. 60.

54. On the failure to observe regulations, see Brant, "Kazarmennoe raspolozhenie," pp. 89–91.

55. TsGVIA, f. 395, op. 248, d. 17, ll. 3ob., 14–15; op. 100, d. 120, ll. 22ob., 26ob.

56. *SVP* (1838), ch. 3, kn. 1, st. 630–34, 638, 648–51, 654–60, 677–78.

57. These duties included reporting, accounting for supplies, and reading military regulations to their subordinates.

58. *SVP* (1838), ch. 3, kn. 1, st. 630–34, 638, 648–51, 654–63, 677–78; "Ob ustroistve shkol dlia rasprostraneniia gramotnosti v voiskakh," *VS* 2, no. 3 (1858): 191; TsGVIA, f. 395, op. 101, d. 232, l. 85ob.

59. Judith Cohen Zacek, "The Lancastrian School Movement in Russia," *SEER* 45, no. 105 (July 1967): 344–46, 360–65; TsGVIA, f. Voenno-uchenyi arkhiv, d. 793, ll. 60–61ob.; *RI*, 13.IV.1819, no. 85, p. 339; 19.IV.1819, no. 90, p. 361; 1.VIII.1819, no. 178, pp. 711–13; 14.I.1820, no. 9, p. 34; 1.VII.1820, no. 154, p. 614.

60. Raevskii was tried for unspecified illegal acts and for a dangerous "way of thinking" that threatened to undermine discipline. His arrest followed disturbances in the Semenovskii Guards (1820) and Kamchatka Infantry (1821) Regiments. Zacek, "The Lancastrian School Movement," pp. 364–65; TsGVIA, f. 801, op. 70/11, d. 42, t. Ia, ch. 1, l. 1.

61. Zacek, "The Lancastrian School Movement," pp. 355–56; B., "Izvestie o zavedenii pri Shtabe Gvardeiskogo korpusa Uchilishcha Vzaimogo Obucheniia," *VZ*, no. 1 (1819): 67–70. M., "O pol'ze obucheniia gramote vsei massy russkikh voisk," *VS* 1, no. 2 (February 1858): 356–58.

62. Following the Crimean War the army once again decided to promote literacy in an effort to improve the army's fighting capability and also provide a means for exerting moral influence over the troops. Estimates on the extent of literacy in the late fifties and early sixties vary from one-tenth to one-half. The lower estimate seems more likely, since several contemporary commentators noted that many soldiers read mechanically without really understanding the meaning of the text. Moreover, the definition of literacy varied. Some commanders designated soldiers who could read, but not write as literate. According to one observer, about half of the soldiers counted as literate could only read the book from which they originally received instruction. See "Ob ustroistve shkol dlia ras-

prostraneniia gramotnosti," p. 191; M., "O pol'ze obucheniia gramote," pp. 354–58; Brant, "Gramotnost' i eia razvitie," pp. 435–36; S.N., "O gramotnosti v voiskakh, pp. 2–5, 11; B.P., "Vzgliad na postepennoe obrazovanie," pp. 517–18; Serebrenitskii, "Postoi v seleniiakh," pp. 315–16.

63. J. A. Houlding, *Fit for Service: The Training of the British Army, 1715–1795* (New York: Oxford University Press).

64. Ibid., pp. 1–2, 38–41, 52, 89–95, 269–70, 276–91, 296–317, 324–48.

65. Ibid., pp. 3, 57–90, 291. Russian historians of the revolutionary era have also raised this problem: William C. Fuller Jr., *Civil-Military Conflict in Imperial Russia, 1881–1914* (Princeton, N.J.: Princeton University Press, 1985), pp. 43, 75–110, 244–58; John Bushnell, *Mutiny amid Repression: Russian Soldiers in the Revolution of 1905–1906* (Bloomington: Indiana University Press, 1985), pp. 12–13, 27–28, 32–33.

66. Houlding, *Fit for Service*, p. 395.

67. Trike, *Pamiatnaia knizhka*; TsGVIA, f. Voenno-uchenyi arkhiv, d. 17533, ch. 1–2.

68. The Second Army occupied the southern borderlands. TsGVIA, f. Voenno-uchenyi arkhiv, d. 792, ll. 19–21; d. 17184, ch. 1, ll. 50–51ob.

69. TsGVIA, f. 36, op. 6, d. 84, ll. 1–7; f. Voenno-uchenyi arkhiv, d. 17533, ch. 1, ll. 142–44ob., 186–89ob.; ch. 2, ll. 118–21.

70. TsGVIA, f. 395, op. 100, d. 120, ll. 22ob.–23.

71. TsGVIA, f. Voenno-uchenyi arkhiv, d. 793, l. 48–48ob.; f. 395, op. 100, d. 120, ll. 4ob.–5; L. Plesterer, *Istoriia 62-go pekhotnogo Suzdal'skogo Generalissimusa Kniazia Italiiskogo Grafa Suvorova-Rymskogo polka*, 6 vols. (Belostok, 1902), 4: 496; *SVM*, vol. 7, pt. 1², bk. 4, sec. 1, ch. 1; appendices 59, 62, 64; pp. 163–66, 180–81, 185.

72. TsGVIA, f. Voenno-uchenyi arkhiv, d. 17533, ch. 1–2.

73. TsGVIA, f. Voenno-uchenyi arkhiv, d. 17533, ch. 1, ll. 14–15ob., 269–70ob., 274–75ob.; ch. 2, ll. 160a–160b, 244–45ob., 251–52.

74. TsGVIA, f. Voenno-uchenyi arkhiv, d. 17533, ch. 1–2.

75. This occurred only in areas with a warm climate, such as the Crimea. It also happened that state works began as early as April 1 and lasted through October. TsGVIA, f. Voenno-uchenyi arkhiv, d. 17533, ch. 1, ll. 44–46ob.; ch. 2, ll. 209–10, 361–63.

76. In 1827 the Iamburg Uhlan Regiment was dispersed over three districts of Tver province at an average distance of six to eight days' march from regimental headquarters; Krestovskii, *Istoriia 14-go Ulanskogo Iamburgskogo polka*, p. 384.

77. TsGVIA, f. Voenno-uchenyi arkhiv, d. 793, ll. 102–103ob.

78. TsGVIA, f. Voenno-uchenyi arkhiv, d. 793, ll. 102–103ob.; d. 17184, ch. 1, l. 35ob.; ch. 3, ll. 136–49.

79. TsGVIA, f. Voenno-uchenyi arkhiv, d. 792, ll. 13–16ob.; d. 17147, ch. 1–3, ll. 1–120ob.; d. 17184, ch. 1, ll. 37–39ob.; ch. 3, ll. 146–47; d. 793, l. 1–1ob.

80. Large-scale maneuvers and exercise camps were a regular feature of military life in the reign of Peter the Great. Following Peter's death, they disappeared

until the 1760s. The Napoleonic Wars caused another disruption, after which regular maneuvers and camps were restored once again in the reign of Nicholas I. See Christopher Duffy, *Russia's Military Way to the West: Origins and Nature of Russian Military Power 1700–1800* (London: Routledge and Kegan Paul, 1981), p. 183; Beskrovnyi, *Russkaia armiia i flot v XIX veke*, pp. 110–16; Krestovskii, *Istoriia 14-go Ulanskogo Iamburgskogo polka*, pp. 499–500, 502–503.

81. TsGVIA, f. Voenno-uchenyĭ arkhiv, d. 17533, ch. 1–2; d. 17184, ch. 3, ll. 136–49; d. 17542, ch. 1, ll. 26–27; ch. 3, ll. 16–18; TsGAOR, f. 48, op. 1, d. 473, ch. 3, ll. 203–42; Ordinator Voskresenskii, "Obzor boleznei, 1835 goda gospodstvovavshikh v voiskakh armii," *VMZ* 30, no. 1 (1837): 3–4, 12.

82. TsGVIA, f. Voenno-uchenyi arkhiv, d. 17533, ch. 1, ll. 14–15ob., 142–44ob., 188–89ob.

83. Following maneuvers, some grenadier regiments performed state works until October 1. TsGVIA, f. Voenno-uchenyi arkhiv, d. 17533, ch. 1, ll. 57–58ob., 238–39ob.; d. 17542, ch. 1, ll. 10ob.–13ob.; ch. 3, ll. 17ob.–18, 21ob.–22.

84. TsGVIA, f. Voenno-uchenyi arkhiv, d. 17533, ch. 1–2.

85. Krestovskii, *Istoriia 14-go Ulanskogo Iamburgskogo polka*, p. 338.

86. Ibid., pp. 520–21.

87. According to one observer, soldiers who spent a lot of time with peasants became lazy and lethargic. *SVM*, vol. 4, pt. 1, bk. 2, sec. 2, p. 76; Serebrenitskii, "Postoi v seleniiakh," pp. 305–44; Enegol'm, *Karmannaia kniga voennoi gigieny*, pp. 8–9.

88. TsGVIA, f. Voenno-uchenyi arkhiv, d. 17184, ch. 1, l. 34.

89. Baraniusa, "Polkovye unter-ofitserskie shkoly," *VS* 44, no. 7 (1865): 105–106.

90. Baraniusa, "Polkovye unter-ofitserskie shkoly," pp. 105–14; "Po povodu stat'i: polkovye unter-ofitserskie shkoly," *VS* 46 (1865): 151–52.

91. Baraniusa, "Polkovye unter-ofitserskie shkoly," pp. 105–106.

92. TsGAOR, f. 48, op. 1, d. 473, ch. 1, l. 12ob.

93. Vorontsov, "Instruktsiia rotnym komandiram," pp. 39, 43; B.P., "Vzgliad na postepennoe obrazovanie," pp. 513–15, 529; "Nachertanie o polevoi egerskoi sluzhbe," *VZ*, no. 5 (1810): 15–16; Serebrenitskii, "Postoi v seleniiakh," pp. 311–14.

94. B.P., "Vzgliad na postepennoe obrazovanie," pp. 512–13.

95. M., "O pol'ze obucheniia gramote," p. 358.

96. Beyrau, *Militär und Gesellschaft*.

97. Duffy, *Russia's Military Way to the West*; Walter M. Pintner, "The Burden of Defense in Imperial Russia, 1725–1914," *RR* 43, no. 3 (July 1984): 231–59.

98. Menzenkampf, "Obzor sistem inspektirovaniia russkoi armii s 1711 goda," *VS*, no. 12 (1862): 399–401, 407–409, 417–26.

99. Inspections became increasingly regularized during the first half of the nineteenth century. TsGVIA, f. Voenno-uchenyi arkhiv, d. 691, l. 2; *SVP* (1838), ch. 3, kn. 1, st. 792; *SVM*, vol. 14, pt. 1, appendices, pp. 14–42; pt. 2, appendices 25–35, 38, 42–43; pp. 112–26, 130, 145–47.

100. TsGVIA, f. Voenno-uchenyi arkhiv, d. 683, 691; 17184, ch. 1, ll. 46ob.–

47; ch. 4, ll. 159–62; 17391; 17542, ch. 1–3; f. 395, op. 101, d. 108, 111, 115, 120, 158, 219, 228, 232, 245, 246; op. 248, d. 17; "Russkaia voennaia istoriia," VS, no. 5 (1908): 288–92.

101. TsGVIA, f. Voenno-uchenyi arkhiv, d. 683, ll. 16–17; d. 691, l. 51ob.; d. 17391, ll. 1–2; f. 395, op. 101, d. 246, ll. 5, 14ob.–15, 24ob.–25; op. 248, d. 17, ll. 13–15ob., 43–44; SVM, vol. 14, pt. 1, appendices, pp. 15–31; "Otryvki iz dnevnika rotnogo komandira I. I. Gladilova, 1841 goda," *Sbornik starinnykh bumag, khraniashchikhsia v muzee P. I. Shchukina* (Moscow, 1901), pt. 8, pp. 174–75; PVM, 11.IV.1809, no. 39; 27.V.1809, no. 67; 14.VII.1809, no. 91; 25.IX.1809, no. 126.

102. In cavalry regiments inspectors also checked riding skills and the performance of the horses. SVM, vol. 14, pt. 1, appendices, pp. 14–42; pt. 2, appendices 25–35, pp. 112–26; TsGVIA, f. Voenno-uchenyi arkhiv, d. 691, l. 51–51ob.; d. 683.

103. Keegan, *The Face of Battle*, pp. 179–81.

104. Lebedev, "Preobrazovateli russkoi armii," pp. 260, 577.

105. Krestovskii, *Istoriia 14–go Ulanskogo Iamburgskogo polka*, p. 105; Dubrovin, "Russkaia zhizn' v nachale XIX veka," p. 477; SVM, vol. 14, pt. 1, appendices, pp. 35–39.

106. SVM, vol. 14, pt. 1, appendices, pp. 14–31; pt. 2, appendix 34, pp. 123–24; TsGVIA, f. Voenno-uchenyi arkhiv, d. 793, ll. 13–14, 37–37ob., 38ob.–39; d. 691, l. 6; d. 17184, ch. 1, ll. 21ob.–22, 30ob., 36; ch. 2, l. 71; d. 17391, l. 3; f. 395, op. 101, d. 111, ll. 29ob.–30; d. 115, ll. 11–11ob., 63–66; Plesterer, *Istoriia 62–go pekhotnogo Suzdal'skogo polka*, 4: 494–95; Brant, "Gramotnost' i eia razvitie," pp. 440–41; Krestovskii, *Istoriia 14–go Ulanskogo Iamburgskogo polka*, pp. 517–18.

107. TsGVIA, f. Voenno-uchenyi arkhiv, d. 17147, ch. 1–3, ll. 1–3; d. 17184, ch. 1, ll. 32ob.–33, 36.

108. The first training units were established in 1808 and 1809. TsGVIA, f. 1, op. 1, d. 1638, 2062; f. Voenno-uchenyi arkhiv, d. 17184, ch. 1, ll. 21ob.–24, 30ob.; d. 17542, ch. 3, l. 19ob.; SVP (1838), ch. 2, kn. 1, appendix to st. 14.

109. SVM, vol. 14, pt. 1, appendices, pp. 35–39; TsGVIA, f. Voenno-uchenyi arkhiv, d. 691, l. 6; d. 17184, ch. 1, ll. 21ob.–24, 30ob., 32ob.–33, 36; d. 17391, l. 3; f. 395, op. 101, d. 111, ll. 29ob.–30; d. 115, l. 11–11ob., 63–66; d. 245, ll. 3–11, 47–49ob.

110. Houlding, *Fit for Service*, pp. 146, 190–92; TsGVIA, f. Voenno-uchenyi arkhiv, d. 17184, ch. 2, l. 71. Krestovskii attributes the tremendous fluctuations in the training and performance of the Iamburg Uhlan Regiment to the character and abilities of individual commanders. Krestovskii, *Istoriia 14–go Ulanskogo Iamburgskogo polka*, pp. 537–42, 546–50, 553–55, 563–66.

111. Houlding, *Fit for Service*, p. 165.

112. E. A. Prokof'ev, *Bor'ba dekabristov za peredovoe russkoe voennoe iskusstvo* (Moscow, 1953), pp. 239–51; SIRIO (St. Petersburg, 1890) 73: 577–78; TsGAOR, f. 48, op. 1, d. 12, l. 80 (1820).

113. TsGVIA, f. Voenno-uchenyi arkhiv, d. 764, ch. 1, l. 26–26ob. (1822).

114. N. Dubrovin, "Graf A. A. Arakcheev," *RS* 101 (January 1900): 98; A. Brikner, "Zapiski grafa Lanzherona o russkom voiske (1796–1824 gg.)," *Russkaia mysl'* 17, no. 9 (1896): 38–39.

115. Brant, "Gramotnost' i eia razvitie," p. 440; Glinoetskii, "Voennaia statistika," pp. 457–58; "Vzgliad na sostoianie russkikh voisk," pp. 8–13; Zaionchkovskii, ed., *Dnevnik D. A. Miliutina*, 2: 29–30; A. A. Kozhevnikov, "Russkaia armiia posle voin 1812–1814 gg.," *OVRO*, 7: 236–37; Alabin, *Chetyre voiny*, 2: 2–5; Krestovskii, *Istoriia 14–go Ulanskogo Iamburgskogo polka*, pp. 387–89, 402–405, 407, 499–500, 517–18, 546–50, 553–54, 563–66, 587–98.

116. Keegan, *The Face of Battle*, pp. 320–31.

117. Ibid., pp. 18–20.

118. "Vzgliad na sostoianie russkikh voisk," pp. 1–15; Alabin, *Chetyre voiny*, 2: 1–10.

119. Sir Robert Thomas Wilson, *A Sketch of the Military and Political Power of Russia in the Year 1817* (London, 1817), pp. 119, 149; idem, *Brief Remarks on the Character and Composition of the Russian Army and a Sketch of the Campaigns in Poland in the Years 1806 and 1807* (London, 1810), pp. 1–2; *VZ*, no. 2 (1855): 183; Brikner, "Zapiski grafa Lanzherona," pp. 30–31; Dubrovin, "Russkaia zhizn' v nachale XIX veka," pp. 482–83. See also Christopher Duffy, *Russia's Military Way to the West*, pp. 89, 234.

120. Brikner, "Zapiski grafa Lanzherona," p. 31; Dubrovin, "Russkaia zhizn' v nachale XIX veke," p. 483.

121. Beyrau, *Militär und Gesellschaft*, pp. 392–405.

122. Vorontsov, "Instruktsiia rotnym komandiram," pp. 35–36; "O tom, chto sleduet soldatu sobliudat' nakhodias' v otpusku," *Chtenie dlia soldat*, no. 1 (1858): 148–50.

123. TsGVIA, f. 16232, op. 1, d. 142, ll. 229–36ob.

124. TsGIA, f. 1284, op. 17, d. 54, l. 10–10ob.; *PVM*, 3.I. 1840, no. 1.

125. Rakhmatullin, "Soldaty v krest'ianskom dvizhenii," pp. 351–58; TsGAOR, f. 48, op. 1, d. 12, ll. 79ob.–80, 83–83ob.; TsGVIA, f. 395, op. 286, d. 215, ll. 116–17; *PVM*, 31.III.1834; *SVM*, vol. 14, pt. 2, appendix 36, pp. 126–28.

126. *PSZ* (II) 7: 5131.

127. *PSZ* (II) 8: 6365.

Four. "Limits of Bureaucratic Regulation"

1. For Russia this relationship has been ably analyzed in Beyrau, *Militär und Gesellschaft*.

2. Pintner, "The Burden of Defense."

3. Lalaev, "Nashi nisshie shkoly voennogo vedomstva i blizkie k nim, po stoimosti soderzhaniia internaty drugikh vedomstv," *Pedagogicheskii sbornik*, no. 4 (March 1866): 293–94; L. Klugin, "Russkaia soldatskaia artel'," *VS*, no. 7 (1861): 129; Armeiskii rotnyi komandir, "Temnaia summa," *VS*, no. 1 (1862): 193–95.

4. On the military economy under Peter the Great, see *SVM*, vol. 5, pt. 1 (St. Petersburg, 1902), pp. 9–35, 89–90; Menzenkampf, "Obzor sistem inspektirovaniia," pp. 399–407; *PSZ* (I) 5: 2621, 2622, 2628; Bogdanovich, *Istoricheskii ocherk*, 2: 123–28.

5. *SVM*, vol. 5, pt. 1, pp. 85–88, 103–11; *Arkhiv Gosudarstvennogo Soveta*, 4, vypusk 2, ch. 2, k. 1915–26, 1945–47, 1959–65, 1976–78; F. A. Leev, "Doreformennaia armiia (Po zapiskam gr. P. D. Kiseleva)," *Vestnik vsemirnoi istorii* 2, no. 11 (1901): 107–109; N. P. Eroshkin, "Voennyi apparat tsarskoi Rossii v period Krymskoi voiny (1853–1856 gg.)," *Trudy Moskovskogo Gosudarstvennogo Istoriko-Arkhivnogo Instituta* 9 (Moscow, 1957): 143–47; TsGVIA, f. 1, op. 1, d. 4060; f. Voenno-uchenyi arkhiv, d. 17147, ch. 1–3, l. 103ob.; Trubnikov, "Staraia i novaia sistema zagotovleniia provianta i furazha dlia armii i flota," *RV* 13 (1858): 186–201; "O pokupke provianta iz pervykh ruk i s torgov," *VS*, no. 6 (1862): 391–410.

6. Eroshkin, "Voennyi apparat," pp. 147–48; Trubnikov, "Staraia i novaia sistema zagotovleniia," pp. 197–99.

7. *VZ*, no. 2 (1857): 212. In 1821 the authorities were still deciding claims from 1812. *RI*, 6.VIII.1821, no. 181, p. 726.

8. *RI*, 16.VIII.1818, no. 188, p. 758; *VZ*, no. 2 (1857): 192–93; *RS* 89 (March 1897): 598; Klugin, "Russkaia soldatskaia artel'," pp. 90–91.

9. TsGVIA, f. Voenno-uchenyi arkhiv, d. 764, ch. 2, ll. 112–26ob.; d. 792, ll. 22–23ob., 26–30ob.; d. 17147, ch. 1–3, l. 103–103ob.

10. TsGVIA, f. Voenno-uchenyi arkhiv, d. 764, ch. 2, ll. 112–26ob.; Leev, "Doreformennaia armiia," p. 107. Kiselev was responding to an 1823 request from St. Petersburg that troops quartered in rich provinces obtain provisions directly from local residents. He concluded that this would be possible only in Kiev and Podolia where the population was occupied mainly with farming. In the other provinces occupied by the Second Army (Kherson, Ekaterinoslav, Tauride, and Bessarabia), the population was sparse and derived its livelihood from raising cattle. In opposition to the proposal, Kiselev also noted that when the troops were concentrated in close quarters or in camp, it would still be necessary to obtain supplies from private traders.

11. *SVM*, vol. 5, pt. 1, pp. 87–94; *Arkhiv Gosudarstvennogo Soveta* (St. Petersburg, 1878) 3: 876; *PSZ* (I) 8: 5864; 37: 28644, 28767; (II) 5: 3658; *SVP* (1838), ch. 4, kn. 3, appendix 15 to st. 483, 502; I. Maslov, "O denezhnom dovol'stvii nizhnikh chinov," *VS* 127, no. 6 (1879): 311; Bogdanovich, *Istoricheskii ocherk*, 2:78–82.

12. *PSZ* (I) 30: 23297, and *SVM*, vol. 5, pt. 1, p. 91.

13. Chernyshev, *Istoricheskoe obozrenie*, p. 56. There were one hundred cups (*charka*) in one *vedro*, which was approximately twenty-one pints; "O udobneishikh sposobakh prodovol'stviia Rossiiskikh voisk za granitseiu," *VZ*, no. 5 (1830): 7. When in camp or concentrated quarters, the troops also received meat and liquor rations. TsGVIA, f. Voenno-uchenyi arkhiv, d. 793, l. 36–36ob.

14. *PSZ* (II) 2: 1004; M. A. Rossiiskii, *Ocherk istorii 3–go pekhotnogo Narvskogo General-Fel'dmarshala Kniazia Mikhaila Golitsyna polka* (Moscow,

1905), p. 419; "O prezhnem i nastoiashchem dovol'stvii soldat," *Chtenie dlia soldat* 7, no. 2 (1859): 33; Miliutin, *Karmannaia spravochnaia knizhka*, p. 207; Trike, *Pamiatnaia knizhka*, p. 66. Salt was considered an important dietary supplement: it was believed to stimulate digestion and protect the body from exhaustion. Miliutin, *Karmannaia spravochnaia knizhka*, p. 832.

15. *PSZ* (I) 17: 12748; (II) 6: 4677; Prokhodtsov, *Riazanskaia guberniia*, 1: 146–47.

16. Chernyshev, *Istoricheskoe obozrenie*, pp. 61–62; *PVM*, 6.XII.1836, no. 131; *PSZ* (II) 11: 9141, 9762; 13: 11478; 17: 15808; 18: 17272; 19: 18096, 18269; TsGVIA, f. 395, op. 100, d. 120, ll. 74–74ob., 79–82ob.

17. *PSZ* (II) 12: 9952; Fedor Zatler, *Zapiski o prodovol'stvii voisk v voennoe vremia* (St. Petersburg, 1860), 1: 274; *Polozhenie o kazennykh zagotovleniiakh vedomstva voennogo ministerstva* (St. Petersburg, 1838), p. 142; "O prezhnem i nastoiashchem dovol'stvii soldat," p. 29.

18. *PSZ* (II) 24: 23702; 26: 25441, 25595; 27: 25991; Trike, *Pamiatnaia knizhka*, p. 66; Miliutin, *Karmannaia spravochnaia knizhka*, pp. 204–206; Klugin, "Russkaia soldatskaia artel'," pp. 91–93.

19. Chernyshev, *Istoricheskoe obozrenie*, pp. 56, 62–63; *PVM*, 1.VIII.1842, no. 69; 6.XII.1849, no. 122; *PSZ* (II) 26: 24941; Bogdanovich, *Istoricheskii ocherk*, 2: 79–81, 91–92; "O rasporiazheniiakh k ustroistvu deistvuiushchei armii k pokhodu 1829 goda," *VS*, no. 2 (February 1905): 63–64, 108.

20. V. M. Anichkov, *Voennoe khoziaistvo. Sravnitel'noe issledovanie polozhitel'nykh zakonodatel'stv Rossii, Frantsii, Prusii, Avstrii, Sardinii, Bel'gii i Bavarii* (St. Petersburg, 1860), pp. 83–85, 559.

21. Ibid., p. 86; TsGVIA, f. Voenno-uchenyi arkhiv, d. 793, l. 37.

22. TsGIA, f. 1409, op. 2, d. 6214, l. 13–13ob.

23. TsGVIA, f. 801, op. 73, d. 32, ll. 138–72, 180–94, 205–15.

24. Anichkov, *Voennoe khoziaistvo*, pp. 397–99.

25. M. Apolev, "Ocherki khoziaistva armeiskogo pekhotnogo polka," *VS*, no. 7 (1859): 7–10; TsGAOR, f. 48, op. 1, d. 473, ch. 1, l. 2–13ob.; TsGVIA, f. Voenno-uchenyi arkhiv, d. 792, ll. 32–36.

26. *SVP* (1838), ch. 4, kn. 4, st. 8, 16, 21, 118; A. M. Zaionchkovskii, *Vostochnaia voina 1853–1856*, 2 vols. (St. Petersburg, 1908), 1: 483; Trike, *Pamiatnaia knizhka*, pp. 64–66.

27. This allowance was not always adequate. TsGAOR, f. 48, op. 1, d. 473, ch. 1, l. 49ob.; Zaionchkovskii, *Vostochnaia voina*, 1: 483; Trike, *Pamiatnaia knizhka*, pp. 64–66; Miliutin, *Karmannaia spravochnaia knizhka*, pp. 210–13, 245; Apolev, "Ocherki khoziaistva," pp. 3, 11–22. For a full account of the soldiers' clothing and equipment, see also K. Kononovich, "Nuzhdy soldata i ego raskhody," *VS*, no. 5 (1862): 135–64; Bogdanovich, *Istoricheskii ocherk*, 2: 128–35; *SVM*, vol. 5, pt. 1, pp. 90–91; *PSZ* (II) 5: 3658; Anichkov, *Voennoe khoziaistvo*, pp. 149–51, 163–66.

28. L. A. Seriakov, "Moia trudovaia zhizn'," *RS* 14 (1875): 179. Regimental commanders were financially responsible for preserving state equipment. TsGAOR, f. 48, op. 1, d. 473, ch. 1, l. 51–51ob.

29. TsGVIA, f. 14414, op. 10/291, sv. 60, d. 326, ch. 12, l. 5–5ob.; ch. 24, l. 52; ch. 35, l. 24. I am grateful to Professor Walter Pintner for sharing these files with me.

30. Each company also supported a sutler who sold the soldiers food products. Although soldiers themselves were forbidden to engage in this trade, their wives could do so. SVM, vol. 5, pt. 1, p. 124; PSZ (I) 24: 17588, 17590; SVP (1838), ch. 4, kn. 4, st. 157–59.

31. Anichkov, *Voennoe khoziaistvo*, p. 543; Leont'ev, *Soldatskaia knizhka* 1: 290–91.

32. The recruitment regulation of 29.IX.1766 also suggests that the artel served an administrative purpose: new recruits were divided into artels of about eight men, which were subdivided into *kapral'stva*. The purpose was to impose collective responsibility (*krugovaia poruka*) on the new recruits in order to prevent desertion. PSZ (I) 17: 12748.

33. The *artel'shchik* purchased supplies only by order of the regimental commander. Anichkov, *Voennoe khoziaistvo*, pp. 543–44, 577–78; Leont'ev, *Soldatskaia knizhka*, 1:302–304.

34. Beyrau, *Militär und Gesellschaft*, p. 347.

35. Anichkov, *Voennoe khoziaistvo*, pp. 543–44; Leont'ev, *Soldatskaia knizhka*, 1: 302–304; Enegol'm, *Karmannaia kniga voennoi gigieny*, p. 27.

36. The *skhodka* could meet only by order of the company commander. Klugin, "Russkaia soldatskaia artel'," pp. 81–82, 109–11.

37. "Zapiski soldata Pamfila Nazarova, v inochestve Mitrofana, 1792–1830 gg.," RS 22 (1878): 549–51.

38. SVM, vol. 5, pt. 1, pp. 123–24; Dmitrii Nikitin, "Zametka polkovogo sviashchennika o russkom soldate," VS 36, no. 3 (March 1864): 136; "Temnaia summa," pp. 169–70; TsGVIA, f. 413, d. 27, l. 8–8ob.

39. SVP (1838), ch. 4, kn. 4, st. 86–121.

40. TsGVIA, f. Voenno-uchenyi arkhiv, d. 764, ch. 2, ll. 187–89; TsGAOR, f. 48, op. 1, d. 473, ch. 4, ll. 305ob.–306ob.; Miliutin, *Karmannaia spravochnaia knizhka*, pp. 255–56.

41. It is likely that in the 1820s the regimental commander made these decisions. TsGVIA, f. Voenno-uchenyi arkhiv, d. 764, ch. 2, ll. 188ob.–189ob.

42. Each soldier was supposed to have at least 7.15 silver rubles in the artel fund. Deductions from the munitions money occurred by decision of the soldiers' assembly (*skhodka*) called together only by the company commander and composed of elected and a few appointed noncommissioned officers and veteran soldiers. Deductions from a soldier's pay occurred only when his artel fund contained under 25 paper rubles and did not exceed 1 ruble every 4 months. The government allocated munitions money for the production and oiling of boots, the cleaning of weapons, and the purchase of soap and other items that the soldier carried in his knapsack. SVP (1838), ch. 4, kn. 4, st. 86–121; Anichkov, *Voennoe khoziaistvo*, pp. 416–19, 458, 517, 545–46, 548–49.

43. In addition, the economic sums were used to clean munitions; repair footwear; buy and maintain artel horses, carts, and cooking utensils; support the company chancery, and for various unspecified needs that might arise. SVP

(1838), ch. 4, kn. 4, st. 122–46; Anichkov, *Voennoe khoziaistvo*, pp. 419–20; Miliutin, *Karmannaia spravochnaia knizhka*, pp. 254–60; "Temnaia summa," pp. 184–87; Klugin, "Russkaia soldatskaia artel'," pp. 79–130; TsGAOR, f. 48, op. 1, d. 473, ch. 4, ll. 307–309ob.; TsGVIA, f. Voenno-uchenyi arkhiv, d. 764, ch. 2, ll. 192–94ob.; f. 413, d. 27, ll. 3–8ob.

44. Anichkov, *Voennoe khoziaistvo*, pp. 421–22; Miliutin, *Karmannaia spravochnaia knizhka*, p. 260; TsGVIA, f. Voenno-uchenyi arkhiv, d. 764, ch. 2, ll. 194–95ob.; TsGAOR, f. 48, op. 1, d. 473, ch. 5, ll. 368–71.

45. One observer noted the existence of a prosperous stratum among the lower ranks composed of artisans, noncommissioned officers, men who received money from home, and married soldiers with working wives who provided additional income. The group reportedly numbered thirty to sixty men per company (about one quarter of a company), and its members were defined as men who spent 15 to 40 rubles a year for personal luxuries like tobacco, tea, sugar, liquor, and refreshments. Kononovich, "Nuzhdy soldata i ego raskhody," pp. 161–62; *SVP* (1838), ch. 4, kn. 4, st. 147; *PSZ* (II) 11: 8808; Anichkov, *Voennoe khoziaistvo*, pp. 420–21.

46. TsGVIA, f. Voenno-uchenyi arkhiv, d. 764, ch. 2, ll. 195ob.–214; d. 17184, ch. 2, l. 68; d. 17542, ch. 2, ll. 21ob.–22; ch. 3, l. 28–28ob.; f. 395, op. 101, d. 108, ll. 173–88, 258–59; d. 111, ll. 84–84ob., 89–89ob., 92, 109ob.–10, 135, 139ob., 143ob., 127ob.–28; d. 115, ll. 13–13ob., 16ob.–17ob.; d. 158, ll. 3–13ob.; d. 228, ll. 11–15, 19ob., 23; d. 232, l. 75–75ob.; d. 245, ll. 12–27ob.; d. 246, ll. 7ob.–8, 12ob.–15.

47. These officials were also supposed to check the artel books monthly and report to their units. TsGVIA, f. Voenno-uchenyi arkhiv, d. 764, ch. 2, ll. 190–92, 194ob., 195ob.; Klugin, "Russkaia soldatskaia artel'," pp. 107–10.

48. Klugin, "Russkaia soldatskaia artel'," pp. 108–11, 114.

49. On the limitations of soldiers' complaints as a check on commanders, see Anichkov, *Voennoe khoziaistvo*, pp. 397–99.

50. *PSZ* (I) 29: 22161; (II) 11: 9549; *SVP* (1838), ch. 3, kn. 2, st. 3, appendix to st. 1.

51. *SVM*, vol. 4, pt. 1, bk. 2, sec. 2, appendix 14, p. 76. In 1823 the two thousand pupils of the Kazan Military Orphanage lived in several villages within a 25-verst area. TsGAOR, f. 990, op. 2, d. 783, ll. 1–3.

52. Krestovskii, *Istoriia 14–go Ulanskogo Iamburgskogo polka*, p. 384.

53. Ibid., p. 516; Rossiiskii, *Istoriia 3–go pekhotnogo Narvskogo polka*, p. 420.

54. Anichkov, *Voennoe khoziaistvo*, p. 223; *SVM*, vol. 4, pt. 1, bk. 2, sec. 2, appendix 2, pp. 15–20.

55. Brant, "Kazarmennoe raspolozhenie," pp. 77–100; Miliutin, *Karmannaia spravochnaia knizhka*, p. 819; TsGVIA, f. Voenno-uchenyi arkhiv, d. 17533, ch. 2, ll. 346–47ob. Cf., Serebrenitskii, "Postoi voisk v seleniiakh," pp. 305–44.

56. TsGVIA, f. 395, op. 100, d. 120.

57. Rossiiskii, *Istoriia 3–go pekhotnogo Narvskogo polka*, p. 420; P. Brant, "Polkovoe i rotnoe khoziaistva," *VS* 29, no. 1 (January 1863): 101.

58. *SVM*, vol. 4, pt. 1, bk. 2, sec. 2, appendix 14, pp. 74–76; Serebrenitskii, "Postoi voisk v seleniiakh," pp. 305–306, 311–19.

59. Krestovskii, *Istoriia 14-go Ulanskogo Iamburgskogo polka*, pp. 516–17; *RI*, 8.VI.1818, no. 130, pp. 526–27; 26.VI.1818, no. 145, p. 586; 3.X.1818, no. 229, pp. 921–22.

60. Rossiiskii, *Istoriia 3-go pekhotnogo Narvskogo polka*, p. 420; TsGAOR, f. 48, op. 1, d. 473, ch. 1, ll. 16ob.–17ob.

61. Beyrau, *Militär und Gesellschaft*, pp. 339–40; Curtiss, *The Russian Army under Nicholas I*, p. 250; Mart'ianov, "Polkovoe i rotnoe khoziaistva," pp. 100–101; Krestovskii, *Istoriia 14-go Ulanskogo Iamburgskogo polka*, p. 517; TsGVIA, f. 395, op. 248, d. 17, ll. 28–31; D. A. Miliutin, *Vospominaniia* (Tomsk, 1919), 1: 202, 232, 246; Keep, "From the Pistol to the Pen," p. 306. Even within a single village, economic conditions could vary; Serebrenitskii, "Postoi voisk v seleniiakh," p. 320.

62. D. V. Fedorov, "Igrushechnaia armiia," *IV* 68 (1899): 151–54, 157–59; M. A. Kretchmer, "Vospominaniia," *IV* 31 (1888): 640–41, 652; 32 (1888): 136.

63. *PSZ* (II) 17: 15867, 16113, 16368.

64. *PSZ* (II) 22: 21248.

65. *PSZ* (II) 25: 24409; 26: 25063.

66. Curtiss, *The Russian Army under Nicholas I*, pp. 246–47.

67. M., "O pol'ze obucheniia," pp. 356–57; Mart'ianov, "Eshche neskol'ko slov," p. 377; TsGVIA, f. Voenno-uchenyi arkhiv, d. 17184, ch. 1–4, ll. 47ob.–48; TsGAOR, f. 48, op. 1, d. 473, ch. 1, ll. 16ob.–17.

68. TsGVIA, f. Voenno-uchenyi arkhiv, d. 683, l. 11; d. 691, l. 6ob.

69. For one case where civilian accusations were judged groundless, see TsGVIA, f. 801, op. 61, d. 34, l. 468.

70. TsGVIA, f. 14414, op. 10/291, sv. 265, d. 147, ch. 2, ll. 88–89ob.; ch. 3, ll. 1–2; *RI*, 15.II.1818, no. 39, p. 154.

71. TsGVIA, f. 405, op. 9, d. 51; f. 801, op. 62, d. 610, ll. 48–50; f. 801, op. 61, d. 34, ll. 506–507ob.

72. TsGVIA, f. Voenno-uchenyi arkhiv, d. 764, ch. 2, ll. 112–26ob.; f. 801, op. 73, d. 32, ll. 138–72, 180–94, 205–15.

73. TsGVIA, f. Voenno-uchenyi arkhiv, d. 764, ch. 2, ll. 112–26ob.; f. 801, op. 73, d. 32, ll. 138–72, 180–94, 205–15.

74. A change of commanders could bring an end to conflicts and complaints. TsGVIA, f. 801, op. 62, d. 610, ll. 48–50.

75. *RI*, 3.X.1818, no. 229, pp. 921–22; 8.VI.1818, no. 130, pp. 526–27; 26.VI.1818, no. 145, p. 586; 21.II.1820, no. 43, pp. 170–71; 30.VI.1820, no. 153, pp. 611–12; 10.VII.1820, no. 162, p. 645; 2.XI.1834, no. 277, p. 1107; 10.XI.1834, no. 285, p. 138; Serebrenitskii, "Postoi voisk v seleniiakh," p. 320.

76. Krestovskii, *Istoriia 14-go Ulanskogo Iamburgskogo polka*, p. 519.

77. TsGAOR, f. 48, op. 1, d. 12, ll. 79–80, 83–83ob. See also Rakhmatullin, "Soldaty v krest'ianskom dvizhenii."

78. TsGVIA, f. 489, op. 1, d. 31; f. Voenno-uchenyi arkhiv, d. 709; d. 793, ll. 13–16; f. 395, op. 100, d. 120, l. 27ob.

79. Bogdanovich, *Istoricheskii ocherk*, 2:17; Lalaev, "Nashi nisshie shkoly voennogo vedomstva," 4: 293–94; Apolev, "Ocherki khoziaistva," pp. 21–22, 35–40; "Temnaia summa," pp. 187–90; TsGVIA, f. 48, op. 1, d. 473, ch. 1, l. 49ob. State monies for repairing equipment did not take into account price fluctuations and regional variations. TsGAOR, f. 48, op. 1, d. 473, ch. 1, l. 49ob. On substandard supplies, see *RI*, 29.V.1824, no. 126, pp. 503–504; "Iz zametok veterana, Sergei Gavrilovich Veselitskii," *RS* 11 (1874): 178–79; TsGVIA, f. Voenno-uchenyi-arkhiv, d. 709; d. 764, ch. 3, ll. 215–31.

80. TsGVIA, f. 48, op. 1, d. 473, ch. 1, ll. 39ob.–40.

81. Klugin, "Russkaia soldatskaia artel'," pp. 96–107, 111–12, 124–25.

82. Bogdanovich, *Istoricheskii ocherk*, 2:176; M. Leliukhin, "Zametka o rotnom khoziaistve po predmetu prodovol'stviia nizhnikh chinov," *VS* 52, no. 12 (1866): 279–82; Klugin, "Russkaia soldatskaia artel'," pp. 88–89, 92–93, 111–13.

83. TsGVIA, f. Voenno-uchenyi arkhiv, d. 793, ll. 13–16; Speransky, *O voennykh poseleniiakh*, pp. 7–8.

84. TsGVIA, f. 413, d. 3, ll. 1–5; Podpolkovnik Averkiev, "Kratkii istoricheskii ocherk razrabotki voprosa o polkovom oboze na Kavkaze," *VS* 152, no. 8 (1883): 304–20.

85. *SVM*, vol. 4, pt. 1, bk. 1, sec. 2, appendix 10, pp. 52–53; Klugin, "Russkaia soldatskaia artel'," p. 113. In summer the government did not provide feed for transport horses. If a unit's horses could not be turned out to pasture, the regimental commander purchased feed out of his own pocket. TsGVIA, f. Voenno-uchenyi arkhiv, d. 793, ll. 42ob.–43ob.

86. Anichkov, *Voennoe khoziaistvo*, pp. 559–60, 576; Klugin, "Russkaia soldatskaia artel'," pp. 88–89; TsGVIA, f. 801, op. 87/32, d. 9, ch. 1–2; f. 395, op. 286, d. 389.

87. Klugin, "Russkaia soldatskaia artel'," pp. 88–89; *SVM*, vol. 14, pt. 2, appendix 30, pp. 117–18.

88. Data from the Second Army illustrate the point. See table.

Annual Cost of Provisioning One Soldier (rounded to the nearest ruble)

Year	Province				
	Podolia	Kiev	Kherson	Ekaterinoslav	Bessarabia
1817	57	49	58		81
1818	58	41	50	30	56
1819	33	33	33	28	36
1820	28	27	31	30	24
1821	31	36	44	43	44
1822	37	37	58	54	44
1823	33	29	36	31	39

SOURCE: TsGVIA, f. Voenno-uchenyi arkhiv, d. 792, l. 60.

89. TsGVIA, f. Voenno-uchenyi arkhiv, d. 792, ll. 22–23ob., 26–30ob.
90. TsGVIA, f. Voenno-uchenyi arkhiv, d. 764, ch. 2, ll. 112–16.
91. Ibid., l. 116–116ob.
92. *PSZ* (II) 16: 14526; 23: 22649; Anichkov, *Voennoe khoziaistvo*, p. 89.
93. TsGVIA, f. Voenno-uchenyi arkhiv, d. 793, ll. 38ob.–39ob.; Anichkov, *Voennoe khoziaistvo*, pp. 504–505; Klugin, "Russkaia soldatskaia artel'," p. 129; Lalaev, "Nashi nisshie shkoly voennogo vedomstva," 3: 251; Fezi, *Byt i nravy russkoi armii posle 1812 goda* (St. Petersburg, 1912), pp. 36, 86; Vorontsov, "Instruktsiia rotnym komandiram," pp. 38–39.
94. Kononovich, "Nuzhdy soldata i ego raskhody," pp. 156–57; Fezi, *Byt i nravy russkoi armii posle 1812 goda* (St. Petersburg, 1912), pp. 36, 86; Vorontsov, "Instruktsiia rotnym komandiram," pp. 38–39.
95. TsGVIA, f. Voenno-uchenyi arkhiv, d. 709.
96. A corrupt officer had bought secondhand uniforms for his men, defrauding both the army and the soldiers. TsGVIA, f. 801, op. 61, d. 34, ll. 509–18, 533–37ob. See also Krestovskii, *Istoriia 14-go Ulanskogo Iamburgskogo polka*, p. 295. See the 1823 case of Lieutenant Colonel Mol'chenko, who took 640 rubles from the soldiers' artel to buy horses, as a result of which the men suffered want. TsGVIA, f. 801, op. 70, d. 25, l. 513–513ob. For an 1856 case of recruits having to use their own money to purchase provisions or beg from their comrades, see TsGVIA, f. 395, op. 213, d. 21, ll. 1088–90ob.
97. In 1843 the Grenadier Corps earned about 7,670 silver rubles from state work and about 20,249 silver rubles from private work. TsGVIA, f. Voenno-uchenyi arkhiv, d. 17542, ch. 1, l. 15ob. That same year the Guards infantry and artillery earned about 38,451 silver rubles and 20,004.25 bushels of potatoes at outside work. TsGVIA, f. Voenno-uchenyi arkhiv, d. 17542, ch. 2, l. 22ob. In 1844 the Grenadier Corps earned about 28,587 silver rubles and the Guards Corps about 44,397 silver rubles and about 6054.75 bushels of potatoes. TsGVIA, f. Voenno-uchenyi arkhiv, d. 17542, ch. 3, l. 34–34ob.
98. TsGVIA, f. Voenno-uchenyi arkhiv, d. 17184, ch. 1, l. 21, and ch. 2, ll. 62ob.–63; Baraniusa, "Polkovye unter-ofitserskie shkoly," p. 110; P. Kartsov, "Neskol'ko myslei o vol'nykh rabotakh i dukhovnykh besedakh v voiskakh," *VS* 186, no. 3 (1889): 133–34.
99. Klugin, "Russkaia soldatskaia artel'," pp. 125–26.
100. TsGVIA, f. Voenno-uchenyi arkhiv, d. 709, l. 1. See also TsGVIA, f. 801, op. 61, d. 11, ll. 242–47.
101. Miliutin, *Karmannaia spravochnaia knizhka*, pp. 664–65.
102. Kononovich, "Nuzhdy soldata i ego raskhody," pp. 156–58.
103. TsGVIA, f. Voenno-uchenyi arkhiv, d. 706, l. 7. By 1844 thirty-seven of forty-two Guards units had vegetable gardens, and by the time of the Crimean War, all had them. In the Grenadier Corps only ten of twenty-one units maintained gardens in 1844. TsGVIA, f. Voenno-uchenyi arkhiv, d. 17542, ch. 3, ll. 32–33ob.; Miliutin, *Karmannaia spravochnaia knizhka*, pp. 251–52.
104. In 1843 the Guards Corps harvested 6,131 barrels (*bochka*) of cabbage, 123,751.5 bushels of potatoes, and 1,388.625 bushels of beets. After meeting the

needs of the troops, the surplus products were sold at a value of 329 rubles, 54 kopecks. In 1844 the Corps earned almost 982 silver rubles from the sale of surplus vegetables. The troops experienced years of bounty and of crop failure. In 1844, which was not considered a particularly good year, the Grenadier Corps earned almost 105 silver rubles from the sale of surplus vegetables. TsGVIA, f. Voenno-uchenyi arkhiv, d. 17542, ch. 2, l. 22–22ob.; ch. 3, ll. 15ob., 32–33ob.

105. In 1845 produce from the gardens of the Moscow Garrison was valued at 11,000 silver rubles. Although the 1846 crop was not considered good, it still yielded 84,000 pints of cabbage and 11,500 bushels of potatoes. TsGVIA, f. 395, op. 101, d. 228, l. 4–4ob. In addition to vegetables, some battalions of the Separate Orenburg Corps were able to plant wheat; because of bad weather, the Fourth and Sixth Battalions suffered crop failures in 1846. TsGVIA, f. 395, op. 101, d. 246, ll. 7ob.–8.

106. Kononovich, "Nuzhdy soldata i ego raskhody," pp. 156–59.

107. *PSZ* (I) 24: 17576; TsGVIA, f. 801, op. 61, d. 31. One critic of outside work claimed that the soldiers did not receive proper military training. Joseph Tanski, *Tableau statistique, politique, et moral du système militaire de la Russie* (Paris, 1833), pp. 77–79.

108. *PSZ* (I) 24: 17856.

109. *PSZ* (I) 27: 20581.

110. *PSZ* (I) 34: 26732. See also TsGVIA, f. 801, op. 70/11, d. 11, ll. 470ob.–472.

111. *PSZ* (I) 27: 20865; 37: 28322; Miliutin, *Karmannaia spravochnaia knizhka*, pp. 664–65.

112. There is no clue as to what action the authorities took on this case. TsGVIA, f. Voenno-uchenyi arkhiv, d. 706, l. 7.

113. The soldiers did not complain about the money they had not received, as the remainder was supposedly forthcoming. TsGVIA, f. 801, op. 70, d. 25, ch. 1. See also the case involving complaints from veterans serving in the Tobol'sk half-battalion of military cantonists who were not paid for services performed for the battalion commander. The commander, who already had retired when the case concluded, received a severe reprimand and was ordered to pay the cost of the case and satisfy the financial claims of the soldiers. TsGVIA, f. 405, op. 9, d. 344. On the coercive nature of outside work, see also Kononovich, "Nuzhdy soldata i ego raskhody," pp. 156–59.

114. TsGVIA, f. 36, op. 6, d. 95, ll. 1–3.

115. TsGVIA, f. 395, op. 325, d. 20, ll. 34–39ob.

116. TsGVIA, f. 801, op. 87/32, d. 9, ch. 1, ll. 19–22; ch. 2, ll. 144–144ob., 299ob.; f. 395, op. 286, d. 389, ll. 11–23.

117. TsGVIA, f. 801, op. 87/32, d. 9, ch. 2, l. 299–299ob.

118. Rothenberg, *The Army of Francis Joseph*, p. 76. In the Russian army, outside work remained an economic necessity in the post-reform period. John Bushnell, "The Tsarist Officer Corps, 1881–1914: Customs, Duties, Inefficiency," *AHR* 86, no. 4 (October 1981): 766–67.

119. Efforts during the 1840s to end outside work in the Guards Corps failed

because of irregular state supplies. Kartsov, "Neskol'ko myslei o vol'nykh rabotakh," pp. 139–45; Anichkov, *Voennoe khoziaistvo*, pp. 576–77.

120. Bogdanovich, *Istoricheskii ocherk*, 2: 165–70; V. I. Chicherin, "O polkovykh komandirakh i ikh khoziaistvennykh rasporiazheniiakh," in A. I. Herzen and I. P. Ogarev, eds., *Golosa iz Rossii*, reprint ed. (Moscow, 1974), vypusk 1: 47–49, 96–97; N. Solov'ev, "Kratkii ocherk veshchevogo dovol'stviia nashei armii v pervoi polovine XVIII stoletiia," *VS* 204, no. 3 (1892): 155–58; Leev, "Doreformennaia armiia," pp. 107–109.

121. Krestovskii, *Istoriia 14-go Ulanskogo Iamburgskogo polka*, pp. 165, 329–31; Leliukhin, "Zametka o rotnom khoziaistve," p. 281; Apolev, "Ocherki khoziaistva," pp. 36–39. On abuses, see Menzenkampf, "Obzor sistem inspektirovaniia," pp. 420–26; Leev, "Doreformennaia armiia," pp. 108–109; Chicherin, "O polkovykh komandirakh," pp. 81–83.

122. TsGAOR, f. 48, op. 1, d. 473, ch. 1, l. 51–51ob. TsGVIA, f. 16231, op. 1, d. 90 (1814).

123. Chicherin, "O polkovykh komandirakh"; Bushnell, "The Tsarist Officer Corps," pp. 770–71; Beyrau, *Militär und Gesellschaft*, pp. 344–46. John Keep has correctly challenged this characterization, stressing the element of collusion between officers and soldiers. See *Soldiers of the Tsar*, pp. 177–78.

124. Chicherin, "O polkovykh komandirakh," pp. 47–98; Bushnell, "The Tsarist Officer Corps," pp. 757, 765–69, 774; Keep, "From the Pistol to the Pen," pp. 313–14; Curtiss, *The Russian Army under Nicholas I*, pp. 202, 212–32; Beyrau, *Militär und Gesellschaft*, pp. 335–61; Tanski, *Tableau statistique*, pp. 213–17; Leev, "Doreformennaia armiia," pp. 109–13, 123–25; I. Z–ii, "Zametki o khoziaistve voisk," *VS* 46 (1865): 169–76; *PVM*, 12.I.1835; Alabin, *Chetyre voiny*, 2: 8–9; see TsGVIA, f. Voenno-uchenyi arkhiv, d. 792, ll. 68–78ob.; f. 1, op. 1, d. 4060. On deals between contractors and state officials, see TsGVIA, f. Voenno-uchenyi arkhiv, d. 17184, ch. 4, ll. 179–179ob. Contractors bribed military officials and commanders to accept goods of substandard quality. Reportedly, because official prices were so low, contractors could turn a profit only by supplying deficient grain. Eroshkin, "Voennyi apparat," pp. 150–51; Trubnikov, "Staraia i novaia sistema zagotovleniia," pp. 194–95.

125. Apolev, "Ocherki khoziaistva," pp. 46–47. On the connection between the financial difficulties of many officers and economic abuses, see Beyrau, *Militär und Gesellschaft*; Keep, "From the Pistol to the Pen," pp. 305–307, 313–14; Bushnell, "The Tsarist Officer Corps," pp. 757–58, 768–71. On pay raises for officers as part of an effort in the reign of Alexander I to regularize the supply system, see Keep, "The Russian Army's Response," p. 511. On the poverty of officers in general during the reign of Alexander I, see TsGVIA, f. 11, op. 6, d. 157, l. 79.

126. Wirtschafter, "Military Justice and Social Relations."

127. I. M. Minaev, "Vospominaniia Ivana Men'shogo 1806–1849," *RS* 10 (1874): 53.

128. TsGVIA, f. 395, op. 213, d. 21, l. 1085–1085ob.

129. TsGVIA, f. 801, op. 73, d. 3 (1856); f. 16233, op. 1, d. 618 (1834).

130. *PVM*, 30.III.1837, no. 19.

131. TsGVIA, f. 801, op. 60, d. 22, l. 13. See also TsGVIA, f. 801, op. 61, d. 11, l. 415–415ob. (1799); d. 34, ll. 227–30, 586–88 (1810).

132. TsGVIA, f. 801, op. 61, d. 34, ll. 586–88.

133. TsGVIA, f. 16232, op. 1, d. 15. See also TsGVIA, f. 31, op. 2, sv. 14, d. 41.

134. TsGVIA, f. 801, op. 90, d. 12, ll. 6–27ob. (Orenburg Line Battalion No. 10). See also TsGVIA, f. 801, op. 61/2, d. 250, ll. 889–942ob. (1855).

135. Curtiss, *The Russian Army under Nicholas I*, pp. 213–14; Chicherin, "O polkovykh komandirakh," pp. 50–76.

136. TsGVIA, f. 801, op. 61, d. 34, ll. 509–18, 533–37ob. (Keksgol'mskii Musketeer Regiment).

137. Kretchmer, "Vospominaniia," 31: 644.

138. TsGVIA, f. 801, op. 70/11, d. 2089, ll. 459–78 (1817–18); op. 61, d. 77, ll. 119–63ob. (1827); f. 395, op. 213, d. 21, ll. 1088–90ob. (1856); f. Voenno-uchenyi arkhiv, d. 709, ll. 1–3ob. (1820–26).

139. TsGVIA, f. 395, op. 213, d. 21. See also TsGVIA, f. 801, op. 61, d. 77, ll. 162ob.–163ob. (1829); d. 202, ll. 402–29 (1843); N.F.T., "Golos iz armii," p. 81. For a case where officers stole outright from recruits, see TsGVIA, f. 801, op. 61, d. 77, ll. 119–63ob. (1827).

140. For an able analysis of the relationship between corruption in the military economy and the broader infrastructure of civilian society and economy, see Beyrau's *Militär und Gesellschaft*, pp. 22–30, 117–27, 335–61.

141. TsGVIA, f. Voenno-uchenyi arkhiv, d. 764, ch. 1, ll. 18–29ob. The future Decembrist P. I. Pestel, who worked with Kiselev at Main Headquarters, expressed a similar view. See TsGAOR, f. 48, op. 1, d. 473, ch. 1, ll. 16–19, 39–52ob. See also "Temnaia summa," pp. 165–96. In another sympathetic account, I. Z-yi argued that because of significant price fluctuations that might occur after state prices for forage were fixed for a specified period, regimental commanders and intendant officials reported higher prices than they in fact found. See "Zametki o khoziaistve voisk," pp. 169–76.

142. TsGVIA, f. 801, op. 61, d. 11, ll. 82–85. See also TsGVIA, f. 801, op. 61, d. 11, ll. 242–47 (1800).

143. The case of F. K. Zatler, who served as general intendant of the Southern and Crimean armies during the Eastern war, further illustrates this point. Although in 1858 Zatler was convicted of economic crimes by a military court, he was fully pardoned in 1869. Public opinion was decidedly against Zatler, but observers sympathetic to his plight argued that whatever irregularities he permitted were unavoidable considering the extremely difficult conditions in which the army found itself in the Crimea. Zatler's first duty was to feed the army, so that the illegal measures he adopted were justified. "F. K. Zatler," *RS* 20 (1877): 127–65.

144. The government distributed money for provisions three times a year, i.e., every trimester (*tret'*).

145. TsGVIA, f. 16232, op. 1, d. 142, ll. 229–60ob.

146. For complaints about rotten meal, see TsGVIA, f. 410, d. 67, l. 20ob. In 1800 Captain von Shitz was acquitted of withholding pay and artel monies, after admitting that he reallocated artel funds to pay senior and noncommissioned officers. He also borrowed (and returned) 150 rubles from the company fund. TsGVIA, f. 801, op. 61, d. 11, l. 32. For an 1829 case where a squadron commander illegally used munitions monies for "various unforeseen needs that arose in the squadron," see TsGVIA, f. 801, op. 61, d. 75, ll. 20–38.

147. On the clergy, see Gregory L. Freeze, *The Russian Levites: Parish Clergy in the Eighteenth Century* (Cambridge, Mass.: Harvard University Press, 1977), and idem, *The Parish Clergy in Nineteenth-Century Russia*.

Five. "Justice with Order"

1. Elise Kimerling Wirtschafter, "The Ideal of Paternalism in the Prereform Army," in Ezra Mendelsohn and Marshall Shatz, eds., *Imperial Russia, 1700–1917: State, Society, Culture. Essays in Honor of Marc Raeff* (Dekalb: Northern Illinois University Press, 1988), pp. 95–114. On the popular myth of the "tsar-batiushka" and its hold over the peasantry, see Daniel Field, *Rebels in the Name of the Tsar* (Boston: Houghton Mifflin, 1976), pp. 1–29. On the origins and implications of the epithet "tsar-batiushka," which was only one aspect of the complex and diversified myth of the ruler, see Michael Cherniavsky, *Tsar and People: Studies in Russian Myths* (New Haven: Yale University Press, 1961).

2. The future Decembrist, P. I. Pestel, argued that commanders should control old uniforms, rather than turn them over to the soldiers as their own property. TsGAOR, f. 48, op. 1, d. 473, ch. 1, ll. 1–8ob. See also "Temnaia summa," p. 171.

3. Khatov 1, "O voinskoi distsipline," VZ (1827) 1: 90–127, 3: 41–79, 4: 38–57; "Nachertanie o polevoi egerskoi sluzhbe," VZ, no. 5 (1810): 15–17.

4. See chapter 6. See also *Russkii invalid*, the organ of the War Ministry, which regularly reported sentences meted out to officers.

5. TsGVIA, f. 801, op. 61, d. 34, ll. 509–10.

6. Ibid., ll. 533–37ob.

7. TsGVIA, f. 801, op. 61, d. 34, ll. 533ob.

8. Sometimes soldiers' offenses were excused because of their "simple-mindedness." TsGVIA, f. 16231, op. 1, d. 26 (1812); f. 16233, op. 1, d. 618 (1834).

9. TsGVIA, f. 801, op. 20, d. 2, ll. 127–32 (Perevalovsk Transport Guard Unit).

10. Ibid., ll. 5–25.

11. Ibid., ll. 5, 31ob.–102ob.

12. Ibid., ll. 127–32.

13. Ibid., ll. 129–30ob.

14. *Imperatorskie ukazy i prikazy voennogo ministerstva za 1809*. Ukaz Ego Imperatorskogo Velichestva from 31.I.1810, iz voennoi kollegii.

15. TsGVIA, f. 801, op. 61, d. 27, ll. 3–6. In a humanitarian case decided by the tsar in 1842, one private was pardoned after deserting to visit his mother who

was seriously ill. M. Sokolovskii, "Imperator Nikolai I v voenno-sudnykh konfirmatsiiakh," *RS* 124 (1905): 420.

16. *PSZ* (II) 1: 538.

17. *PSZ* (II) 5: 3675, 3978; 7: 5278; 10: 8658; 11: 8794; 13: 11409; 15: 13263; *SVP* (1838), ch. 2, kn. 1, st. 1420–22, 1462–68; *PVM*, 6.XII.1835; 20.I.1836, no. 36; 21.III.1836, no. 39; 29.IX.1836, no. 110; 20.XII.1837, no. 133.

18. *PSZ* (II) 5: 4008; *PVM*, 22.VII.1837, no. 84.

19. *PSZ* (II) 13: 11680, 11681.

20. *PSZ* (II) 15: 13708.

21. *PSZ* (II) 18: 16455; 19: 17805, 18507; TsGVIA, f. 801, op. 61/2, d. 335, ll. 336–37.

22. TsGVIA, f. 395, op. 286, d. 368.

23. TsGVIA, f. 395, op. 286, d. 250, ll. 52–91.

24. *PSZ* (II) 16: 14460; TsGVIA, f. 801, op. 60, d. 40, ll. 11ob.–12ob.

25. *PVM*, 12.VI.1841, no. 52; 8.VIII.1841, no. 75; *PSZ* (II) 16: 14525. For the amnesty of 1826, see *PSZ* (II) 1:29, 548, 549, 704, 789; 2: 1033; 3: 1847; 6: 4254.

26. *PSZ* (II) 30: 29167–68, 29531; *PVM*, 2.III.1855, no. 68; TsGVIA, f. 801, op. 73, d. 3, ll. 253ob.–58ob., 260–62ob.

27. For a summary of military judicial procedure, see Bogdanovich, *Istoricheskii ocherk*, 2: 412–32; John P. LeDonne, "The Administration of Military Justice under Nicholas I," *CMRS* 13, no. 2 (April–June 1972): 182–83; Keep, "Justice for the Troops," p. 32.

28. The extent to which commanders employed these methods is at this time impossible to determine. Reports of the Guards and Grenadier Corps indicate that in 1843, 208 lower ranks from the Guards were punished with birches for minor infractions without trial or investigation by order of the regimental commander or a higher authority. In 1844, 201 lower ranks in the Guards and 175 in the Grenadier Corps were punished in like manner. TsGVIA, f. Voenno-uchenyi arkhiv, d. 17542, ch. 2, l. 13–13ob.; ch. 3, l. 9ob. Birches represented the lightest form of corporal punishment. For a detailed description of the various types of corporal punishment, see A. G. Timofeev, *Istoriia telesnykh nakazanii v russkom prave* (St. Petersburg, 1904), pp. 219–308.

29. *PSZ* (II) 5: 3835; Sokolovskii, "Imperator Nikolai I," p. 412.

30. *PSZ* (I) 16: 12289.

31. The "light punishments" included running the gauntlet and beatings with sticks. *PSZ* (I) 29: 22322; N. Vish., "Telesnye nakazaniia v voiskakh i ikh otmena," *VS*, no. 10 (October 1904): 140.

32. *SVM*, vol. 12, pt. 1, bk. 1, pp. 155–58; *PSZ* (I) 24: 17588.

33. *PSZ* (I) 28: 21904. Guards regiments were excluded from this rule.

34. *SVM*, vol. 12, pt. 1, bk. 1, pp. 161–63; *PSZ* (I) 26: 19265. Beginning in 1797 the establishment of a military court required either an imperial order or the tsar's confirmation for cases involving all senior (*ober*) and field (*shtab*) officers. *SVM*, vol. 12, pt. 1, bk. 1, p. 186.

35. *PSZ* (I) 27: 20230.
36. *SVM*, vol. 12, pt. 1, bk. 1, pp. 179, 186; *PSZ* (I) 27: 20250.
37. *SVM*, vol. 12, pt. 1, bk. 1, pp. 186–88; *PSZ* (I) 29: 22322; *PVM*, 14.V.1809, no. 63.
38. Regimental commanders generally imposed punishments with birches or sticks without convening a court.
39. *PSZ* (I) 32: 25195.
40. *SVM*, vol. 12, pt. 1, bk. 1, pp. 188–89; *PSZ* (I) 31: 24628.
41. *PSZ* (I) 32: 24975.
42. Commanders-in-chief and commanders of separate corps exercised judicial authority through a field judicial apparatus (*polevoi auditoriat*). See I. Shendzikovskii, "O voennom sude v voennoe vremia," *VS* 206, no. 8 (1892): 315–16.
43. *PSZ* (I) 33: 26022; 34: 26845; 35: 27274, 27420; (II) 7: 5636; 8: 6520; 13: 10873; 21: 20670.
44. *SVP* (1838), ch. 5, kn. 2, st. 388–402; *PSZ* (II) 18: 16491; 19: 17653; LeDonne, "The Administration of Military Justice," pp. 180–91.
45. The General Auditoriat was revived in 1832. *SVP* (1838), ch. 5, kn. 2, st. 421–26; LeDonne, "The Administration of Military Justice," p. 189.
46. *PSZ* (I) 16: 12289.
47. TsGVIA, f. Voenno-uchenyi arkhiv, d. 17184, ch. 2, l. 82.
48. Vorontsov, "Instruktsiia rotnym komandiram," pp. 45–46; *SVM*, vol. 12, pt. 1, bk. 1, pp. 151–52.
49. "Pravila dlia obkhozhdeniia s nizhnimi chinami 12-i pekhotnoi divizii. (Prikaz nachal'nika 12-i divizii, general-leitenanta, grafa Mikhaila Semenovicha Vorontsova)," *VS*, no. 2 (1859): 495–502.
50. Ibid., p. 497.
51. The limits Vorontsov placed upon regimental and brigade commanders fell below those allowed by the 1806 law.
52. The regiments also were required to keep a record of all punishments that were carried out. Vorontsov, "Pravila dlia obkhozhdeniia," pp. 498–502. For a similar effort to limit corporal punishment in the Second Army around 1820, see TsGVIA, f. 16231, op. 1, d. 430, ll. 1–15.
53. Bogdanovich, *Istoricheskii ocherk*, 2: 415.
54. *PSZ* (II) 30: 29218; Bogdanovich, *Istoricheskii ocherk*, 2: 414–15. According to Klugen, formal legal restrictions existed since 1845, though even earlier some commanders had limited punishments by senior officers to twenty-five blows with birches (*rozgi*). L. Klugen, "Neskol'ko slov o telesnom v russkikh voiskakh nakazanii, po pravilam voennoi distsipliny," *VS*, no. 9 (1859): 200, 205–206.
55. Vish., "Telesnye nakazaniia," 10: 137–38; Timofeev, *Istoriia telesnykh nakazanii*, pp. 102–56, 285–87.
56. *SVM*, vol. 12, pt. 1, bk. 1, p. 173; *PSZ* (I) 26: 19814, 20022; Sokolovskii, "Imperator Nikolai I," pp. 399–400, 404.
57. *SVM*, vol. 12, pt. 1, bk. 1, p. 178; *PSZ* (I) 27: 20115; Vish., "Telesnye nakazaniia," 10: 142; Timofeev, *Istoriia telesnykh nakazanii*, p. 244.

NOTES TO CHAPTER 5

58. TsGVIA, f. 801, op. 60, d. 30, l. 11; Klugen, "Neskol'ko slov o telesnom nakazanii," pp. 198–99; Vish., "Telesnye nakazaniia," 11: 117. After execution and maiming, the knout was the harshest form of punishment applied in Russia. Particularly painful and life threatening, the knout was a type of whip with an iron ring and hard, sharp lash at the end. Peter the Great replaced the knout with running the gauntlet for soldiers. Unlike punishment with the knout, which was carried out by a professional executioner and therefore considered dishonorable, running the gauntlet was carried out by the victim's fellow soldiers. Timofeev, *Istoriia telesnykh nakazanii*, pp. 119–29, 218–50, 287–88.

59. Punishment with the knout still applied to host cossacks, but was not to exceed fifty blows. TsGVIA, f. 801, op. 61/2, d. 335, ll. 26–27; *PSZ* (I) 40: 30324; (II) 1: 33; Klugen, "Neskol'ko slov o telesnom nakazanii," pp. 198–99; "O tom, chto ozhidaet soldata za neispravnosti po voennoi sluzhbe," *Chtenie dlia soldat* no. 4 (1857): 42.

60. TsGVIA, f. 801, op. 61/2, d. 335, ll. 141–42ob.; Klugen, "Neskol'ko slov o telesnom nakazanii," p. 199.

61. TsGVIA, f. 801, op. 60, d. 36, l. 12–12ob.; *PSZ* (II) 12: 10815.

62. On Austria, see Rothenberg, *The Army of Francis Joseph*, p. 83; Alan Sked, *The Survival of the Hapsburg Empire* (New York: Longman, 1979), pp. 39–41. On Prussia, see Martin Kitchen, *A Military History of Germany* (Secaucus, N.J.: The Citadel Press, 1976), pp. 44–45. On England, see Roy Palmer, ed. *The Rambling Soldier* (Harmondsworth, Eng.: Kestrel Books, 1977), pp. 65–69. By 1855 the maximum number of lashes that any court-martial could assign was fifty.

63. *SVP* (1838), ch. 5, kn. 1, st. 248–54, 500–502.

64. Vish., "Telesnye nakazaniia," 11: 117.

65. TsGVIA, f. 801, op. 60, d. 38, ll. 13ob.–14ob.

66. Kozhevnikov, "Russkaia armiia posle voin 1812–1814 gg.," *OVRO*, 7: 240; Sokolovskii, "Imperator Nikolai I," pp. 397–420.

67. *PSZ* (I) 30: 23296.

68. *PSZ* (II) 6: 4677.

69. Once the victim recovered, he would undergo the remainder of his sentence. *Imperatorskie ukazy i prikazy voennogo ministerstva za 1809 g.*, Imianyi ukaz from 6.VI.1809, no. 743; *PSZ* (I) 26: 20070; 30: 23691; Timofeev, *Istoriia telesnykh nakazanii*, p. 282.

70. *PVM*, 5.VI.1853, no. 39; *PVM*, 11.II.1855, no. 27.

71. TsGVIA, f. 801, op. 61/2, d. 250; Plesterer, *Istoriia 62-go pekhotnogo Suzdal'skogo polka*, 4: 510–11; "Ivan Skobelev," *RS* 1 (1870): 605; Sokolovskii, "Imperator Nikolai I," p. 404. According to Timofeev, a punishment of three thousand blows by running the gauntlet was tantamount to death; see *Istoriia telesnykh nakazanii*, pp. 284–85. On the reluctance to impose capital punishment, see TsGVIA, f. 801, op. 61/2, d. 335, ll. 242–43ob.

72. *PSZ* (I) 31: 24312; *SVM*, vol. 12, pt. 1, bk. 1, p. 181.

73. *PSZ* (I) 34: 27091; 35: 27528.

74. *PSZ* (II) 5: 3926; 15: 13707; TsGVIA, f. 395, op. 208, d. 66, ll. 48–51ob.

75. TsGVIA, f. 395, op. 208, d. 66, l. 1; *PSZ* (II) 26: 25180; 30: 29424.
76. *PSZ* (I) 26: 20061.
77. TsGVIA, f. 395, op. 178, d. 1181; op. 286, d. 368, ll. 1–41ob.; f. 801, op. 60, d. 28, ll. 4ob.–5 (1823); *PSZ* (I) 35: 27528; 37: 28323, 28841; (II) 17: 15701.
78. *SVP* (1838), ch. 2, kn. 1, st. 967.
79. TsGVIA, f. 395, op. 286, d. 442.
80. TsGVIA, f. 801, op. 61/2, d. 335, l. 351. See also *PSZ* (I) 43: 27091; (II) 22: 20940.
81. Each regiment supposedly kept a record of the punishments meted out to its members (*shtrafnaia kniga*).
82. Bogdanovich reports that crime statistics were kept since 1831 (*Istoricheskii ocherk*, 2: 432).
83. The figures on desertion are probably low. Since officers faced punishment for high rates of desertion, they may have suppressed the actual numbers. The law defined desertion as unauthorized absence for more than three days. *PSZ* (II) 21: 10216.
84. TsGVIA, f. 801, op. 61/2, d. 335, ll. 242–43ob., 254; *PSZ* (I) 37: 28151; (II) 16: 14217; 24: 23514.
85. TsGIA, f. 1286, op. 3, d. 105, ll. 39ob.–40ob., 47–49; *PSZ* (I) 25: 19014; (II) 18: 16655, 16760, 16792, 17011.
86. TsGVIA, f. 14414, op. 10/291, sv. 60, d. 326, ch. 35, ll. 16–17. I am grateful to Professor Walter Pintner for sharing with me the files from fond 14414.
87. *PSZ* (I) 24: 17588; 25: 18319; (II) 18: 16834; *TsGVIA*, f. 801, op. 61, d. 11, l. 192; op. 62, d. 746, l. 15ob.; d. 787, ll. 21ob., 27, 31–31ob.
88. *PSZ* (II) 18: 16455; 19: 17805.
89. *PSZ* (II) 19: 17805.
90. *PSZ* (II) 18: 16455; 19: 17805.
91. *PSZ* (II) 19: 17805; *PVM*, 3.II.1846, no. 29.
92. *PSZ* (II) 21: 20615; *PVM*, 16.XI.1846, no. 179.
93. Legislation clearly suggests that desertion was more likely among unseasoned recruits, but data from the Guards and Grenadier Corps show that in 1843 and 1844, the majority of deserters were older soldiers. Even so, the rate of desertion among recruits still could have been higher. TsGVIA, f. Voenno-uchenyi arkhiv, d. 17542, ch. 2, l. 13ob.; ch. 3, ll. 9ob.–10.
94. TsGVIA, f. 16231, op. 1, d. 2, 118, 139, 195, 196, 251.
95. Only one category of economic crime mentions the lower ranks: "use of lower ranks for private work without pay."
96. Bogdanovich, *Istoricheskii ocherk*, 2: 415; Krestovskii, *Istoriia 14-go Ulanskogo Iamburgskogo polka*, pp. 362–64, 405, 535.
97. A. Kudriavtsev, "O distsiplinarnom ustave izdaniia 1879 goda," *VS*, no. 1 (January 1886): 91.
98. TsGVIA, f. 36, op. 1, d. 605, ll. 31–37ob. (1818); f. 801, op. 61/2, d. 250 (1850); Timofeev, *Istoriia telesnykh nakazanii*, p. 301. Punishments for minor crimes recorded in the reign of Nicholas I include: eighteen men demoted; one received 25 blows with sticks; three received under 100 blows with birches; four-

teen received 100–199 blows; forty-one received 200–299 blows; twenty-four received 300–399 blows; one received 400–499 blows; and three were punished with 500 blows by running the gauntlet, though two of these had also made false claims against superiors. TsGVIA, f. 16232, op. 1, d. 1040; f. 395, op. 286, d. 368; Krestovskii, *Istoriia 14–go Ulanskogo Iamburgskogo polka*, pp. 332, 535.

99. M. Sokolovskii, "Iz russkoi voenno-ugolovnoi stariny," *RS* 119 (August 1904): 365–66.

100. Krestovskii reports that on August 9, 1821, two privates were punished with five hundred blows with birches without a trial for the theft of property valued at about 222 rubles. On August 10, 1821, two other privates were punished by running the gauntlet through five hundred men three times on the basis of a court decision for the theft of property valued at about 263 rubles. Similarly, on October 4, 1821, by order of the regimental commander, again without a court decision, three privates were punished by running the gauntlet through five hundred men two times for the theft of property valued at about 457 rubles; *Istoriia 14–go Ulanskogo Iamburgskogo polka*, p. 535.

101. The following sources record a variety of punishments: TsGVIA, f. 489, op. 1, d. 31, l. 140; f. 395, op. 286, d. 368; d. 442, ll. 2–3; op. 178, d. 1181; f. 801, op. 66, otd. 1, stol 1, d. 1, 14, 24, 38, 45; op. 61/2, d. 250; f. 16232, d. 565, 589, 665, 1009, 1073.

102. John Keep has stressed the important role that maintaining discipline played in the practice of military justice during the reign of Nicholas I ("Justice for the Troops," pp. 26–32).

Six. "Soldiers in Service"

1. *SVP* (1838), ch. 3, kn. 1, st. 792; N.G., "O pretenziiakh nizhnikh chinov," *VS* 46 (1865): 155.

2. TsGVIA, f. Voenno-uchenyi arkhiv, d. 17184, ch. 1, ll. 45ob.–47ob.

3. The transfer, removal, or retirement of a commander also prompted soldiers to express grievances. TsGVIA, f. 801, op. 61, d. 11, l. 32; op. 70/11, d. 11, ll. 459–78; f. 16231, op. 1, d. 90; N.G., "O pretenziiakh nizhnikh chinov," p. 156.

4. Krestovskii, *Istoriia 14–go Ulanskogo Iamburgskogo polka*, p. 369.

5. TsGVIA, f. 16231, op. 1, d. 164, ll. 5–8.

6. Ibid., ll. 15, 19.

7. The emperor considered the officer's punishment insufficient and in February 1819 ordered a trial. As a result, he had to satisfy monetary claims amounting to 4,551 rubles, was arrested for one month, and lost the right to command before receiving special recognition from the authorities. TsGVIA, f. 16231, op. 1, d. 164, ll. 26–29, 49–52, 59, 62–63.

8. TsGVIA, f. Voenno-uchenyi arkhiv, d. 764, ch. 1, ll. 26ob.–27.

9. TsGVIA, f. 410, d. 67, ll. 44–47.

10. TsGVIA, f. 801, op. 20, d. 2, ll. 63ob.–64ob.

11. TsGVIA, f. 801, op. 61/2, d. 250, l. 889.

12. TsGVIA, f. 395, op. 213, d. 21, l. 1089 (1856).

13. Ibid., l. 1084–87. See also Menzenkampf, "Obzor sistem inspektirovaniia," pp. 420–26; TsGVIA, f. Voenno-uchenyi arkhiv, d. 17184, ch. 1, ll. 16ob.–20ob.; d. 764, ch. 1, ll. 22, 26ob.–27.

14. N.G., "O pretenziiakh nizhnikh chinov," p. 156.

15. TsGVIA, f. 801, op. 61, d. 11, l. 32.

16. An ukase of 1796 forbade the use of soldiers' artel and personal funds for other regimental requirements. TsGVIA, f. 801, op. 70/11, d. 25, ch. 4, l. 512. In 1809 the war minister confirmed this law and ordered that pay and munitions money be immediately distributed to soldiers upon receipt by the regiments, forbidding its use for outside purposes. *PVM*, 30.IX.1809, no. 129.

17. The fact that von Shitz could freely borrow 150 rubles from the company fund reflected the vast economic power held by the officers.

18. TsGVIA, f. 16232, op. 1, d. 142, ll. 229–36ob.

19. On the soldiers' suspicions about the economic honesty of superiors, see "Temnaia summa," pp. 170, 192–93; A. Mart'ianov, "Obiazatel'nye vychety iz zhalovan'ia nizhnikh chinov," *VS* 29, no. 1 (January 1863): 114–16.

20. TsGVIA, f. 801, op. 61, d. 11, l. 415–415ob. (Major General Vedemeier's Jager Regiment).

21. TsGVIA, f. 801, op. 61, d. 34, ll. 227–30 (Tambov Garrison Battalion).

22. TsGVIA, f. 801, op. 61/2, d. 250, ll. 889–942ob. (Bilimbaevskii Mounted Transport Guard Unit).

23. Given the soldiers' wishes, Tishchenko's good service, and the fact that when the regimental commander was informed about the money, Tishchenko immediately began an investigation, his sentence was light. In addition to the year he had already spent under arrest, Tishchenko faced another month in the fortress. The soldiers, who were guilty of not informing the authorities when they did not receive the munitions money, received pardons based on the amnesty of 22.VIII.1826. TsGVIA, f. 801, op. 61, d. 75, ll. 28–30 (Second Burgskii Uhlan Regiment).

24. TsGVIA, f. 801, op. 62, d. 66, ll. 8–11ob.

25. Other officers leading parties of recruits repeatedly used the situation for personal gain. TsGVIA, f. 801, op. 61, d. 77, ll. 119–63ob. (1829); f. 395, op. 213, d. 21, ll. 1088–90ob.

26. TsGVIA, f. 801, op. 60, d. 11, l. 364–364ob. (Tsaritsyn Artillery Garrison).

27. TsGVIA, f. 801, op. 61, d. 11, ll. 242–47.

28. The archival file does not indicate the final outcome of this case. TsGVIA, f. 801, op. 61, d. 11, ll. 242–47 (Pushchin Garrison Regiment).

29. The authorities found Siziakov guilty only of granting leaves for illegal periods and of releasing soldiers for improper work. As punishment he lost his rank and received the title of inactive veteran. TsGVIA, f. 801, op. 70/11, d. 11, ll. 459–78. Similar complaints by other lower ranks are found in TsGVIA, f. 801, op. 71/11, d. 11, l. 294ob.; op. 20, d. 2, ll. 5ob.–102ob. (Perevalovsk Transport Guard Unit, 1834); f. 405, op. 9, d. 344, ll. 1–10, 32–33ob. (Tobol'sk cantonist half-battalion, 1839); d. 519, ll. 41–48 (Vitebsk region of ploughing soldiers, 1841).

30. TsGVIA, f. 395, op. 286, d. 389, ll. 4–7; f. 801, op. 61/2, d. 250, ll. 514–19; f. 801, op. 87/32, d. 9, ch. 1–3.
31. TsGVIA, f. 801, op. 61/2, d. 250, ll. 518–19; f. 395, op. 286, d. 389, ll. 4–7.
32. TsGVIA, f. 801, op. 87/32, d. 9, ch. 3, ll. 148–52.
33. Ibid., l. 149.
34. Sokolovskii, "Imperator Nikolai I," pp. 399–400, 404.
35. Vish., "Telesnye nakazaniia," 10: 137–38, 142; Timofeev, *Istoriia telesnykh nakazanii*, pp. 102–19.
36. Vorontsov, "Instruktsiia rotnym komandiram," p. 46.
37. Ibid., p. 39. See also TsGVIA, f. Voenno-uchenyi arkhiv, d. 17817, ll. 1–2.
38. Wirtschafter, "Military Justice and Social Relations," pp. 74–76.
39. *SVM*, vol. 12, bk. 1, appendix 4, pp. 29–30.
40. Ibid.
41. Ibid.
42. Wirtschafter, "Military Justice and Social Relations," p. 75.
43. Dubrovin, "Russkaia zhizn' v nachale XIX veka," pp. 476–82; Brikner, "Zapiski grafa Lanzherona," pp. 33–34; Kozhevnikov, "Russkaia armiia posle voin 1812–1814 gg.," pp. 237–39.
44. Vorontsov, "Pravila dlia obkhozhdeniia," pp. 496–500.
45. TsGVIA, f. Voenno-uchenyi arkhiv, d. 691, l. 9.
46. S. S. Volk and P. V. Vinogradov, "Dva prikaza M. F. Orlova po 16-i divizii (1820–21)," *Literaturnoe nasledstvo* 60, no. 1 (Moscow, 1956): 7–12; TsGVIA, f. 801, op. 70/11, d. 42 (delo Raevskogo); E. A. Prokof'ev, *Bor'ba dekabristov za peredovoe russkoe voennoe iskusstvo* (Moscow, 1953); V. F. Raevskii, "O soldate," *Krasnyi arkhiv* 13 (1925): 309–14.
47. Volk and Vinogradov, "Dva prikaza M. F. Orlova," pp. 8–9; TsGVIA, f. 801, op. 70/11, d. 42, t. 12–V, ch. 1, ll. 75–76.
48. Volk and Vinogradov, "Dva prikaza M. F. Orlova," pp. 7–8; TsGVIA, f. 801, op. 70/11, d. 42, t. 7–V, l. 104–104ob.
49. TsGVIA, f. 16231, op. 1, d. 430, l. 1–1ob.; Leev, "Doreformennaia armiia," pp. 98–100, 105–106, 123.
50. TsGVIA, f. 16231, op. 1, d. 430, ll. 2–3; f. Voenno-uchenyi arkhiv, d. 17184, ch. 1, ll. 45ob.–46ob.
51. "Prikaz 2–i armii," *VS*, no. 4 (1858): 477–79.
52. TsGVIA, f. Voenno-uchenyi arkhiv, d. 17184, ch. 1, l. 45ob.
53. L.K., "Soldat i ofitser," *VS* 4, no. 8 (1858): 345; Joseph Tanski, *Tableau statistique*, pp. 268–69.
54. TsGVIA, f. 801, op. 70/11, d. 42, t. 2, 7–V.
55. TsGVIA, f. 801, op. 60, d. 11, ll. 29–29ob. (Plutalov Garrison Regiment). Sviatikhin was sentenced to loss of noble patents and dismissal from the service.
56. TsGVIA, f. 801, op. 91, d. 28, ll. 65–70 (Black Sea Line Battalion No. 8).
57. TsGVIA, f. 801, op. 91, d. 28, ll. 15–16, 66–67ob.
58. TsGVIA, f. 801, op. 91, d. 28, l. 65.
59. TsGVIA, f. 801, op. 91, d. 28, l. 85ob.
60. TsGVIA, f. 801, op. 61/2, d. 250 (Samara Veterans' Company).

61. TsGVIA, f. 801, op. 62, d. 720, ll. 43–54; op. 60, d. 11, ll. 449–50 (Shreider 2's Dragoon Regiment).
62. Nineteen men from the squadron were punished with sticks or by running the gauntlet for previous crimes. TsGVIA, f. 801, op. 62, d. 720, ll. 52–54.
63. Lachin was guilty of conducting exercises at an illegal time, but did not receive any punishment beyond the arrest of four months and three weeks he already had served. TsGVIA, f. 801, op. 60, d. 11, ll. 449ob.–50; op. 62, d. 720, l. 4.
64. TsGVIA, f. 36, op. 1, d. 605, ll. 4–7ob.
65. Ibid., ll. 8ob.–12.
66. TsGVIA, f. 36, op. 1, d. 605, ll. 8–12.
67. TsGVIA, f. 36, op. 1, d. 605, ll. 12ob.–13.
68. Ibid., ll. 21–25.
69. TsGVIA, f. 36, op. 1, d. 605, ll. 31–37ob.
70. Ibid., ll. 39–41.
71. For this view, see Lalaev, "Nashi nisshie shkoly voennogo vedomstva," 4: 289; Kutuzov, "Sostoianie gosudarstva v 1841 godu," pp. 523–24.
72. Shchigolev was eventually stripped of all ranks and demoted to private. TsGVIA, f. 801, op. 61, d. 34, ll. 254–62. For a similar case, see TsGVIA, f. 801, op. 61, d. 34, ll. 351–53.
73. V. Matveev, "O telesnom nakazanii," VS no. 4 (1858): 480–82; L.K., "Soldat i ofitser," pp. 333–46; Klugen, "Neskol'ko slov o telesnom nakazanii," pp. 191–210; Dubrovin, "Russkaia zhizn' v nachale XIX veka," p. 476; Brikner, "Zapiski grafa Lanzherona," p. 33.
74. TsGVIA, f. Voenno-uchenyi arkhiv, d. 17184, ch. 1, l. 45ob.
75. TsGVIA, f. 16231, op. 1, d. 360, ll. 2–5 (Starol'skii Infantry Regiment).
76. The use of rods was illegal.
77. TsGVIA, f. 16231, op. 1, d. 360, ll. 1–1ob., 17. For another case where a private shot and killed himself after a noncommissioned officer illegally dealt him one hundred blows with sticks for theft and threatened to repeat this if he did not return the stolen goods, see TsGVIA, f. 16233, op. 1, d. 563 (Poltava Infantry Regiment, 1834).
78. TsGVIA, f. 801, op. 60, d. 11, ll. 350–51.
79. TsGVIA, f. 16232, op. 1, d. 142.
80. TsGVIA, f. 801, op. 62, d. 746.
81. TsGVIA, f. 801, op. 62, d. 787.
82. Vorontsov, "Pravila dlia obkhozhdeniia," p. 499.
83. TsGVIA, f. Voenno-uchenyi arkhiv, d. 709, l. 2.
84. TsGVIA, f. 16231, op. 1, d. 430, ll. 1–3.
85. TsGVIA, f. Voenno-uchenyi arkhiv, d. 17184, ch. 1, l. 45ob.; Leev, "Doreformennaia armiia," pp. 98–100, 105–106; Kozhevnikov, "Russkaia armiia posle voiny 1812–1814 gg.," p. 241.
86. Iu. G. Oksman, *Dekabristy. Sbornik otryvkov iz istochnikov* (Moscow and Leningrad, 1926), pp. 60–62; Volk and Vinogradov, "Dva prikaza M.F. Orlova," pp. 7–12.

NOTES TO CHAPTER 6

87. TsGVIA, f. Voenno-uchenyi arkhiv, d. 709, l. 2–2ob.; *Arkhiv Grafov Mordvinovykh*, 8: 400–404.

88. TsGVIA, f. 395, op. 101, d. 111, ll. 81ob., 87, 41ob.–42, 49ob.–50, 67ob., 133, 137, 141.

89. *PVM*, 7.I.1841, no. 2; TsGVIA, f. 395, op. 101, d. 115, l. 121; d. 228, l. 3.

90. TsGVIA, f. 16232, op. 1, d. 1022, 1040.

91. TsGVIA, f. 801, op. 62, d. 805, ll. 3–6ob. For later cases of soldiers fleeing under the influence of comrades, see TsGVIA, f. 16232, op. 1, d. 982 (1828); f. 801, op. 66, otd. 1, stol 1, d. 14 (1842).

92. TsGVIA, f. 14414, op. 10/291, sv. 60, d. 326, ch. 10, 16. For similar cases, see TsGVIA, f. 16232, op. 1, d. 984, 990, 1040; f. 16233, op. 1, d. 565, 589, 1009; f. 801, op. 66, otd. 1, stol 1, d. 1, 38.

93. TsGVIA, f. 14414, op. 10/291, sv. 60(273), d. 326, ch. 47, l. 7ob.

94. The private, aged 56, was sentenced to running the gauntlet. TsGVIA, f. 16233, op. 1, d. 1073.

95. This private, aged 25, was sentenced to 1,500 blows by running the gauntlet followed by lifelong assignment to a convicts' company. TsGVIA, f. 801, op. 66, otd. 1, stol 1, d. 38 (1842).

96. TsGVIA, f. 14414, op. 10/291, sv. 60(273), d. 326, ch. 10.

97. TsGVIA, f. 16233, op. 1, d. 1033 (1829); d. 565 (1834); f. 801, op. 66, otd. 1, stol 1, d. 5 (1842).

98. TsGVIA, f. 14414, op. 10/291, sv. 60(273), d. 326, ch. 32 (Twelfth Infantry Division).

99. Sokolovskii, "Imperator Nikolai I," p. 420.

100. TsGVIA, f. 14414, op. 10/291, sv. 60, d. 326, ch. 12, l. 5–5ob. (Tatar Uhlan Regiment).

101. Ibid., sv. 60, d. 326, ch. 24, l. 52; ch. 35, l. 24.

102. Ibid., sv. 60, d. 326, ch. 4, l. 2.

103. Ibid., sv. 60, d. 326, ch. 47, l. 6 (Kavlergard Regiment).

104. TsGVIA, f. 36, op. 1, d. 1109, ll. 21–22ob.

105. TsGVIA, f. 14414, op. 10/291, sv. 60(273), d. 326, ch. 26, l. 2 (Dneprovskii Infantry Regiment). See also TsGVIA, f. 16233, op. 1, d. 665.

106. TsGVIA, f. 801, op. 61, d. 202, ll. 390–93 (Second Training Carabineer Regiment).

107. Ibid., ll. 472–519ob. (Orenburg Line Battalion No. 1).

108. See also TsGVIA, f. 14414, op. 10/291, sv. 60, d. 326, ch. 21, ll. 4–11 (1832); f. 801, op. 61, d. 202, ll. 390–93 (1850).

109. TsGVIA, f. 801, op. 62, d. 226, ll. 375–82ob. (Azov Regiment).

110. Ibid., ll. 375, 388–89.

111. TsGVIA, f. 801, op. 61, d. 34, ll. 509–18, 533–37ob. (Keksgol'mskii Regiment).

112. TsGVIA, f. 395, op. 286, d. 250, ll. 57–58.

113. TsGVIA, f. 395, op. 286, d. 389, ll. 4–7; f. 801, op. 61/2, d. 250, ll. 514–19.

114. TsGVIA, f. 395, op. 286, d. 389, ll. 4–7; f. 801, op. 87/32, d. 9, ch. 1–3.

115. Eight lower ranks were prosecuted: one sergeant major for not restraining the men, when they announced a desire to complain to Loman, and seven others for "inappropriate statements" made when they returned to the barracks. Due to their good behavior during the lengthy trial and in recognition of their previously unblemished records, their sentences were light: demotion to gunner and transfer to various garrisons. TsGVIA, f. 395, op. 286, d. 389, ll. 4–7; f. 801, op. 61/2, d. 250, ll. 518–19; op. 87/32, d. 9, ch. 3, ll. 46–48, 148–52,

116. TsGVIA, f. 801, op. 73, d. 32, ll. 138–72, 180–94, 205–15.

117. The bombardier and seventeen gunners from Company No. 4 were found guilty of "overt disobedience." Except for four gunners, deemed medically unfit to undergo corporal punishment, and one gunner who had died, all were sentenced to run the gauntlet through one hundred men two to four times, followed by three to five years in a convicts' company. The four gunners also faced three years in a convicts' company. Eighteen gunners from Companies No. 5 and 6, who had returned to their quarters on October 17, faced punishment with birches and lost the right to obtain leaves or retire "until they atone for their crime with zealous service and irreproachable behavior." Two noncommissioned officers were demoted to gunners and transferred to another artillery garrison for failing to ensure that the men of Companies No. 5 and 6 returned to work. Shchetinin faced two weeks' arrest in the guardhouse for "inefficiency" in provisioning his unit.

118. There are several adequate accounts of these events. See V. A. Fedorov, *Soldatskoe dvizhenie v gody dekabristov, 1816–1825 gg.* (Moscow, 1963).

119. Anatole G. Mazour, *The First Russian Revolution, 1825* (Stanford, Calif.: Stanford University Press, 1937), pp. 518–63; Fedorov, *Soldatskoe dvizhenie*, pp. 72–160; Kozhevnikov, "Russkaia armiia posle voin 1812–1814 gg.," pp. 241–48; Timofeev, *Istoriia telesnykh nakazanii*, pp. 258–60.

120. In 1823 Schwarz was appointed a captain in the military colonies; but in 1850 he was again found guilty of cruelty, permanently dismissed from the service, and forbidden to reside in the capitals. Mazour, *The First Russian Revolution*, p. 60; Fedorov, *Soldatskoe dvizhenie*, p. 157.

121. A. Shebalov, "Soldaty Moskovskogo polka o 14 Dekabria 1825 g.," *Krasnyi arkhiv* 13 (1925): 288–92; V. Syroechkovskii, "Vosstanie Chernigovskogo polka v pokazaniiakh uchastnikov," *Krasnyi arkhiv* 13 (1925): 1–67; "Rasskaz I. Ia. Telesheva o 14 Dekabria 1825 g.," *Krasnyi arkhiv* 13 (1925): 284–88; V. Ia. Bogucharskii, "Den' 14 dekabria 1825 goda v Peterburge," *OVRO*, 7: 262.

122. The soldiers received punishments of one thousand to three thousand blows by running the gauntlet followed by transfer to the Caucasus Corps. TsGVIA, f. 14414, op. 1, d. 202, ll. 4–7, 11.

Conclusion. "The Semi-Standing Army"

1. Bushnell, *Mutiny amid Repression*.

SELECT BIBLIOGRAPHY

This bibliography is selective and does not include individual files from archival collections or articles from prerevolutionary Russian journals. These references are too numerous to list, though they are cited in the footnotes.

Archives

Central State Military Historical Archive, Moscow (TsGVIA)

f. 11	Inspectors' Department (*ekspeditsiia*) of the War College
f. 395	Inspectors' Department of the War Ministry (*inspektorskii departament*)
f. 801	Military Judicial Department of the War Ministry (*auditoriatskii departament*)
f. 16231	Chancery of the Commander of Main Headquarters of the First Army
f. 16232	Chancery of the Commander of Main Headquarters of the Second Army
f. 16233	Field Judicial Department (*polevoi auditoriat*) of the First Army
f. 14014	Main Headquarters of the First Army
f. 14414	Main Headquarters of the Second Army
f. 489	Collection of service lists (*formuliarnye spiski*)
f. 1	Chancery of the War Ministry
f. 36	Chancery of the General of the Day of His Imperial Majesty's Main Headquarters
f. 405	Chancery of the War Ministry, Section of the Ober-Auditor of the Department of Military Settlements
f. 413	Materials on military theory (*teoriia voennogo iskusstva*) and construction of the armed forces of Russia
f.	Voenno-uchenyi arkhiv

Central State Archive of the October Revolution, Moscow (TsGAOR)

f. 48	Decembrists

Personal fonds:

f. 672	Emperor Nicholas I
f. 825	Bakunin
f. 917	P. G. Divov
f. 990	B. L. Mansurov
f. 1053	N. F. Romanchenko
f. 1155	Ia. I. Rostovtsev

SELECT BIBLIOGRAPHY

Central State Historical Archive, Leningrad (TsGIA)
f. 1262   Recruitment Committee of the Second Department of His Majesty's Personal Chancery
f. 1281   Governors' reports
f. 1284   Governors' reports
f. 1286   Department of Executive Police (*departament politsii ispolnitel'noi*)
f. 1287   Governors' reports

Printed Sources

Alabin, P. *Chetyre voiny. Pokhodnye zapiski v 1849, 1853, 1854–56 i 1877–78 godakh*. 4 parts. Moscow, 1890.
Aleksandrov, V. A. *Obychnoe pravo krepostnoi derevni Rossii. XVIII–nachalo XIX v*. Moscow, 1984.
Aleksandrov, V. A. *Sel'skaia obshchina v Rossii (XVII–nachalo XIX v.)*. Moscow, 1976.
Anichkov, Viktor. *O khoziaistve voisk v voennoe vremia*. St. Petersburg, 1863.
Anichkov, V. M. *Voennoe khoziaistvo. Sravnitel'noe issledovanie polozhitel'nykh zakonodatel'stv Rossii, Frantsii, Prusii, Avstrii, Sardinii, Bel'gii i Bavarii*. St. Petersburg, 1860.
Arkhiv Gosudarstvennogo Soveta. 5 vols. St. Petersburg, 1869–1904.
Arkhiv Grafov Mordvinovykh. 10 vols. St. Petersburg, 1901–1903.
Baiov, A. *Kurs istorii russkogo voennogo iskusstva*. Vypusk VII. St. Petersburg, 1913.
Bairashevskii, O. A. *Organizatsiia sanitornoi sluzhby (mirnogo vremeni) v glavneishikh evropeiskikh armiiakh*. St. Petersburg, 1910.
Belovinskii, L. V. "Russkaia gvardiia v XVIII–XIX vekakh," *Voprosy istorii*, no. 9 (September 1983): 94–105.
Beskrovnyi, L. G. *Ocherki po istochnikovedeniiu voennoi istorii Rossii*. Moscow, 1957.
Beskrovnyi, L. G. *Russkaia armiia i flot v XVIII veke*. Moscow, 1958.
Beskrovnyi, L. G. *Russkaia armiia i flot v XIX veke*. Moscow, 1973.
Best, Geoffrey, and Wheatcroft, Andrew, eds. *War, Economy, and the Military Mind*. Totowa, N.J.: Rowan and Littlefield, 1976.
Beyrau, Dietrich. "La formation du corps des officiers russes au XIXe siècle: De la 'militarisation' à la 'professionalisation,'" *Cahiers du monde russe et soviétique* 19, no. 3 (July–September 1978): 309–10.
Beyrau, Dietrich. *Militär und Gesellschaft im Vorrevolutionären Russland*. Cologne: Bohlau Verlag, 1984.
Beyrau, Dietrich. "Von der Niederlage zur Agrarreform: Leibeigenschaft und Militärverfassung in Russland nach 1855," *Jahrbücher für Geschichte Osteuropas* 23, no. 2 (1975): 191–212.
Blum, Jerome. *Lord and Peasant in Russia from the Ninth to the Nineteenth Century*. Princeton, N.J.: Princeton University Press, 1971.

SELECT BIBLIOGRAPHY

Bobrovskii, P. O. *Perekhod Rossii k reguliarnoi armii*. St. Petersburg, 1885.
Bogdanov, L. P. *Russkaia armiia v 1812 godu*. Moscow, 1979.
Bogdanovich, M. I., ed. *Istoricheskii ocherk deiatel'nosti voennogo upravleniia v Rossii (1855–1880 gg.)*. 6 vols. St. Petersburg, 1879–81.
Bohac, Rodney D. "The Mir and the Military Draft," *Slavic Review* 47, no. 4 (Winter 1988): 652–66.
Bois, Jean-Pierre. "Les anciens soldats de 1715 à 1815. Problèmes et methodes," *Revue historique* 265 (1981): 81–102.
Borisevich, A. I. "Istoricheskoe obozrenie deiatel'nosti intendanstva v 1825–1850," *Intendantskii zhurnal*, no. 6 (June 1905) and no. 7 (July 1905): 15–30.
Brett-James, Antony. *Life in Wellington's Army*. London: George Allen and Unwin, 1972.
Brooks, E. Willis. "Reform in the Russian Army, 1856–1861," *Slavic Review* 43, no. 1 (Spring 1984): 63–82.
Büsch, Otto. *Militärsystem und Sozialleben im Alten Preussen, 1713–1807: Die Anfange der Sozialen Militärisierung der preussisch-deutschen Gesellschaft*. Berlin: De Gruyter, 1962.
Bushnell, John. *Mutiny amid Repression: Russian Soldiers in the Revolution of 1905–1906*. Bloomington: Indiana University Press, 1985.
Bushnell, John. "Peasants in Uniform: The Tsarist Army as a Peasant Society," *Journal of Social History* 13, no. 4 (Summer 1980): 565–76.
Bushnell, John. "The Tsarist Officer Corps, 1881–1914: Customs, Duties, Inefficiency," *The American Historical Review* 86, no. 4 (October 1981): 753–80.
Charukovskii, A. A. *Voenno-pokhodnaia meditsina*. 5 parts. St. Petersburg, 1836.
Cherniavsky, Michael. *Tsar and People: Studies in Russian Myths*. New Haven: Yale University Press, 1961.
Chernov, S. N. *Iz istokov russkogo osvoboditel'nogo dvizheniia*. Saratov, 1960.
Chernyshev, A. I. *Istoricheskoe obozrenie voenno-sukhoputnogo upravleniia s 1825 po 1850 god*. St. Petersburg, 1850.
Corvisier, André. *L'armée française de la fin du XVIIe siècle au ministère du Choiseul: Le Soldat*. 2 vols. Paris: Presses universitaires de France, 1964.
Corvisier, André. *Armies and Societies in Europe, 1494–1789*. Trans. Abigail T. Siddall. Bloomington: Indiana University Press, 1979.
Craig, Gordon A. *The Politics of the Prussian Army, 1640–1945*. New York: Oxford University Press, 1956.
Cross, A. G., ed. *Russia and the West in the Eighteenth Century*. Newtonville, Mass.: Oriental Research Partners, 1983.
Curtiss, John Shelton. *The Russian Army under Nicholas I, 1825–1855*. Durham, N.C.: Duke University Press, 1965.
Curtiss, John Shelton. *Russia's Crimean War*. Durham, N.C.: Duke University Press, 1979.
Davydov, Denis. *Voennye zapiski*. Moscow, 1982.

SELECT BIBLIOGRAPHY

Denikin, A. I. *The Career of a Tsarist Officer.* Trans. Margaret Patoski. Minneapolis: University of Minnesota Press, 1975.

Druzhinin, I. M. *Gosudartsvennye krest'iane i reforma P. D. Kiseleva.* 2 vols. Moscow and Leningrad, 1946 and 1958.

Duffy, Christopher. *Russia's Military Way to the West: Origins and Nature of Russian Military Power, 1700–1800.* London: Routledge and Kegan Paul, 1981.

Dvenadtsat' soldatskikh pesen. St. Petersburg, 1898.

Enesol'm, I. I. *Karmannaia kniga po voennoi gigiene, ili zamechaniia o sokhranenii zdorov'ia russkikh soldat.* St. Petersburg, 1813.

Eroshkin, N. P. "Voennyi apparat tsarskoi Rossii v period Krymskoi voiny (1853–1856 gg.)," *Trudy Moskovskogo Gosudarstvennogo Istoriko-Arkhivnogo Instituta* 9 (Moscow, 1957): 138–76.

Esper, Thomas. "The Odnodvortsy and the Russian Nobility," *Slavonic and East European Review* 45, no. 104 (1967): 124–34.

Fadeev, R. *Vooruzhennye sily Rossii.* Moscow, 1868.

Fedorov, A. V. *Obshchestvenno-politicheskoe dvizhenie v russkoi armii.* Moscow, 1958.

Fedorov, A. V. *Russkaia armiia v 50–70 gg. XIX veka.* Leningrad, 1959.

Fedorov, V. *Vooruzhennye sily russkoi armii v XIX stoletii.* St. Petersburg, 1911.

Fedorov, V. A. *Soldatskoe dvizhenie v gody dekabristov, 1816–1825 gg.* Moscow, 1963.

Fezi. *Byt i nravy russkoi armii posle 1812 goda.* St. Petersburg, 1912.

Field, Daniel. *Rebels in the Name of the Tsar.* Boston: Houghton Mifflin, 1976.

Filimonov. *Postepennoe razvitie meropriiatii po mobilizatsii russkoi kadrovoi armii v XIX stoletii.* St. Petersburg, 1908.

Flisfish, Emmanuel. *Kantonisty.* Tel Aviv: Effect Publications, 1983.

Freeze, Gregory L. *The Parish Clergy in Nineteenth-Century Russia: Crisis, Reform, Counter-Reform.* Princeton, N.J.: Princeton University Press, 1983.

Freeze, Gregory L. *The Russian Levites: Parish Clergy in the Eighteenth Century.* Cambridge, Mass.: Harvard University Press, 1977.

Freeze, Gregory L. "The *Soslovie* (Estate) Paradigm and Russian Social History," *The American Historical Review* 91, no. 1 (February 1986): 11–36.

Frey, Sylvia R. *The British Soldier in America.* Austin: University of Texas Press, 1981.

Fuller, William C., Jr. *Civil-Military Conflict in Imperial Russia, 1881–1914.* Princeton, N.J.: Princeton University Press, 1985.

Fuller, William C., Jr. "Civilians in Russian Military Courts, 1881–1904," *The Russian Review* 41, no. 3 (July 1982): 288–305.

Gertsen, A. I., and Ogarev, N. P., eds. *Golosa iz Rossii.* 4 vols. Reprint ed. Moscow, 1974.

Gessen, S. *Soldatskie volneniia v nachale XIX veka.* Moscow, 1929.

Gessen, S. *Soldaty i matrosy v vosstanii dekabristov.* Moscow, 1930.

Gilbert, Felix, ed. *The Historical Essays of Otto Hintze.* New York: Oxford University Press, 1975.

Glinka, F. N. *Podarok russkomu soldatu*. St. Petersburg, 1818.
Haythornthwaite, Philip J. *Weapons and Equipment of the Napoleonic Wars*. Poole, Dorset, U.K.: Blanford Press, 1979.
Hirschbiel, Henry. "The District Captains of the Ministry of State Properties in the Reign of Nicholas I: A Case Study of Russian Officialdom, 1838–1856." Ph.D. dissertation. New York University, 1978.
Houlding, J. A. *Fit for Service: The Training of the British Army, 1715–1795*. New York: Oxford University Press, 1981.
Ivanov, A., and Ianovskii, A. *Uchebnaia kniga dlia chteniia voennym kantonistam*. St. Petersburg, 1850.
Jones, Robert E. *The Emancipation of the Russian Nobility*. Princeton, N.J.: Princeton University Press, 1973.
Kaminskii, L. S., and Novosel'skii, S. A. *Poteri v proshlykh voinakh*. Moscow, 1947.
Kartsov. *Istoriia Leib Gvardii Semenovskogo polka*. St. Petersburg, 1852.
Keegan, John. *The Face of Battle*. New York: Penguin, 1978.
Keep, John L. H. "Catherine's Veterans," *The Slavonic and East European Review* 59, no. 3 (July 1981): 385–96.
Keep, John L. H. "From the Pistol to the Pen: The Military Memoir as a Source on the Social History of Pre-Reform Russia," *Cahiers du monde russe et soviétique* 21, no. 3–4 (July–December 1980): 295–320.
Keep, John L. H. "Justice for the Troops: A Comparative Study of Nicholas I's Russia and France under Louis-Philippe," *Cahiers du Monde russe et soviétique* 27, no. 2 (1986): 26–48.
Keep, John L. H. *Soldiers of the Tsar: Army and Society in Russia, 1462–1874*. New York: Oxford University Press, 1985.
Keep, John L. H. "The Case of the Crippled Cadet: Military Justice in Russia under Nicholas I," *Canadian Slavonic Papers* 28, no. 1 (March 1986): 35–51.
Keep, John L. H. "The Russian Army's Response to the French Revolution," *Jahrbücher für Geschichte Osteuropas* 28 (1980): 500–23.
Kenez, Peter. "A Profile of the Prerevolutionary Officer Corps," *California Slavic Studies* 7 (1973): 121–58.
Kimerling [Wirtschafter], Elise. "A Social History of the Lower Ranks in the Russian Army, 1796–1855." Ph.D. dissertation. Columbia University, 1983.
Kimerling [Wirtschafter], Elise. "Soldiers' Children, 1719–1856: A Study of Social Engineering in Imperial Russia," *Forschungen zur osteuropäischen Geschichte* 30 (1982): 61–136.
Kiraly, Bela K., ed. *East Central European Society and War in the Era of Revolutions, 1775–1856*. New York: Brooklyn College Press, 1984.
Kitchen, Martin. *A Military History of Germany*. Secaucus, N.J.: The Citadel Press, 1975.
Klochkov, M. V. *Ocherki pravitel'stvennoi deiatel'nosti vremeni Pavla I*. Petrograd, 1916.
Komarov, A. A. "Razvitie takticheskoi mysli v russkoi armii v 60–90–kh godakh

XVIII v.," *Vestnik Moskovskogo Universiteta*, Series 8, History, no. 3 (May–June 1982): 57–66.

Korneev, V. M., and Mikhailov, L. V. *Meditsinskaia sluzhba v Otechestvennuiu voinu 1812 goda.* Leningrad, 1962.

Kratkoe izvlechenie iz zakonov sluzhashchee rukovodstvom pri proizvodtsve i reshenii voenno-sudnykh del. St. Petersburg, 1818.

Kratovskii, Vladimir. *Obzor rasporiazhenii po prodovol'stvii deistvuiushchei armii v 1831, 1848, 1849 i 1853–1855 godakh.* St. Petersburg, 1874.

Krestovskii. *Istoriia 14-go Ulanskogo Iamburgskogo eia imperatorskogo vysochestva velikoi kniazhny Marii Aleksandrovny polka.* St. Petersburg, 1873.

Krieger, Leonard. *Kings and Philosophers, 1689–1789.* New York: W. W. Norton, 1970.

LeDonne, J. P. "The Administration of Military Justice under Nicholas I," *Cahiers du monde russe et soviétique* 13, no. 2 (April-June 1972): 180–91.

LeDonne, J. P. "Civilians under Military Justice during the Reign of Nicholas I," *Canadian American Slavic Studies* 7, no. 2 (Summer 1973): 171–87.

LeDonne, John P. "Outlines of Russian Military Administration, 1762–1796. Part I: Troop Strength and Deployment," *Jahrbücher für Geschichte Osteuropas* 31, no. 3 (1983): 321–47.

LeDonne, John P. "Outlines of Russian Military Administration, 1762–1796. Part II: The High Command," *Jahrbücher für Geschichte Osteuropas* 33, no. 2 (1985): 175–204.

LeDonne, John P. "Outlines of Russian Military Administration, 1762–1796. Part III: Military Finance: The Commissary Budget of 1780," *Jahrbücher für Geschichte Osteuropas* 34, no. 2 (1986): 188–214.

Leont'ev, A. N. *Soldatskaia knizhka.* 2 vols. 2d ed. St. Petersburg, 1866.

Le Roy Ladurie, Emmanuel. "The Conscripts of 1868," in *The Territory of the Historian.* Chicago: University of Chicago Press, 1979.

McFarlin, H. A. "Recruitment Norms for the Russian Civil Service in 1833: The Chancery Clerkship," *Societas: A Review of Social History* 3, no. 1 (Winter 1973): 61–73.

McFarlin, H. A. "The Extension of the Imperial Russian Civil Service to the Lowest Office: The Creation of the Chancery Clerkship, 1827–1833," *Russian History* 1, no. 1 (1974): 1–17.

McNeal, Robert H. *Tsar and Cossack, 1855–1914.* New York: St. Martin's Press, 1985.

Makhotin, N. A. *Karmannaia spravochnaia knizhka dlia russkikh ofitserov.* 3d ed. St. Petersburg, 1861.

Mavrodin, V. V. "K voprosu o perevooruzhenii russkoi armii v seredine XIX veka," in *Problemy istorii feodal'noi Rossii.* Leningrad, 1971.

Mazour, Anatole G. *The First Russian Revolution, 1825.* Stanford, Calif.: Stanford University Press, 1937.

Miliutin, D. A. *Karmannaia spravochnaia kniga dlia russkikh ofitserov.* St. Petersburg, 1856.

SELECT BIBLIOGRAPHY

Miliutin, D. A. *Vospominaniia*. Tomsk, 1919. Reprint ed., Newtonville, Mass.: Oriental Research Partners, 1979.

Mudrov, M. *Slovo o pol'ze i predmetakh voennoi gigieny ili nauka sokhranit' zdorovie voenno-sluzhashchikh*. Moscow, 1809.

Obrazovanie intendantskogo upravleniia. St. Petersburg, 1812.

Obzor rasporiazhenii po prodovol'stviiu deistvuiushchei armii v 1831, 1848, 1849 i 1853–55 godakh. St. Petersburg, 1874.

Oksman, Iu. G. *Dekabristy. Sbornik otryvkov iz istochnikov*. Moscow and Leningrad, 1926.

O polevoi sluzhbe sobstvenno k voennomu vremeni otnosiashcheisia. St. Petersburg, 1827.

Orlovsky, Daniel. "Recent Studies on the Russian Bureaucracy," *The Russian Review* 35, no. 4 (October 1976): 448–67.

Otechestvennaia voina i russkoe obshchestvo. 7 vols. Moscow, 1911–12.

"Otryvki iz dnevnika rotnogo komandira I. I. Gladilova, 1841 goda," *Sbornik starinnykh bumag khraniashchikhsia v muzee P.I. Shchukina* 8 (Moscow, 1901): 171–85.

Palmer, Roy, ed. *The Rambling Soldier*. Harmondsworth, Eng.: Kestrel Books, 1977.

Pavlenko, N. I. *Petr Pervyi*. Moscow, 1975.

Petrov, A. N. *Russkaia voennaia sila*. 2 vols. Moscow, 1892.

Pintner, Walter M. "The Burden of Defense in Imperial Russia, 1725–1914," *The Russian Review* 43, no. 3 (July 1984): 231–59.

Pintner, Walter McKenzie, and Rowney, Don Karl, eds. *Russian Officialdom: The Bureaucratization of Russian Society from the Seventeenth to the Twentieth Century*. Chapel Hill: University of North Carolina Press, 1980.

Pipes, Richard. *Russia under the Old Regime*. New York: Scribner, 1974.

Pipes, Richard. "The Russian Military Colonies, 1810–1831," *Journal of Modern History* 22, no. 3 (September 1950): 205–19.

Plesterer, L. *Istoriia 62-go pekhotnogo Suzdal'skogo Generalissimusa Kniazia Italiiskogo Grafa Suvorova-Rymskogo polka*. 6 vols. Belostok, 1902.

Polevoi, I. A. *Rasskazy russkogo soldata*. St. Petersburg, 1852.

Polnoe sobranie zakonov rossiiskoi imperii. First series, 1649–1825, 45 vols. St. Petersburg, 1830; Second series, 1825–81, 55 vols. St. Petersburg, 1830–84.

Polozhenie o kazennykh zagotovlenniiakh vedomstva voennogo ministerstva. St. Petersburg, 1838.

Popov, G. M. *Sbornik boevykh bytovykh i pliasovykh soldatskikh pesen*. 2 parts. Khar'kov, 1888.

Prikazy voennogo ministra. St. Petersburg, 1809–68.

Prokhodtsov, I. I. *Riazanskaia guberniia v 1812 godu*. 2 vols. Riazan, 1913.

Prokof'ev, E. A. *Bor'ba dekabristov za peredovoe russkoe voennoe iskusstvo*. Moscow, 1953.

Prokof'eva, L. S. *Krest'ianskaia obshchina v Rossii vo vtoroi polovine XVIII–pervoi polovine XIX veka*. Leningrad, 1981.

Prudnikov, Iu. F. "K voprosu komplektovaniia russkoi armii (1794–1796 gg.),"

Vestnik Moskovskogo Universiteta, Series 8, History, no. 4 (July–August 1970): 15–25.

Rabinovich, M. D. "Sotsial'noe proiskhozhdenie i immushchestvennoe polozhenie ofitserov reguliarnoi armii v knotse Severnoi voiny," in N. I. Pavlenko, ed., *Rossiia v period reform Petra I*. Moscow, 1973.

Radishchev, A. N. *A Journey from St. Petersburg to Moscow*. Ed. Roderick Page Thaler, trans. Leo Wiener. Cambridge, Mass.: Harvard University Press, 1958.

Radozhitskii, I. *Pokhodnye zapiski artillerista, s 1812 po 1816 god*. 4 parts. Moscow, 1835.

Raeff, Marc. *Origins of the Russian Intelligentsia*. New York: Harcourt, Brace and World, 1966.

Raeff, Marc. *The Well-Ordered Police State: Social and Institutional Change through Law in the Germanies and Russia, 1600–1800*. New Haven: Yale University Press, 1983.

Ransel, David L., ed. *The Family in Imperial Russia*. Urbana-Champaign: University of Illinois Press, 1978.

Ransel, David L. *Mothers of Misery: Child Abandonment in Russia*. Princeton, N.J.: Princeton University Press, 1988.

Rediger, A. *Komplektovanie i ustroistvo vooruzhennoi sily*. St. Petersburg, 1900.

Rediger, A. *Uchebnye zapiski po voennoi administratsii*. St. Petersburg, 1888.

Rediger, A. *Ustroistvo polevogo upravleniia v nashei armii*. St. Petersburg, 1890.

Rieber, Alfred J., ed. *The Politics of Autocracy*. Paris: Mouton, 1966.

Roberts, J. M. *The French Revolution*. Oxford: Oxford University Press, 1978.

Rossiiskii, M. A. *Ocherk istorii 3–go pekhotnogo Narvskogo General-Fel'dmarshala Kniazia Mikhaila Golitsyna polka*. Moscow, 1905.

Rothenberg, Gunther E.; Kiraly, Bela K.; and Sugar, Peter F., eds. *East Central European Society and War in the Pre-Revolutionary Eighteenth Century*. Boulder, Colo.: Social Science Monographs, 1982.

Rothenberg, Gunther E. *The Army of Francis Joseph*. West Lafayette, Indiana: Purdue University Press, 1976.

Rothenberg, Gunther E. *The Art of Warfare in the Age of Napoleon*. Bloomington: Indiana University Press, 1978.

Sbornik voenno-istoricheskikh materialov. Vypusk XVI. St. Petersburg, 1904.

Screen, J.E.O. *The Helsinki Yunker School, 1846–1879: A Case Study of Officer Training in the Russian Army*. Studia Historica 22. Helsinki: Painokaari, 1986.

Screen, J.E.O. "Russian Officer Training in the 1860s–70s: The Helsinki Yunker School," *The Slavonic and East European Review* 65, no. 2 (April 1987): 210–17.

Semevskii, M. I., ed. *Graf Arakcheev i voennye poseleniia, 1809–1831*. Reprint ed. Cambridge, Eng.: Oriental Research Partners, 1973.

Shepelev, L. E. *Otmenennye istoriei—chiny, zvaniia, i tituly v Rossiiskoi imperii*. Leningrad, 1977.

Shtraikh, S. *Brozhenie v armii pri Aleksandre I*. Petrograd, 1922.

Sked, Alan. *The Survival of the Hapsburg Empire*. New York: Longman, 1979.

Skobelev, I. *Podarok tovarishcham, ili perepiska russkikh soldat v 1812 godu.* St. Petersburg, 1833.

Smirnov, Ia. *Istoriia 65-go Pekhotnogo Moskovskogo Ego Imperatorskogo Vysochestva Gosudaria naslednika tsesarevicha polka, 1642–1700–1890.* Warsaw, 1890.

Sobranie zakonov i postanovlenii do chasti voennogo upravleniia otnosiashchikhsia. St. Petersburg, 1816–30.

Sosedko, F. D. *Istoriia 72-go pekhotnogo Tul'skogo polka, 1769–1901.* Warsaw, 1901.

Sovetskaia voennaia entsiklopediia. 8 vols. Moscow, 1976–80.

Speransky, M. M. *O voennykh poseleniiakh.* St. Petersburg, 1825.

Stanislawskii, Michael. *Tsar Nicholas I and the Jews. The Transformation of Jewish Society in Russia, 1825–1855.* Philadelphia: The Jewish Publication Society, 1983.

[Statistik]. *Naem rekruta v polovine XIX-go stoletiia v Arkhangel'skoi gubernii.* Arkhangel'sk, 1912.

Stefanovskii, N., and Solov'ev, N. *Ocherk sanitarnogo sostoianiia Krymskoi armii v kampaniiu 1854–1856 gg.* Moscow, 1972.

Stein, Hans-Peter. "Der Offizier des Russischen Heeres im Zeitabschnitt zwischen Reform und Revolution (1861–1905)," *Forschungen zur osteuropäischen Geschichte* 13 (1967): 346–507.

Stoletie voennogo ministerstva. 13 vols. St. Petersburg, 1902–14.

Stolpianskii, N. P. *Soldatskaia azbuka.* St. Petersburg, 1873.

Sviachenko. "Khronika zhizni soldatskogo syna Dmitriia Zhurby," *Sovremennik* 110, no. 9 (1865): 33–113; no. 10: 283–361.

Svod rossiiskikh uzakonenii po chasti voenno-sudnoi. St. Petersburg, 1820.

Svod voennykh postanovlenii. 12 vols. St. Petersburg, 1838.

Svod zakonov rossiiskoi imperii. 15 vols. St. Petersburg, 1842.

Tanski, Joseph. *Tableau statistique, politique et moral du système militaire de la Russie.* Paris, 1833.

Tikhov, P. I. *Meditsina v Rossii v epokhu Napoleonovskikh voin.* St. Petersburg, 1913.

Timofeev, A. G. *Istoriia telesnykh nakazanii v russkom prave.* St. Petersburg, 1904.

Torke, Hans-Joachim. "Das russische Beamtentum in der ersten Hälfte des 19. Jahrhunderts," *Forschungen zur osteuropäischen Geschichte* 13 (1967): 7–345.

Trike, I. *Pamiatnaia knizhka dlia nizhnikh chinov, napominaiushchaia im o znachenii i dolge russkogo soldata i o glavnykh obiazannostiakh ego v razlichnye periody sluzhby.* St. Petersburg, 1853.

Vagts, Alfred. *A History of Militarism.* Revised ed. New York: Meridian Books, 1959.

Verzhbitskii, V. G. *Revoliutsionnoe dvizhenie v russkoi armii s 1826 po 1859 g.* Moscow, 1964.

Voennaia entsiklopediia. 18 vols. (incomplete). St. Petersburg, 1911–15.

SELECT BIBLIOGRAPHY

Voennaia sluzhba spaseniiu dushi ne pomekha ili soldat vozvrativshiisia posle pokhoda na rodinu. Povest'. St. Petersburg, 1850.

Voinskii ustav o pekhotnoi sluzhbe. St. Petersburg, 1848.

Volk, S. S., and Vinogradov, P. V., eds. "Dva prikaza M. F. Orlova po 16–i divizii (1820–21)," *Literaturnoe nasledstvo* 60, no. 1 (Moscow 1956): 7–12.

Voprosy voennoi istorii. Moscow, 1965.

Vysochaishie kofirmovannye doklady o snabzhenii i usilenii vydelki v gosudarstve sukon i o obrazovanii Glavnogo pravleniia manufaktur. St. Petersburg, 1808.

Wildman, Allan K. *The End of the Russian Imperial Army.* Princeton, N.J.: Princeton University Press, 1980.

Wilson, Sir Robert Thomas. *Brief Remarks on the Character and Composition of the Russian Army and a Sketch of the Campaigns in Poland in the Years 1806 and 1807.* London, 1810.

Wilson, Sir Robert Thomas. *A Sketch of the Military and Political Power of Russia in the Year 1817.* London, 1817.

Wirtschafter, Elise Kimerling. "The Ideal of Paternalism in the Prereform Army," in Ezra Mendelsohn and Marshall Shatz, eds., *Imperial Russia, 1700–1917: State, Society, Opposition. Essays in Honor of Marc Raeff.* Dekalb: Northern Illinois University Press, 1988.

Wirtschafter, Elise Kimerling. "The Lower Ranks in the Peacetime Regimental Economy of the Russian Army, 1796–1855," *The Slavonic and East European Review* 64, no. 1 (January 1986): 40–65

Wirtschafter, Elise Kimerling. "Military Justice and Social Relations in the Prereform Army, 1796 to 1855," *Slavic Review* 44, no. 1 (April 1985): 67–82.

Woloch, Isser. *The French Veteran from the Revolution to the Restoration.* Chapel Hill: University of North Carolina Press, 1979.

Wrigley, E. A. *Population and History.* New York: McGraw-Hill, 1969.

Zacek, Judith Cohen. "The Lancastrian School Movement in Russia," *The Slavonic and East European Review* 45, no. 105 (July 1967): 343–67.

Zaionchkovskii, A. M. *Vostochnaia voina 1853–1856.* 2 vols. St. Petersburg, 1908.

Zaionchkovskii, P. A., ed. *Dnevnik D. A. Miliutina.* 4 vols. Moscow, 1947–50.

Zaionchkovskii, P. A. *Pravitel'stvennyi apparat samoderzhavnoi Rossii v XIX v.* Moscow, 1978.

Zaionchkovskii, P. A. *Voennye reformy 1860–1870 godov v Rossii.* Moscow, 1952.

Zaitsov, Pavel. *Kurs voennoi administratsii.* Moscow, 1867.

Zatler, Fedor. *O gospitaliakh v voennoe vremia.* St. Petersburg, 1861.

Zatler, Fedor. *Uchast' ranenykh i bol'nykh vo vremia voiny,* 2d ed. St. Petersburg, 1868.

Zatler, Fedor. *Zapiski o prodovol'stvii voisk v voennoe vremia.* 4 vols. St. Petersburg, 1860–65.

Zolotarev, V. A.; Mezhevich, M. N.; and Skorodumov, D. E. *Vo slavu otechestva rossiiskogo.* Moscow, 1984.

INDEX

Åbo, 145
Academy of Arts, 168n
Active Army, 31, 80, 103, 144
Åland, 77, 145
Aleksei Mikhailovich, Tsar, 12
Alexander I, Tsar, xvi, xviii, 4, 6, 48, 61, 64, 70, 76, 88, 97, 103–105, 118, 127–28, 135, 186n
Alexander II, Tsar, 101, 130, 163n
Arkhangel'sk, 13, 17, 19; garrison, 108
army, xiii–xiv, xix, 111, 149–51, 153–54n; combat readiness, 69–70; guard duty, 65–66; manpower problem, 15–18, 24–25, 31, 107–108, 161n; reserves, 161n; social relations, 149–50; state works, 66, 174–75n, 184n
artel, 38, 69, 77–81, 83, 87, 94–95, 123–25, 143, 180–81n, 188n, 194n. *See also* regimental economy
artel'shchik, 78–79, 81, 180n
artillery, 37, 40–41, 43, 64, 80, 165n
Artillery Half-Company No. 1, 89
artisans, 63–64, 87, 165n, 181n
Astrakhan (province), 156n
Astrakhan Grenadier Regiment, 132–33
Austria, 13, 44, 84, 90, 106, 140, 154n, 191n
Azov Infantry Regiment, 11, 46, 197n

Baltic: provinces, 12, 160n; Sea, 156n. *See also* Estland; Kurland; Lithuania
Barclay de Tolly, M. B., 28
barracks. *See* quartering
Bessarabia, 12–13, 15, 73, 75, 83, 86, 138, 156n, 178n, 183n
Bilimbaevskii Mounted Transport Guard Unit, 194n
Biretov, Captain, 138
Black Sea, 12, 162n; Line Battalion No. 8, 195n
Bzhetsk, 81

cantonists. *See* soldiers' children
carabineer, 108

Catherine the Great, Empress, 6, 36, 102, 104, 127
Caucasus, xviii, 3, 13, 38, 82, 86, 100, 156n; Corps, 36, 108–109, 115, 198n; Division, 93–94
cavalry, 37, 40, 86, 115, 176n
Central Asia, 3
Chernyshev, A. I., 65–66, 89
Chtenie dlia soldat, 55, 59
clergy, 11, 18, 44–46, 59, 156n, 166n
Commissariat Department, 90; *prikaz*, 74
Committee of Ministers, 156n
Congress of Vienna, 3, 70
conscription, 3–25; evasion, 5–9, 12, 17–20, 155n; exemptions, 11–15, 156n, 159–60n; government policy, 9–20; popular attitudes toward, 4–9, 164n; process of, 8, 18–25, 156n, 158–61n. *See also* recruits
Constantine Pavlovich, 147
convicts' companies, 7, 101, 108, 197–98n
corporal punishment. *See* military justice; noncommissioned officers; officers; soldiers
cossacks, 17, 44, 46–47, 93–94, 191n; Don, 140; Ukrainian, 164n
courts-martial. *See* military justice
crime, 108–16, 192n. *See also* military justice; officers; regimental economy; soldiers
Crimea, 76, 174n, 187n
Crimean War, xvi, xviii, 3, 8, 15–16, 19, 23, 34, 50–51, 69, 71–72, 75, 156n, 160n, 173n, 184n, 187n
cruelty. *See* military justice; noncommissioned officers; officers; soldiers
cuirassiers, 108, 139

Daghestan, 83
Danubian Army, 97
Decembrist revolt, 100
Decembrists, xviii, 147–48
decorations (military orders, monetary awards, etc.), 51–53, 78, 100, 104, 130

INDEX

demotion. *See* military justice
Denikin, A. I., 167n
desertion, 32–33, 69–70, 77, 99–100, 108–15, 129, 133, 137–42, 180n, 192n; and abuses by officers, 138–39; reasons for, 137–42, 188–89n, 197n
diad'ka ("uncle," older soldier), 56; role in training, 58, 171n
Dibich, I. I., 59, 132–33, 135
Dinaburg Garrison Regiment, 123
discipline. *See* military justice; training
disobedience, 115–16, 142–48, 198n
Dneprovskii Infantry Regiment, 197n
Dreniakin, Colonel, 137
drunkenness, 98, 117, 129, 133, 135, 137–39, 140–41, 143. *See also* desertion; military justice

Eastern War. *See* Crimean War
economic fund (*s"estnaia, kharchevaia summa*). *See* artel
Ekaterinoslav, 86, 93, 178n, 183n
Eliseev, Captain, 131
emancipation, 161n
engineering troops, 37, 40, 43, 64, 80, 108
England, 84, 106, 191n
equipment, 77. *See also* regimental economy
Estland, 14

feldsher, 131, 165n
Fifth Infantry Corps, 83
Finland, 12, 166n
Finnish Corps, 80, 108
First Army, 128, 132, 147
First Carabineer Regiment, 108
folklore, 154n
Forty-third Jager Regiment, 92
France, 44, 61, 64, 84, 106, 154n, 169n
Frederick the Great, 60, 72
"free farmers," 155n
French revolution, 170n
fusiliers, 133–34

garrisons, 108. *See also* Internal Guards Corps
general staff (*glavnyi shtab*). *See* Main Headquarters
Georgia, 12–13, 80
Glinka, F. N., 163n
Great Reforms, xvi, 54

grenadier, 100, 108, 135, 142, 144, 175n; Corps, 32, 61, 67, 80, 88, 184–85n, 189n, 192n
Grodno, 15
guards, 40–41, 49, 51, 76, 81, 86, 100, 166n; Corps, 32, 61, 64, 80, 88, 106, 108, 111, 112, 115, 172n, 184–86n, 189n, 192n
Guards Grenadier Regiment, 62, 101
health. *See* medical facilities; soldiers; training
hospitals. *See* medical facilities
Hungary, 3

Iakovlev, Sergeant Major, 97
Ialutorovskii Veterans' Unit, 89
Iamburg Uhlan Regiment, 67, 81, 174n, 176n
Iaroslavl, 10, 19, 37, 63; Demidov School of Higher Education, 48
infantry, 37, 40, 44, 51, 61, 115, 143–44
inspections, 57–58, 69–71, 83–84, 121–22, 175–76n
Inspectors' Department, xvii, 12, 19, 39, 89, 108, 161n
Internal Guards Corps, 48–49, 51, 91, 108, 115

Jager Regiment No. 35, 46
jagers, 45
Jews, 154–56n. *See also* conscription; minorities
junkers (*iunker*), 42–45

Kamchatka Infantry Regiment, 173n
Kavlergard Regiment, 197n
Kazan, 158n; military orphanage, 181n
Keksgol'mskii Musketeer Regiment, 87, 97, 187n, 197n
Kherson, 76, 86, 137, 178n, 183n
Kiev, 10, 12, 37, 48, 63, 86, 178n, 183n
Kiliia, 73, 94
Kinburn Artillery Garrison, 38, 89–90, 126, 144–45
Kirghiz, 141
Kiselev, P. D., xvii, xviii, 13, 27–28, 62, 65, 67–68, 71, 75, 86, 93, 128–29, 139, 178n, 187n
Kniazhnin, Colonel, 97–98, 143
knout, 143, 191n. *See also* military justice
Korf, Baron M. A., 22

INDEX

Kostroma, 10, 37, 63
Kovno, 19
Kridner, Major, 132–36
Krymaium, Field Captain, 134
Kurland, 12
Kursk, 10, 37, 63

Lachin, Field Captain, 131–32, 196n
Lancastrian schools, 64
Larionov, Lieutenant, 4
Light Company No. 34, 121
line system. *See* conscription
literacy. *See* noncommissioned officers; officers; soldiers; training
Lithuania, 13, 83
Loginov, Border Guard, 140
Loman, Lieutenant Colonel, 89–90, 126, 144, 198n
lottery system. *See* conscription
lower ranks (*nizhnie chiny*), 41–42. *See also* noncommissioned officers; soldiers
Lubenskii Hussar Regiment, 46

Main Headquarters (*glavnyi shtab*), xvii, 105
maneuvers. *See* training
Mart'ianov, Colonel, 125
medical facilities, 28–29, 76
merchants, 11–12, 18, 75
military colonies, 13, 25, 38, 164n
Military Judicial Department (*general auditoriat*), 91–92, 102–104, 109, 131–32, 146, 190n
military justice, 28, xvii, 57; courts-martial, 189n; government policy, 96–102; mercy, 99–101, 188–89n, 194n; punishments, 52–53, 97–100, 102–109, 118–19, 132–37, 140–44, 189n, 190–93n, 196–98n
Military Medical Academic Committee, 131
military orphanage, 64
military society, xvi, 40–45, 150; social mobility, 53–54
militia, 14
Ministry of Interior, 6, 8, 156n
Ministry of State Domains, 22
minorities, 7–15, 17, 44–46, 82–84, 156n, 158n, 166n
modernization, xiii, xvi, 54
Mordvinov, N. S., 4, 9

Moscow, 20, 140; Foundling Home, 36, 39; Garrison, 88, 185n; University, 48
musketeers. *See* infantry

Napoleonic Wars, xviii, 3, 15, 50, 69–70, 84, 103, 128, 175n. *See also* War of 1812
Nazarov, P., 78
Nepenin, A. G., 128
Nicholas I, Tsar, xvi–xviii, 5, 13, 20, 22, 29, 34, 43, 48, 54, 61–62, 67, 70, 76, 82, 89, 97, 100, 104–106, 108–109, 118, 130, 140–41, 163–64n, 175n, 192–93n
Nikanov, Private, 137
nobles, 10–11, 14, 18, 44–50, 114, 117, 124, 141, 159n. *See also* officers; personal nobles
noncommissioned officers, 37, 42–47, 52, 60, 133–35, 153n, 166n, 180–81n, 188n, 198n; duties of, 173n; powers, 196n; qualifications, 42–43, 167n; social mobility, 44–45. *See also* junkers; officers; *podpraporshchiki*; training
Novgorod, 9–10, 20, 37, 63

Obreskov, M. A., 155n
Odessa, 83
odnodvortsy (single householders), 19, 34, 44–47, 49, 159n
officers, xiv, 27, 44, 189n; cruelty, 117–18, 126–36, 141–42, 144, 198n; economic crimes, 80–81, 88–89, 91–94, 97–99, 117–18, 181n, 184n, 187n, 194n; judicial powers, 102–107, 109, 118–19, 169n, 188n, 190n; poverty of, 186n; promotion to, 40–41, 45–52, 166n, 168–69n; punishment of, 111–12, 115, 124, 130, 193–96n, 198n; relations with soldiers, 88, 91, 135–36. *See also* military justice; regimental economy; soldiers; training
Okerman, Captain, 144
Okhotsk Jager Regiment, 83
Oranienbaum Veterans' Unit, 125
Orel, 77
Orenburg, 92; Cavalry Inspectorate, 56; Corps, 49, 80, 88, 108, 111, 115, 165n, 185n; Line Battalion No. 10, 187n, 197n
Orlov, M. F., 64, 128, 139
Ostrog, 83

INDEX

pakhatnye soldaty (ploughing soldiers), 100, 194n
Papsuev, Lieutenant, 138
paternalism, 58, 96–97, 127
Paul, Tsar, xvi, 50, 70, 102, 124, 143
Pavlov, Major, 130
peasants, 10–11, 19, 44–47, 58, 61, 68, 73, 75, 82–85, 91, 99, 118–20, 134, 138, 159–60n, 166n, 170n, 175n
Penza, 4
Perevalovsk Transport Guard Unit, 194n
Perm, 17
Persia, 3, 83
personal nobles, 41
Pestel, P. I., xvii, 39, 71, 128, 160n, 170n, 187–88n
Peter the Great, Tsar, xiii, xvi, 9, 11, 28, 54, 74, 174n, 178n, 191n
Petrov, Private, 143
Pisanskii, Captain, 142–43
pioneers (*pionery*). *See* engineering troops
Plutalov Garrison Regiment, 195n
Podolia, 86, 178n, 183n
podpraporshchiki, 44, 46. *See also* junkers; noncommissioned officers
Podzhio, A. V., 71
Poland, 3, 14, 141, 156n
Polevoi, N. A., 170–71n
Polizeistaat, xiii, 59, 171n
Poltava, 27; Infantry Regiment, 196n
Potemkin, G. A., 36
Preobrazhenskii Guards Regiment, 88–89
prikazy obshchestvennogo Prizreniia, 165n
promotion, 38–40. *See also* officers
Prussia, 13, 84–85, 106, 139, 154n, 156n, 191n
Pskov, 6, 10, 14, 37, 63; Infantry Regiment, 33
Pushchin Garrison Regiment, 194n

quartering, 70, 81–85, 174–75n. *See also* regimental economy; training

Raevskii, V. F., xvii, 128, 130, 173n
raznochintsy, 46, 48
rebellion, 115, 147–48. *See also* Decembrist revolt
recruiting station (*rekrutskoe prisutstvie*), 5, 7, 23
Recruitment Committee, xviii, 6, 16–18, 24

recruits, 3, 106–107, 122, 125, 138, 180n, 194n; and desertion, 192n; physical requirements, 11, 15–18, 24, 157–58n, 161n; social data, 10–11, 160n; substitutes, 19–20, 158–60n. *See also* conscription; training
regimental economy: and company commander, 77–79, 87, 180n; corruption, 80–81, 88–95, 186–88n; government policy, 94–95; local variations, 82–83, 85–87, 149, 182–83n, 187n; pay, 53, 76, 78, 180n, 188n, 194n; and quartering, 75, 77, 82; rations, 75–77, 145–47, 178–79n; and regimental commander, 77, 79, 179–80n, 183n; self-sufficiency, 85–90, 184–85n; sources of supply, 74–77, 83–85, 178–80n, 183n, 187–88n, 194n; subsistence, 74, 80. *See also vol'nye raboty*
reserve depots (*zapasnye depo*), 57
Riazan, 5, 7, 10, 37, 63; Garrison Battalion, 47; Veterans' Unit, 47
Riga, 19, 138
Russkii invalid, 84, 188n
Rybinsk (Iaroslavl province), 165n

Sacen, General, 128
sacristans (*tserkovniki*), 41, 43–47
St. Petersburg, 6, 10, 20, 37–38, 62–63, 71, 87, 108, 178n; Engineering Unit, 88; Foundling Home, 36, 39; Main Pedagogical Institute, 48
Samara Veterans' Company, 195n
sapper. *See* engineering troops
Saratov, 10, 35, 37, 63, 73
Schwarz, Colonel, 147, 198n
Second Army, 27, 59, 62, 64, 67–68, 75, 86–87, 94, 128–29, 138–39, 174n, 178n, 183n, 190n
Second Burgskii Uhlan Regiment, 194n
Second Carabineer Company, 123–24
Second Training Carabineer Regiment, 197n
Sedikin, Lieutenant, 98–99
self-mutilation. *See* conscription
self-sufficiency. *See* regimental economy
Semenovskii Guards Regiment, 173n; rebellion in, 147
Senate, 5, 18, 103
senior officers' children (*ober-ofitserskie deti*), 44–45

212

INDEX

serfs. *See* peasants

service: burden of, 16–20, 24–25; indefinite leaves, 34, 161n, 164–65n; terms of, 33–34, 155n. *See also* noncommissioned officers; officers; soldiers

Sevastopol, 36, 100

Seventeenth Infantry Division, 67

Shchetinin, Ensign, 145–47, 198n

Shchigolev, Major, 136, 196n

Sheniavskii, Private, 141

Sheremetev estate, 159n

Shreider 2's Dragoon Regiment, 196n

Siberia, 3, 5, 7, 13, 38, 86, 101, 124, 143, 156n, 165n

Siberian Cavalry Inspectorate, 56

Siberian Corps, 49, 108, 115

Simbirsk, 6

single householders. *See odnodvortsy*

Sixteenth Infantry Division, 128, 139

Sixth Infantry Corps, 32, 67, 73, 80, 111

Siziakov, Second Lieutenant, 125–26, 194n

skhodka. See artel

Smolensk, 10, 37, 63, 89; Garrison, 65–66

social mobility. *See* promotion

soldiers, xiii–xiv, xix, 153n; attitudes toward service, 132–33; bravery of, 55, 72–73, 151; family life, 36–38, 46–47, 165–66n, 181n; government expectations, 69–70, 73; grievances, 120–23, 136, 142–44, 149–50, 193n; health of, 26–33, 62, 69–70, 81–82, 107–108, 161–64n; legal status, 32–36, 39–40, 150, 165–66n; leisure activities, 60; noncombat, 37, 41–42; and peasant rebellion, 73, 84; relations with civilians, 75, 83–85, 135, 182n; relations with officers, 60, 69, 123–36, 182n, 194n; retirement, 34–35, 100, 164–65n; suicide, 30, 137–38, 196n. *See also* army; *diad'ka*; military justice; officers; regimental economy; service; soldiers' children; soldiers' wives; training

soldiers' children (*soldatskie deti*), 11, 27, 35–40, 44–48, 57, 64, 77, 82, 93, 157n, 162–63n, 166n, 185n

soldiers' monies. *See* artel

soldiers' wives (*soldatki*), 35–38, 180n

soslovie (status group), xv, 9, 32–36, 40, 49–51, 54, 64–65, 166n

Southern Artillery Region, 90

Speransky, M. M., 4, 25

standing army. *See* army

Staraia Rusa, 100

Starol'skii Infantry regiment, 196n

State Council, 5, 36, 155n

state works. *See* army; regimental economy; training

Suzdal Infantry Regiment, 46

Sviatikhin, Second Lieutenant, 130, 195n

Sweden, 3

szlachta. See nobles

Table of Ranks, 41

tactics, 60–61, 70. *See also* training

Tambov Garrison Battalion, 194n

Tatars, 125. *See also* minorities

Tatar Uhlan Regiment, 197n

Tauride, 13, 86, 178n; Garrison, 66, 82

theft, 110, 112–14. *See also* crime; military justice; officers; quartering; regimental economy; soldiers

Thirteenth Infantry Division, 67

Thirty-second Jager Regiment, 94, 123, 128, 138

Timofeev, Lieutenant, 124

Tishchenko, Captain, 124–25, 194n

Tiumen, 98–99

Tobol'sk, 27, 162n, 185n, 194n; Treasury, 99

Tokovnik, Private, 98–99

Tomsk, 10, 37, 63

townspeople (*meshchane, posadskie*), 10–11, 166n. *See also* urban society

training, 28, 134–35; of artisans, 63–64; and company commander, 58, 61; and daily routines, 172n; and discipline, 60, 62, 68; drills, 60–62, 70, 126–28, 131–32, 135, 138, 141, 173n, 196n; hygiene, 57–59, 162n; inadequacies, 65–69, 71–72; literacy, 11, 46–50, 53, 63–64, 173n; maneuvers, 66–67, 174–75n; marksmanship, 61, 172n; and noncommissioned officers, 58, 61, 68; official expectations, 60, 69–73; and quartering, 65–67, 82; of recruits, 55–58, 63, 66, 170n; and regimental economy, 68; religion, 57, 59, 170n; standardization, 70–71, 176n

training troops (*uchebnye voiska, obraztsovye voiska*), 43, 176n

tsar-batiushka, 188n

Tsaritsyn Artillery Garrison, 194n

INDEX

Tsebel'dinsk, 130
Tula, 135, 165n
Turgenev, S. I., 64
Turkey, 3, 15, 83, 140
Tutorin, Private, 140–41
Tver, 20, 81, 174n
Twelfth Infantry Division, 197n

Uglich Infantry Regiment, 46
uhlan, 139
Ukraine, 17, 156n
uniforms. *See* artisans; equipment; regimental economy
urban society, 19, 44–47

Vedemeier's Jager Regiment, 194n
Vel'iaminov, Major General, 97–98
veterans' companies (*invalidnye roty*), 51, 122, 164n
Viatka, 19
Vitebsk, 67, 194n
Voenno-meditsinskii zhurnal, xviii
Voennyi sbornik, xviii
Voichulionis, Private, 131
voiskovye obyvateli, 34
vol'nye raboty (outside/private work), 60, 68, 78–79, 86, 87–90, 98–99, 125–26, 184–86n, 192n. *See also* regimental economy
Vologda, 17
"volunteers" (*vol'noopredeliaiushchiesia*), 45, 47, 49–50, 167–68n
Von Shitz, Captain, 123, 188n, 194n
Voronezh, 10, 27–28, 37, 63; Garrison Battalion, 47; Veterans' Unit, 47
Vorontsov, M. S., 104–105, 128, 138
Vorontsov, S. R., 104, 127
vospitanniki, 46
Vyborg Infantry Regiment, 101

war, xvii, 8, 14–15, 30
War College. *See* War Ministry
War Council, 5
War of 1812, 5, 14
War Ministry, xvii, 9, 29, 78, 84, 102–103, 188n. *See also* Inspectors' Department; Military Judicial Department
weapons, 60–61. *See also* training
Wittgenstein, P. Kh., 129

Zatler, F. K., 187n

GPSR Authorized Representative: Easy Access System Europe - Mustamäe tee 50, 10621 Tallinn, Estonia, gpsr.requests@easproject.com

www.ingramcontent.com/pod-product-compliance
Lightning Source LLC
Chambersburg PA
CBHW082036300426
44117CB00015B/2502